Knowledge is of two kinds.
We know a subject ourselves or we
know where we can find
information upon it

– Samuel Johnson

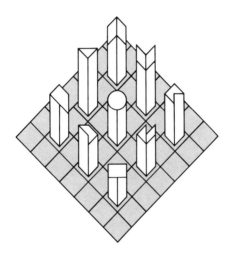

Only those who have the
patience to do simple things
perfectly will acquire the skill to
do difficult things easily

– Friedrich von Schiller

THE HOW TO
MANAGE
HANDBOOK

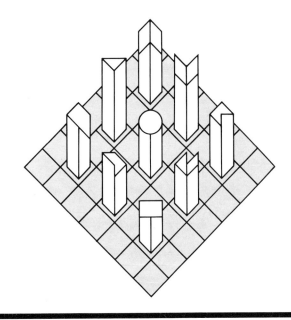

Publisher: York Management Services Limited
Design: Creative Communications
Typesetting: Jet Set Photosetting
Printer: CTP Book Printers
Distributed in the British Isles by:

CONTENTS

1   **PREFACE**

2   **DEVELOPING PERSONAL SKILLS**
3   How to plan for a successful career *ED.*
5   Beyond Management: Mastering the art of leadership
7   Assess your leadership potential
9   Profile of a motivating manager
10   How to tell a winner from a loser
11   How to identify 7 basic personality attitudes
12   Is there a boss lurking inside you?
13   What you should know about negotiating
16   20 Ways to get a bright idea
20   How to improve your memory
22   Coping with executive stress   *Copy Ramesh*
25   How well can you handle stress? Test yourself
26   A ten-point plan for dealing with stress
27   Coping with criticism
28   How to be assertive without being aggressive
30   How to turn an interview into a job   *ED.*
33   How to ask for a promotion or a pay rise

35   **MANAGING YOUR TEAM**
36   The art of delegation
39   How effectively do you delegate?
40   Managing your boss   *ED.*
41   Guidelines for working with your secretary
43   Decision-making and problem-solving   *Kelloggs*
45   Solid solutions vs quick fixes   *Copy.*
47   Performance coaching: targets, guidance and feedback
49   Attributes of a good training programme   *for BK — Checklist*

51   **MANAGING YOUR TIME**
52   Techniques for organising a busy day
54   How to run a meeting
56   How to make time for you and your family   *— Ramesh*
58   Are you wasting time?

59   **THE ART OF COMMUNICATING**
60   Improve the way you speak
62   A brief guide to speech-making

64 How to approach speech-making

66 How to use the telephone successfully — BK

69 The importance of listening

71 The manager's guide to dictation

73 Clear rules for effective written communication

77 A practical guide to letter-writing

82 Sharpen your report-writing techniques

84 How to write concise and accurate minutes

85 An editing checklist

86 Standard correction marks for proofreading

87 Guide to writing a curriculum vitae

89 Guidelines for effective graphic and tabular communication

92 Getting the message across with visual aids

97 All the basics for a successful conference

100 How to meet the media

103 Body language: the importance of non-verbal communication

108 The manager's guide to dressing for success

110 Cross-cultural communication

112 Guidelines for improving customer care

114 Correct forms of address

116 **ORGANISING YOUR HUMAN RESOURCES**

117 How to interview and select staff

119 Employment application form

122 Interviewer's assessment form

123 Tips on induction of new staff

124 Checklist for new personnel

125 Guidelines for writing a job description

126 Evaluating employee performance

129 What to do about high staff turnover

130 Effective use of temporary staff

132 **DEALING WITH PERSONNEL ISSUES**

133 Dealing with employee complaints

134 Poor work deserves fair criticism

135 Dealing with difficult people

137 Conflict management: how to defuse explosive situations

139 The right approach when dismissing an employee

142 How to control absenteeism and improve attendance

144 Some aspects of employment law in the UK

146   RUNNING YOUR OFFICE

147   Designer office - the easy way

148   How to make better use of available office space

149   How to make office moves easier

150   How secure is your office?

154   Office security — 10 points to remember

155   A practical guide to computer security

157   Setting up a filing system that works

160   Tips on printing office stationery

161   International paper sizes

162   A checklist for form design and examples of some useful forms

163   *Leave application*

164   *Leave record*

165   *Transmittal slip*

166   *Message slip*

167   *Despatch request*

168   *Supplies requisition*

169   *Payment voucher*

170   *Petty cash voucher*

171   Keeping costs down

172   USEFUL REFERENCES

173   A comprehensive travel checklist

178   Keep fit in your seat ✳ NB ✳

179   Dealing with jet lag

181   Temperatures you can expect elsewhere in the world

183   World times related to UK times

191   Perpetual calendar

192   How to calculate the number of days between dates

193   Ideas on selecting gifts for all occasions

194   Conversion tables

195   Weights and measures

196   Glossary of common administrative and business terms

210   BIBLIOGRAPHY

PREFACE

The revolution in the technical transfer of information has been one of the outstanding features of the twentieth century. Yet with all this hi-tech growth in the world, the communications gap within offices and between organisations has been constantly widening.

One of the main reasons is the scant training in practical management and communication which men and women receive during their first years after full-time education. Moreover, the books available to trainee accountants, bankers, company secretaries, solicitors, sales personnel, technicians, etc. tend to concentrate virtually exclusively on theory.

But what happens when they are now confronted daily with tasks outside their normal sphere of expertise? When their original tightly-defined job specifications broaden out into a more general management function? Imagine the qualified specialist who is now required to interview, appoint, induct, motivate and evaluate personnel; or arrange conferences; or supervise time management; deal with difficult people; make presentations; prepare for a business trip; write letters, job descriptions, minutes, CVs ...

"Nobody has considered preparing me for this" might well be the unspoken reaction.

This valuable new practical desk-top aid should be welcomed by all levels of administrators, and particularly by newly-appointed and *de facto* managers. It has been carefully researched and compiled with the assistance of editors worldwide. Leaders in various management fields have also made invaluable contributions. We are truly indebted to their enthusiastic support.

Although the publishers may be accused of re-inventing common sense, "The How to Manage Handbook" has a very basic objective – to get every job done well! True excellence and true professionalism in the working environment is dependent on the following five explicit principles:

- care in simplifying the complex details of execution,

- enthusiastic interest in all the people in the organisation,

- commitment to being close to customers and suppliers,

- genuine concern for superior service and quality,

- recognition of the importance of growth and profits.

This handbook concentrates on summarising, as succinctly as possible, many of the important areas of skill and knowledge that contribute to executing these principles successfully. It also illustrates that management tasks can give great enjoyment!

You may find it interesting from time to time just to browse through these pages. But this book's main aim is to be an authoritative and practical desk-top guide to help you to cope with the myriad of challenging situations with which you are confronted daily. Its scope is broad and its aim is to put at your fingertips the exact information you are seeking, rapidly and succinctly. It does not contain superfluous management theory and you don't have to wade through a sea of prose to find the solid, practical information you are seeking. Comprehensive yet concise copy makes the book a useful and an easy work of reference.

We believe it will become an indispensable communication aid in the office, helping busy professional people – from the personal assistant to the accountant, the production supervisor to the human resources manager, and every office and departmental manager – by simultaneously reducing their frustration and enhancing their efficiency.

THE PUBLISHERS

Publishers' Note

It is important to note that in the editorial copy we have chosen to use 'him' rather than 'her'. This is a grammatical choice and does not imply sexual bias.

DEVELOPING PERSONAL SKILLS

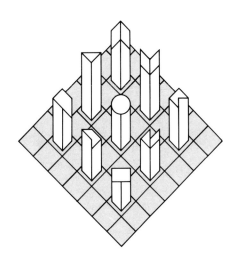

Where are you and where are you going?

Are you satisfied with your life style? Are you heading towards success? mediocrity? failure? Success, mediocrity or failure are relative and may be perceived differently by you or others. How do you see yourself? Are there indications that others don't see you in the same light as you see yourself? Are your perceptions compatible with your goals? Perhaps a hard and objective look at what you've done, what you are doing, and what you think your future prospects might be, could provide focus and guidance.

Assess your situation

Firstly, do you have life and career goals? What do you actually expect from life? Are your goals realistic and compatible with your abilities and interests? What are your abilities? What extra abilities are needed to give you a reasonable chance of your reaching goals? Now, answer this critical question: Are you willing to do what has to be done to make your goals achievable? It is simple to talk and fantasise about doing something; it is something else to take the time and effort to actually do what should be done. Are your aspirations incompatible with your abilities or dedication? To be successful you have to work at it!

Rather than go for "all or nothing", it might be more realistic to set attainable and less ambitious goals. Such objectives do not necessarily mean capitulation and final career compromise. They can subsequently become the stepping stones to a higher achievement. Most people have an amazing and often untapped talent for continued growth and accomplishment. What might at one time in your career appear to be an insurmountable obstacle can subsequently become just another minor difficulty, which can be overcome with reasonable effort. An important variable which often separates the successful person from the also-ran, is motivation.

Life experiences generally follow a varying pattern of ups and downs with plateaux in between. The plateaux are career periods where we regroup, consolidate, and prepare for the climb to the next level. Long plateau periods lead to career inertia. By lingering too long in one situation, there is a tendency to lose momentum and upward mobility.

Secondly, what type of organisation are you in? Do you know what the goals, strategies, and policies of the organisation are? Is the organisational setting compatible with your personal ambitions? Does it provide the means for you to further your ambitions? Can you reconcile its objectives and methods of operation with your sense of values? Do you find that on many occasions you are forced to compromise your values to achieve job objectives? You must periodically assess your values and if, after examination, you conclude that survival within the organisation is contingent on action which is personally repugnant to you, then you are in the wrong organisation, activity, or profession.

Thirdly, assuming there is no ethical incompatibility between your life style and the organisation's operational philosophy: What have you done and what are you doing to make yourself more valuable to your organisation and yourself more marketable as an individual? Are you growing in the same direction as the organisation? Are you a leader or follower? A contributor or hanger-on? In short, are you an asset or liability? Why? What are your prospects? What can or should be done to improve them?

How to proceed

Let's move from the general to the specific. If you look, there are many clues which will indicate how well you're moving towards your career objectives. The following are a few suggestions. Undoubtedly, based on your own experience, you can embellish, eliminate, or add relevant clues which can give you further indications of your progress and prospects.

Are you in the decision chair? How much decisional latitude do you have? Are you an initiator and innovator? Or, are you placed in a position where you are primarily a mechanic implementing other people's ideas and decisions? If so, how good a mechanic are you? It is not uncommon to start as an organisational mechanic and use this as a learning process en route to the role of initiator and innovator. A worse situation is where you have in effect been ostracised and sent to an organisational Siberia where you are neutralised and impotent in the decision-making process. You can determine where you fit into the decision-making spectrum by objectively answering the following:

- Are you given encouragement and a free hand to initiate new projects?
- Are you consulted by your superiors, peers, and subordinates for ideas and suggestions involving organisational activities?
- Do your ideas or suggestions have any impact?
- Is your freedom to decide restricted by your superior's instructions to check with him or her before you act?
- Are you ignored, bypassed, and avoided when it is apparent that the time has come for action?

Information is also vital to decision-making. Your position in the hierarchy of information can be a most telling indicator of your place in the organisation. Are you privy to current, accurate, relevant, action-directed, and privileged communication? If not, enough said!

Next, you should look at your career progression in the light of your age, number of years of experience, and as member of your current organisation. In the present job arena there is a fetish for youth. There are also the old clichés that you must pay your dues, you're too young, etc. and then, all of a sudden they tell you that you are too old. You're passed up for someone younger, more aggressive, and possibly cheaper.

Even though there can be exceptions, as a generalisation you should be well-established career-wise by the time you are 35 years old. Career shifts or job changes normally get progressively more difficult after your 35th birthday. Executive recruiters usually look for pertinent experience, levels of responsibility, extent of tangible accomplishments including career progression, and indicators of professional growth and involvement.

You must avoid career obsolescence. Don't allow yourself to get dead-ended in functions, organisations, or industries which are static or becoming obsolete. Being oblivious to changing requirements can result in serious damage to your career. People may get into a position where they feel they have 10 years' experience when in fact they have one year's experience 10 times. A positive response to the following can be an indicator that you are moving in the right direction: Have you grown within your activity, profession, organisation? Is there tangible evidence to support your assertion? Can you cope with emerging developments, or better yet, are you capable of initiating relevant innovations? Where and at what time intervals have you

made significant contributions? Are new opportunities evolving?

Your salary is another important clue. Do you feel your earnings are commensurate with your contributions? Have there been instances where you have received compensation beyond normal expectations in recognition of superior performance? Have there, on the other hand, been occasions where no salary increases have been forthcoming? Why? Some managers or organisations revel in underpaying their people. They may not realise that the "cheap" employee is not really cheap at all because he or she may be disgruntled and not very productive. Periodic testing of the job market will give you an indication of your personal saleability. You may be pleasantly surprised or unpleasantly shocked at your marketability. A worse possibility is that you may have become vulnerable by pricing yourself out of the market. Your skills and potential may lag behind your salary. Younger and more technically competent people may be available for your job at less money.

Tying the pieces together

If, after you have candidly evaluated your position and if you feel less than satisfied with your progress and prospects, you might want to effect a career transition. To do so a few suggestions might be in order:

- *Education:* Consider acquiring skills in new areas which are intellectually and professionally promising. Such added educational attainment should offer economic and psychological rewards.

- *Career research:* Research different industries and organisations which you think can provide a challenging opportunity for creative development.

- *Mobility:* Are you where the

action is within a growing industry? Are you in a stagnant area of a dynamic organisation, or are you progressing within a receding area of the economy? It is important to know where you are at present so that you can realistically plan where you want to be in the future. If you are moving upward in your present organisation, your career planning at this stage may be satisfactory. On the other hand, if your analysis indicates that you are in a dead-end job with little or no likelihood for upward progression within your present organisation, it may be time to begin looking elsewhere.

In the long run it is best to be your own agent of change. Don't wait until you're called into the boss's office and then react to his or her criticism. Make your own initial analysis. After all, who knows you better than yourself! It must be recognised that changing a career can be difficult. Usually there are short-term sacrifices, but at times it is necessary to take one step back to move two steps forward. A career should enhance life satisfaction; it is an integral part of our lives. It should provide challenge, interest, growth, self-respect, satisfaction, fun and enjoyment.

Career pressure is a constant process. Career progression and accomplishment usually entails pressure. Some people thrive and respond productively to pressure; other people are unable to cope with or function effectively under stress. The amount of non-detrimental pressure varies from person to person. Your career choice may ultimately be determined by the types of pressure involved and your responsiveness to such pressure.

In conclusion, our dynamic and highly competitive society means you can't rest on past accomplishment. The past is only a prologue to the present and the future.

BEYOND MANAGEMENT: MASTERING THE ART OF LEADERSHIP

"Leadership is the ability to get other people to do what they don't want to do, and like it."
— Harry S. Truman

Management and leadership

Moving beyond management into the realm of business leadership, has been one of the causes most fervently advocated by many corporate philosophers over the past few years. But what exactly does this transition entail?

Leadership is different from management, but not for the reasons most people think. Leadership isn't mystical and mysterious. It does not necessarily have to do with charisma or other exotic personality traits. Nor is leadership necessarily better than management or an absolute replacement for it.

Rather, leadership and management are two distinctive and complementary systems of action. Each has its own function and characteristic activities. Both are necessary for success in an increasingly complex and volatile business environment.

Management is about coping with complexity. Its practices and procedures are largely a response to one of the most significant developments of the 20th century: the emergence of large organisations. Without good management, complex enterprises tend to become chaotic in ways that threaten their very existence. Good management brings a degree of order and consistency to key dimensions like the quality and profitability of products.

Leadership, by contrast, is about coping with change. Part of the reason it has become so important in recent years is that the business world has become more competitive and more volatile. Faster technological change, greater international competition, the deregulation of markets, overcapacity in capital-intensive industries, and the changing face of the work force are among the many factors that have contributed to this shift. The net result is that doing what was done yesterday, or doing it 5 percent better, is no longer a formula for success.

In these circumstances, many corporations today are overmanaged and underled. They need to develop their capacity to exercise leadership. However, successful corporations don't wait for leaders to come along. They actively seek out people with leadership potential and expose them to career experiences designed to develop that potential.

Creating a culture of leadership

Recruiting people with leadership potential is only the first step. Equally important is managing their career patterns. Individuals who are effective in large leadership roles often share a number of career experiences.

Perhaps the most typical and most important is significant challenge early in a career. Leaders have almost always had opportunities during their 20s and 30s to actually try to lead, take a risk, and to learn from both triumphs and failures. Such learning seems essential in developing a wide range of leadership skills and perspectives. It also teaches people something about both the difficulty of leadership and its potential for producing change.

Two more attributes of leaders are their breadth of knowledge and their network of relationships acquired both inside and outside the company. However, developing people for important leadership positions requires work on the part of senior executives, often over a long period of time. That work begins with efforts to spot people with great leadership potential early in their careers and to identify what will be needed to stretch and to develop them.

From a different perspective, it seems essential for young, aspiring business leaders to recognise the keys to dynamic business leadership.

Seven keys to developing business leadership

How can corporate executives and managers go beyond managing and learn to inspire through effective leadership? Kenneth Labich of *Fortune Magazine* spoke to some of America's most prominent corporate executives and identified the following seven keys to inspiring business leadership:

1. Trust your subordinates
Managers have been hearing it for years, yet many of them either still don't believe it or only pay lip service to it: the corporate command-and-control structure, with virutally all authority and responsibility residing in a chief executive at the top of a management pyramid, is fast giving way. Instead, it is being replaced by what is called the high-commitment organisation. This requires pushing responsibility down the ladder and relying far more on the energy and talent of the entire work force. The key to making a high-commitment organisation work is mutual trust between managers and employees. The ability to engender that trusting relationship has become the number one leadership test.

2. Develop a vision
In today's business, people are looking for leaders with a vision which will reflect and pre-empt their own way of working and progressing. This is very different from times past when people had to take a job and comply with the way managers organised the job whether they liked it or not.

With the increased level of education and freedom of mobility between one organisation and another, employees increasingly look to work with managers with whom they have compatibility. Therefore we are likely to see a new approach to leadership emerge. The effective leader will have a team of people who do not just respond to orders, but work enthusiastically with him. They will share a vision with the leader. They will be consulted by the leader. They will have respect for the leader. Of course a leader must be able to sell his vision, and that can be difficult. The best way to do this, however, is to set the tone and pace, define objectives and strategies, and to demonstrate by personal example what you expect from others. Finally, a leader should never underestimate the power of vision.

3. Keep your cool

While crisis isn't the only test of leadership, it's the acid test. By demonstrating grace under pressure, the best leaders inspire those around them to stay calm and act intelligently. Genuine leadership necessarily involves stepping forward in a crisis, whether you like it or not. While the natural inclination is to hide in a hole for a while, you can create a serious credibility gap if you do not face the issues and problems at hand.

4. Encourage risks

Effective corporate leaders encourage employees not only to take calculated chances in the interest of the organisation, but also to accept error readily. They make clear to one and all that the future of the enterprise rests on a willingness to experiment, to push in new and untested directions. And the best way for a leader to convey that message – or any message – is by leading the charge personally. One of the key policies of an effective and inspir-ing leader should clearly be that fear of failure must never be a reason not to try something different.

5. Be an expert

Another hallmark of successful corporate leaders is that they do their homework. The troops will follow a lot more willingly if they are confident that the man or woman in front knows at least as much as they do. Many senior executives, especially those in family-dominated companies, were educated in their respective industries virtually from birth. However, most managers don't have that advantage, and many have parachuted into companies with which they are only passingly familiar. For such managers it is absolutely essential to be armed with the proper mindset which spurs them to fill the gaps in their knowledge and master the company's area and mode of operations to such an extent that they are looked upon as experts to be followed with confidence.

6. Invite dissent

A company run by an effective leader is a place where dissent is desirable. Well-known organisational analyst and longtime leadership scholar Warren Bennis contends that smart leaders tend to hire people of youth and vitality, people who are chronic critics of the status quo. Such leaders are not afraid to encourage controversy and to encourage people to say what they think. They constantly entertain often quite sharply differing opinions about what should be done, and are prepared to accept that better decisions can be made as a result.

7. Simplify

Effective leaders possess an extraordinary ability to focus on what is important and reach elegant, simple answers to complex questions. It is not a matter of settling for an easy answer or a quick fix, but of homing in on the esssentials. They demonstrate an exceptional knack of locking onto the most vital parts of a problem and executing deceptively simple solutions.

Summary

There is a need for companies to help create a corporate culture where people value strong leadership and strive to create it. Just as we need more people to provide leadership in the complex organisations that dominate our world today, we also need more people to develop the cultures that will create that leadership. Institutionalising a leadership-centred culture is the ultimate act of leadership.

Read the statements below carefully. After each statement, circle whether you agree or disagree. Do this for all eleven statements before you look at the answers.

1.	Good leaders are born, not made.	Agree	Disagree
2.	I tend to treat my subordinates well as long as they do what I say.	Agree	Disagree
3.	Good leaders depend on their followers as much as they depend on themselves.	Agree	Disagree
4.	As a leader, I would always include the reasons why when asking a subordinate to perform a task.	Agree	Disagree
5.	A good leader will achieve his or her objectives at any cost.	Agree	Disagree
6.	As a group manager, I would never entrust an important project to anyone but myself, even if it means working overtime.	Agree	Disagree
7.	A key to good leadership is being consistent in how one leads.	Agree	Disagree
8.	If justified, I would recommend a subordinate for a promotion to a position equal to or even higher than my own position.	Agree	Disagree
9.	Some subordinates can participate in the decision-making process without threatening a leader's position.	Agree	Disagree
10.	If my group failed to achieve an objective because of a group member's failure, I would explain it as such to my superiors.	Agree	Disagree
11.	I consider myself indispensable to the company in my present position.	Agree	Disagree

Scoring your responses

A point value has been assigned to each statement. To determine your score, simply total the values of your responses.

1.	Agree	0	Disagree	1
2.	Agree	0	Disagree	1
3.	Agree	0	Disagree	1
4.	Agree	0	Disagree	1
5.	Agree	0	Disagree	1
6.	Agree	0	Disagree	1
7.	Agree	0	Disagree	1
8.	Agree	1	Disagree	0
9.	Agree	1	Disagree	0
10.	Agree	0	Disagree	1
11.	Agree	0	Disagree	1

To facilitate understanding, the scoring is now briefly explained.

1. Although some leaders are born, for the most part, leadership is an acquired management skill.

2. The thinking expressed in this statement is similar to the Machiavellian concept of the benevolent dictator. Although such behaviour can be useful, it tends not to be successful.

3. Mutual dependence is important. The best results cannot be achieved single-handedly.

4. Here "always" is the key word. Subordinates do not always need nor should they always be given the reasons why. For example, when a company is negotiating to acquire another business, the confidentiality of the situation does not allow the leader to give reasons for certain actions.

5. Whilst achieving one's objectives is important, it should not be done at any cost. Sometimes the costs may outweigh the value of the goal. Also, if a manager achieves a goal at the expense of his subordinates, it could lead to failure in achieving subsequent objectives.

6. A good leader recognises the need to delegate responsibility to competent subordinates. When justified, this should include responsibility for important projects.

7. There is no one way of being an effective leader. The effective leader is flexible, and changes his approach to meet the needs of the par-ticular employee and/or situation.

8. A successful leader is also a successful trainer. One result of effective leadership is the ability to promote qualified subordinates to any level.

9. In participative decision-making, by experienced and knowledgeable subordinates, the leader's role is not usurped.

10. An effective leader always takes responsibility for a subordinate's actions, whether those actions result in successes or failures. The ineffective leader blames everyone and everything except himself.

11. No one is or should be indispensable. If you feel that this is the case, you have succeeded in locking yourself into a situation, from which you cannot progress. Stagnation is the result.

Assessing your potential

In assessing your score, bear in mind that this device is not a test but an indicator of your leadership potential. If your score was 11 to 9, you have excellent potential; indeed, your leadership ability is probably already self-evident. A score of 8 to 6 shows good potential but that some thinking needs to be sharpened or changed. A score of 5 to 0 suggests that drastic changes are needed and now.

How did you do?

It is important to recognise that individuals can change over time. What you scored today is not necessarily what you will score tomorrow. It could be better, but it could also be worse. That's why you need to monitor periodically your thinking about leadership style.

There are three ways you can manage this monitoring process. Firstly, you can look at other supervisors and managers and decide which of them you would follow. Why would you follow them? Is their behaviour consistent with the responses to the 11 statements discussed? Consider, too, those whom you would not follow and why. How does their behaviour differ from those individuals whom you would follow? Answering these questions can provide a better understanding about your own leadership style because the type of leader you would follow is the type of leader you would most want to be.

Secondly, you should go back and review the statements. Do the explanations make sense to you? Could you successfully apply them to situations at work? If not, why not? In answering this last question, try to be as specific as possible. Listing all the negative reasons is a worthwhile exercise since these reasons probably reflect your own behaviour.

Leadership, itself, is a positive force. It's a positive force for your subordinates and your organisation. But to be effective, leadership has to be monitored periodically by the one person it will most benefit – you.

PROFILE OF A MOTIVATING MANAGER

What sort of manager are you?

Do you qualify as a motivator who consciously and deliberately does all he can to inspire his subordinates with a sense of excitement and job-satisfaction? Or are you, sadly, a member of the de-motivating brigade?

A well-motivated department or business is one in which employees work with initiative, enthusiasm and with due regard to the company's goals and aspirations. A **de-motivated** department or business is characterised by a lack of care, by a "so-what" attitude that is as destructive as it is difficult to change.

By and large **managers** are responsible for the level of their subordinates' commitment to the firm or the department. What managers **do** and **say** will determine the degree to which their subordinates are motivated or de-motivated. As a manager, naturally you would not deliberately set out to de-motivate your staff, and yet perhaps you are not doing as much as you could be doing to motivate them positively. We list the following pointers for careful consideration:

Motivators	De-motivators
Managers who make reasonable efforts to supply staff with the tools needed to perform their functions.	Managers who have the attitude: "If I could do without it in my day, *you* can do without it today".
Managers who provide appropriate training so that staff are capable of performing in a professional manner.	Managers who are "too busy" to train their people how to perform in the appropriate manner.
Managers who are trained in supervisory and management skills.	Managers who have received no training in management skills.
Managers who are sincerely interested, and who assist their subordinates in career development and advancement, even if it means losing good people to other departments.	Managers who selfishly hold their people back from job enrichment and advancement opportunities.
Managers who reinforce the company's staff training programmes.	Managers who don't let employees use the new skills they learn.
Managers who take the time to get more people involved in special assignments and projects.	Managers who use only a chosen few for special projects and assignments.
Managers who take the time to coach their staff for improved performance.	Managers who do not coach or do so in a way that the subordinate's self-esteem is damaged.
Managers who are fair to their employees.	Managers who are inconsistent in their dealings with staff and exhibit signs of favouritism.
Managers who are promoted to their positions because they have performed well and shown signs of leadership.	Managers who are promoted to their positions for reasons of seniority without regard for their leadership abilities.
Managers who sincerely care about staff and demonstrate this attitude. They treat subordinates as mature adults. Staff feel comfortable, important, co-operative and motivated.	Managers who rule by fear, threats, and intimidation, ignoring employees' need for feelings of safety, belonging and self-esteem.

Developing personal skills

Motivators	De-motivators
Managers who **communicate** on a regular basis with subordinates. Members of staff feel that they are part of a team and well-informed. Employees feel comfortable because they are not embarrassed by customer enquiries about matters of which they should be aware but aren't.	Managers who do not take the time and interest to keep their staff informed. Another de-motivator is lack of uniformity in the information disseminated to staff. A person's self-esteem is attacked when a customer learns of changes before members of staff are informed.
Managers who defend and protect their staff's self-esteem in problems and conflicts.	Managers who embarrass their employees in front of others, especially in situations where the person on the staff is following established procedures.
Managers who encourage and seriously consider the ideas and suggestions of employees.	Managers who always respond or react negatively to the ideas and suggestions of employees.
Managers who sincerely compliment staff for jobs well done. The compliments are given immediately, whenever a situation warrants praise.	Managers who never say thanks, or who wait for the annual appraisal to do so.
Managers who take the time and interest to place each employee in the job for which he is most suited and in which he is most interested.	Managers who fill slots with people not equipped with the appropriate talents or dispositions to achieve success and happiness.
Managers who take the time simply to say "Hello" to their subordinates.	Managers who seldom chat to their subordinates.

Which column rings more bells for **you**? If you think you may be a de-motivating manager, console yourself with the thought that, with awareness of your problem, there's still time to do something about it!

HOW TO TELL A WINNER FROM A LOSER

A Winner says: "Let's find out!"
A Loser says: "Nobody knows!"

A Winner makes a mistake and says: "I was wrong!"
A Loser makes a mistake and says: "It wasn't my fault!"

A Winner goes through a problem.
A Loser goes around it – and never gets past it.

A Winner makes commitments.
A Loser makes promises.

A Winner says: "I'm good, but not as good as I ought to be."
A Loser says: "I'm not as bad as a lot of other people."

A Winner tries to learn from those who are superior to him.
A Loser tries to tear down those who are superior.

A Winner says: "There ought to be a better way to do it!"
A Loser says: "That's the way it's always been done here!"

A Winner says: "I'm going to do it!"
A Loser says: "Forget it. It won't work!"

HOW TO IDENTIFY 7 BASIC PERSONALITY ATTITUDES

There are seven basic attitudes that all individuals display in various forms and at various stages of their lives. These attitudes have a marked effect on everything the individual does, whether in relation to career, marriage or other spheres of life.

With specific emphasis on your career, you can become more aware of your attitude by picking the one that is closest to yours at the moment, and those you've had over the past 12 months. If in doubt, ask a friend or colleague. An objective opinion can often reveal an attitude buried so deep that you no longer recognise it, even though it may be holding you back from achieving real job satisfaction.

• The first attitude is **idealistic, superficial**. This is a "new beginning" attitude, marked by high hopes and enthusiasm, often occurring at the onset of a new career.

• What often follows on the first attitude is the second – **frustrated, anxious** when you begin to see a gap between personal expectations or desires and present circumstances. You might find difficulty in coping with your new job, for example. Anxiety sets in and momentum slows down. This is a time of troublesome indecision brought about by fear that things may not work out as well as expected. Frustration is the breeding ground for the next attitude.

• **Defiant, angry**. After frustration comes a conclusion that things clearly won't work out as expected unless something definite is done. Often this happens when a long time goes by with no change in a positive direction. There are two levels of defiance. The first is overt (maybe leading to a direct confrontation, which will probably be governed by emotion), the other covert (burying your anger, allowing it to simmer). Neither is constructive, but covert defiance is especially unproductive, even destructive, in the long run. Covert defiance is often not recognised and personal anger can be buried for days, months and even years. Long-service employees are particularly prone. This buried defiance can lead to attitude number four, resigned.

• The **resigned, uninvolved** attitude happens when you feel there is no longer any use in trying to change things. You could resign mentally from your job, while your body carries out what is required and little more. There are several symptoms of this: a sudden preference for working or being alone, missed schedules or appointments, a pattern of unaccountable absence, increased drinking, irritability or fault-finding.

The resigned attitude is always serious especially as it is contagious! However, the next attitude can help.

• **Aware, accepting**. You reach this attitude when you see you must be willing to change. There is no real awareness without an honest acceptance of personal responsibility and need for personal change. Personal awareness can usually be reached in one of two ways: by someone else's honesty, which is risky as it's not always wanted, or by looking squarely in the mirror and accepting yourself for what you are. It is taking stock and accepting the possibility that nothing good can come unless there's change. It is a constructive attitude that sets the stage for the next attitude.

• **Decisive, changing**. This is an active, productive attitude. A conscious decision is made and decisive steps are taken away from a negative attitude. It is often easier to decide to do something different in a small, safe area of work before tackling a main area.

However, its the final attitude that sustains the vitality started by decisiveness.

• **Commitment**. You become committed when you don't expect perfection from your job, or yourself, yet you want to make things work. You strive for excellence, knowing that perfection is often idealistic. The committed attitude is not a reaction to things that are going wrong but an active, working desire to help out. There is a practical understanding that people must work together. Things become workable when you get the stars out of your eyes and push on towards your goals. These must be attainable, challenging and worthwhile for commitment to remain.

These attitudes need not follow immediately on one another, but may be spread out over many years in your career. Knowing what your attitude is, however, can be the starting point in understanding yourself and your needs and can help to create and maintain a positive attitude towards your job.

IS THERE A BOSS LURKING INSIDE YOU?

Business is always looking for good management material and rarely finding it.

One reason: most workers are not qualified. Another: many qualified people just aren't ambitious enough to take on the added responsibility; they just want to do their job, collect their pay and not worry.

As a result, many middle management jobs are held by people who are not really qualified. But at least they were willing to take a shot at the extra responsibility. (How often do you hear people saying: "My boss isn't really qualified. I know more than he does, but who wants the headaches?")

Maybe you'd like to move up the ladder in your present firm or somewhere else. If so, answer the questions below and see – Is there a boss lurking inside you?
Choose one:

1. Do you hate to make mistakes on the job and consequently are very careful about checking your work?
Yes ☐   No ☐   Yes & No ☐

2. Are you curious enough about various aspects of the business you're in, to ask questions even about things unrelated to your job?
Yes ☐   No ☐   Yes & No ☐

3. When colleagues are confused about how to handle an out-of-the-ordinary situation on the job, do they often ask your advice?
Yes ☐   No ☐   Yes & No ☐

4. Do you make suggestions to your supervisor on how to smooth out some bottleneck?
Yes ☐   No ☐   Yes & No ☐

5. Are you generally well-liked and respected by colleagues and superiors?
Yes ☐   No ☐   Yes & No ☐

6. Have you ever voluntarily cut your lunch time short because it was busy that day, and you wanted to help get the work done?
Yes ☐   No ☐   Yes & No ☐

7. When you're not busy, do you offer to help a colleague who is extra busy?
Yes ☐   No ☐   Yes & No ☐

8. Have you ever offered to take on added responsibility as a regular part of your job, because you felt it would improve the efficiency of your department?
Yes ☐   No ☐   Yes & No ☐

9. Have your superiors ever asked your opinion or advice about a problem concerning one or more of your colleagues?
Yes ☐   No ☐   Yes & No ☐

10. Do you enjoy having to think your way through a problem when something unusual occurs on the job?
Yes ☐   No ☐   Yes & No ☐

11. Are you more likely than not to be even-tempered on days when everything seems to go wrong?
Yes ☐   No ☐   Yes & No ☐

12. When you come across a newspaper or magazine article about the business your company is in, do you read it?
Yes ☐   No ☐   Yes & No ☐

13. Do you feel that the quality of work done in your department or office is important and should be kept at a high standard?
Yes ☐   No ☐   Yes & No ☐

14. Do you frequently go to lunch with one or more of your colleagues?
Yes ☐   No ☐   Yes & No ☐

15. Do you maintain a social relationship with any of your colleagues beyond working hours?
Yes ☐   No ☐   Yes & No ☐

16. If a colleague was shirking responsibility and lowering the efficiency of the department, would you speak to him about it?
Yes ☐   No ☐   Yes & No ☐

17. Are you familiar enough with the job of one or more of your colleagues, so that you could fill in when necessary?
Yes ☐   No ☐   Yes & No ☐

18. Have you a good enough command of the English language to write a report or memo that is easy to read and understand?
Yes ☐   No ☐   Yes & No ☐

19. Do you feel comfortable about explaining to a new employee how certain things are done and why they are done that way?
Yes ☐   No ☐   Yes & No ☐

20. Do you actively pursue one or more hobbies?
Yes ☐   No ☐   Yes & No ☐

21. Does your circle of friends include people of various backgrounds and ethnic origins?
Yes ☐   No ☐   Yes & No ☐

22. Are you patient with people who are slow to understand, so that you don't make them feel stupid or uncomfortable?
Yes ☐   No ☐   Yes & No ☐

23. Are you usually on time for work?
Yes ☐   No ☐   Yes & No ☐

24. When a new system is planned at work and you see a potential problem for your department, do you bring it to the attention of your superiors?
Yes ☐   No ☐   Yes & No ☐

Answers

SCORE POINTS:
Yes & No = 2   Yes = 4   No = 0

IF your BOSS POTENTIAL score is:

0–18:
Just doing a job and collecting your pay is where you are now. If it's not where you want to stay, a big rethink about your attitude towards work and responsibility is essential.

50-74:
At this point you have untapped potential for being a good boss. Check your No answers and see in how many cases you can change your attitude or behaviour to a Yes in the future.

76 plus:
There's a BOSS lurking inside of you! You possess the very qualities that make for a good one. To use that talent to best advantage, start looking for challenges with more responsibility.

WHAT YOU SHOULD KNOW ABOUT NEGOTIATING

Whenever people exchange ideas with the specific intent of changing relationships or situations they are negotiating.

Of all executive skills, the ability to negotiate seems to be increasingly essential to success. For example, when times are tough managers must negotiate better deals for their companies. Growth, profitability and even survival can depend on the ability of a company's managers across the board to negotiate better deals for it.

Inter-departmental relationships will also benefit from improved negotiation. The bigger the organisation the more each department and/or subsidiary company sees itself in competition with other departments or companies. Each competes for a share of the limited resources of the organisation. This competition tends to be of a non-productive, political and back-biting kind.

The following five strategies are the result of much reflection and research into what really works when skilled negotiators from the widely different fields of commerce, politics and industrial relations are faced with very difficult deals to negotiate:

- **Generate** as many negotiable issues/alternative solutions as possible.
- **Refuse** to engage in personal attacks or dirty tricks.
- **Explore** the real interests/needs of both parties.
- **Agree** to objective principles for evaluating alternatives.
- **Tie down** the implementation clearly and carefully.

How to use these strategies

Generate as many negotiable issues/alternative solutions as possible

Analyse the situation in and around the area needing negotiation and list as many negotiable issues as possible. Skilled negotiators are very good at this: they literally do **generate** long lists of negotiable issues. It's as though there is a virtue in sheer quantity. Also, they include not only their own main issues but also any that the other party may raise. The reason for this strategy is that it ensures maximum flexibility. The more negotiable issues there are the more chance there is for creative trade-offs on both sides.

The second part of this first key strategy is **"generate as many alternative solutions as possible"**. Here we still have an emphasis on the quantity, but equally an emphasis on creativity. Skilled negotiators, when faced with difficult situations, tend to think laterally. This means including solutions which may initially be unpalatable to you in your full list of possible solutions. Thinking laterally often means you must obtain a flexible mandate from the group on whose behalf you are negotiating, rather than locking yourself into a set of inflexible demands. Finally, thinking laterally entails keeping an open mind and exercising your creativity from the planning right through to the implementation of the negotiated deal.

Refuse to engage in personal attacks or dirty tricks

This sounds like a simple strategy to follow, but it is not always an easy one.

Turbulence in the spheres of economic, political and industrial relations creates conditions of stress and threat and it is very easy, indeed natural, to become emotional and personal under such conditions. Further, it is very tempting to use dirty tricks when you perceive the other party as "the enemy", or where you suspect them of using dirty tricks on you.

One of the things skilled negotiators seem to achieve in using this great strategy is to separate the people from the issues. They put conscious energy into self-control and as a matter of strategy, try not to react to any personal attacks that may be levelled at them by the other side. One way of doing this is to focus or refocus the conversation constantly on the **issues** at hand. Another way of de-escalating personal antagonisms is to talk about them openly and specifically as an issue to be handled separately from the other substantive issues being negotiated.

Then, as a matter of strategy, most masters of the art of negotiation never use dirty tricks themselves. There are very good reasons for this. One pragmatic reason is that, by and large, dirty tricks can only be used once – and once discovered, you will never be trusted again as a negotiator.

Some examples of dirty tricks are: The "rolling concession", in which the other party leads you to believe that if only you agree to this last point you have a deal. You agree. And then the party introduces a further concession that they want. Or the "nice guy – nasty guy" routine, in which the nice guy appeals to you to give way on a little point just to appease the "difficult" member in his team. The list of dirty tricks is almost unending.

Another good reason for refusing to play games or use dirty tricks is that our society seems to be so constituted that in business, as in life, ethics tend to outlast dirty dealing – the honest players have a higher survival value than the cheats. Having said that, skilled negotiators do, however, take active steps to protect themselves against dirty tricks that the other party may be tempted to use.

Explore the real interests/needs of both parties

Turbulence of any kind can obscure the real needs of groups in conflict. Upheaval, crises or threats tend to polarise parties in a negotiation, and people become locked into "bargaining positions", which usually result in a win or lose struggle which carries painful consequences for both parties.

The experts go about implementing this key strategy by analysing their own real interests and needs. They establish very carefully, but in broad terms, what it is that they really need.

So, as well as being clear about your own interests/needs, this third strategy requires that you try to uncover the interests and needs of the other party. This means doing your homework and planning prior to the negotiation, as well as taking the trouble to clarify and confirm your assumptions and understanding during the negotiation.

Focus on the real interests and needs that lie behind the stated positions.

Agree on objective principles for evaluating alternatives

The conflicts that arise from difficult situations in economic, political and industrial relations can be pretty intense, and there is often a feeling of warfare surrounding the negotiations that take place under such conditions. Power struggles can become the norm, resulting too often in the best actors and the hardest bargainers "winning" the negotiation. The problem with such outcomes is that they are nearly always very costly to both parties, for the "losing" side will do everything possible to get back their losses during the implementation of the deal, and will be heavily prepared

to "win" the next negotiation – if there is one.

An alternative to engaging in damaging power struggles is to search for some objective criteria which both parties can accept as means of evaluating any proposed settlements. There is a need to search for standards of fairness and efficiency, for principles of merit against which the proposals of both parties can be measured. So the first thing to negotiate is agreement on which objective principles will apply in each case.

Once you have agreed on the objective criteria for evaluating the deal, it should help you to avoid having to yield to pressure, because agreed principles become the things to which you "yield". Finally, in striving for a solution based on principle, you are being open to reason, and not to threats – which is a pretty good way to avoid being caught up in power games during negotiations.

Tie down the implementation clearly and carefully

The best negotiators are calm, clear and careful people, and because of these characteristics, when they make a deal – it works, it sticks.

The rapidity of change means that unforeseen circumstances can hamper the implementation of the deals that you might be making. Clarity and care is much needed as people approach the euphoria of reaching agreement. The fifth key strategy requires that you think through the threats to implementation very carefully. Take the trouble to list all possible events that could derail the implementation of the agreement, and evaluate the probability that they might occur.

Deals may be **concluded** by those who play the negotiating game, but they are **implemented** in the everyday world with all its

harsh realities. It is therefore important that both parties to an agreement should be informed and clear about any threats to its successful implementation. To gain the full commitment of the other party to implementation of the agreement, it is advisable to share your thinking about the threats with him and jointly develop strategies to ensure smooth implementation. And throughout this final phase at the negotiating table, the masters of the art take pains to maintain clarity – to ensure that the agreement and its implementation are fully understood. Too often implementation becomes bogged down because mediocre negotiators have not clarified it sufficiently, and so leave the table with genuinely different perceptions of how things are going to be implemented.

The costs of using these negotiating strategies

The first cost of these strategies is that you must take **the interests of the other party seriously**. It means being committed to going for a sound, win-win agreement that will really benefit both parties and which is therefore unlikely to equate with your most optimistic outcome. Some people find this hard to do. They love achieving a big killing.

The second cost is that you must **remain open and flexible**. This means not simply accepting the starry-eyed expectations of the group you are negotiating for, but rather being willing to enter into tough internal negotiations with them to get a reasonable range of expectations before the external negotiation. It also means being willing to come back and renegotiate your mandate, should this seem appropriate in the light of new information or creative and as yet unconsidered solutions which arise during the negotiating process itself. It also means that inflexibility and stubborn pride are luxuries that you can't afford.

The third cost is that you must be **cool and patient**. The five great strategies absolutely demand coolheadedness. They cannot be implemented without it. Don't under-estimate this cost. It really is a price to pay. It takes great patience to operate according to the five strategies. Self-control is neither easy nor enjoyable, but is a *sine qua non* of skilled negotiation. Skilled performance is often not doing what comes naturally, but rather the exact opposite – controlling what comes naturally! And there are many successful, powerful people who find such self-control, such patience and coolheadedness an impossibly high price to pay. They are so used to exercising the power of their positions or organisations to get what they want, that they can't adjust to negotiations where the power is more or less equal.

The benefits of the five suggested strategies

These strategies do increase the odds in favour of arriving at sound, wise agreements. The strategies work because they aim at recognising the real interests of both parties, and at striving to take these interests into account in the solutions that the strategies help create. Also, because the strategies require clarity about, and commitment to, the implementation of agreements, such agreements stand a pretty good chance of survival.

The next benefit that flows from use of the five strategies is that they tend to lead to creative solutions to conflicts of interest rather than to battles and wars. They lead to agreements based on principle, not power, and help the parties to avoid the adversarial, antagonistic stances that are so imbedded in many negotiation rituals and practices, as found for example in the industrial relations of many countries.

Finally, the strategies provide some protection from "the powerful" and from "the bad" – dirty trick artists. By following the five strategies you can avoid the temptation of giving in to pressure and agreeing to damaging deals that should have been rejected. And, of no small importance, they are strategies that enhance your own dignity, maintain your integrity and in the process, build your self-esteem.

It's only the people with push that have pull!
- Lord Dewar

Leaders must be seen to be up front, up to date, up to their job and up early in the morning
- Marcus Sieff

Ever since people began to think, our progress has depended on the development of bright ideas. The invention of the wheel, plough, printing press, steam engine, light bulb and many other products, illustrates the power of the human mind to create bright ideas. Our lives have been enriched by our ability to come up with the right idea at the right time. And, from time to time, our very survival has depended on our capacity to generate creative solutions.

An idea is an odd sort of creature. It flits around in our minds looking for problems to solve. It bounces against other ideas and sometimes merges to form a new idea - a bright one. Bright ideas can become contagious and generate more bright ideas, until eventually a complete solution to your problem is produced. However, if you don't know where you are going when trying to solve a problem, the ideas you produce will quickly lose their brilliance. Following are 20 guidelines to help you to use the ideas you have productively.

1. What do you know about the problem?

This question is the most basic question. It is the one question that you should always ask yourself before attempting to redefine a problem or generate ideas. In responding to this question, you should write down - without evaluation - every bit of information you possess or can collect in a reasonable period of time. Scanning this information can clarify the problem situation and suggest possible redefinitions.

2. What don't you know about the problem?

Your responses to this question can be equally if not more valuable than your responses to question 1. Aspects of the problem that initially are hidden from view or unknown to you can increase your understanding of the problem considerably once they are revealed. Furthermore, the fact that these aspects are initially hidden or unknown to you makes them unique bits of information that can clarify the problem or prompt unique solutions. At the moment you uncover such information, you will often have an "Aha!" reaction that immediately suggests a new problem perspective or potential solution.

3. Who needs to solve the problem more than you?

If someone else has a stronger need to solve the problem than you do, they are likely to be more motivated. And, if they are more motivated, the chances are they have devoted considerable effort to digging out information and looking for solutions. Consulting such individuals can often provide valuable new insights as well as ideas.

Even if you don't know any individuals with a greater need to solve the problem you can still receive some benefit from this question. Imagine how highly motivated people you know might solve the problem. In particular, think about how much effort they would invest, where they would look for information, and what types of ideas they might generate for solving the problem.

4. What are your major objectives in solving the problem?

It has been said many times before, but it bears repeating: "If you don't know where you're going, you probably won't get there".

In order to bring out all relevant information about a problem, you need to develop clear statements about what you hope to accomplish. Without such statements, the information you collect about your problem can have no meaning. The situation is something like setting out on a trip in your car. If you don't know your destination, then no road sign will be able to point you in the right direction. You can't expect to understand your problem unless you first understand your objectives.

5. Incubate

A partially developed idea is like an unhatched egg. The chick can't break out of its shell unless the egg is incubated. Ideas too need incubating so that your subconscious mind can work on them. Your subconscious mind likes to take partial ideas and whirl them around hoping that a connection can be made with some information you have suppressed and perhaps forgotten.

Whenever you are trying to solve a problem you should allow some time for incubation. You never know when a connection will be made, but it does not usually occur when you are concentrating intensely on the problem. Concentration helps to start incubation, which in turn brings into play your subconscious thinking process.

To incubate an idea, all you must do is engage in some activity other than work on the problem. If possible, you should do something that is relaxing. Relaxation takes your mind off your problem and allows your subconscious to work more effectively.

6. Set aside a specific time

Designate a specific time that you can work on producing your ideas. The time you set aside for your conscious idea-generation activity should be a time when you won't be subject to the pressures of everyday life. It should also be a time when you are at your emotional and psychological peaks. This can be early morning, afternoon, or late evening. You know when you are most productive – choose your time accordingly. Ensure that the time set aside is sufficient for you to give adequate attention to idea generation. Whatever time period you decide upon, try to be consistent in using it. Establish a schedule and stick to it as much as possible. If you view this time as your time, it will be much easier for you to maintain your schedule.

7. Use an idea diary

Because ideas are so fleeting, you have to capture them before they get away. You can't trust your memory since it is usually preoccupied with other things. Bright ideas tend to peek out of your subconscious mind briefly and then retreat to the nether regions inside you. Grab them immediately because they may not appear again.

The best way to ensure that your bright ideas don't slip away is to write them down as soon as they emerge. Even if they are not highly polished, you should write them down. The core of a potential bright idea might yield something that you can modify and polish until some degree of brilliance is achieved.

If you automatically reject some of the ideas that slip out of your subconscious, you won't have another chance at them. Thus, instead of evaluating emerging ideas and rejecting some without writing them down, view everything you think of as a possible stimulator of bright ideas.

8. Think up a set number of ideas

An old trick used by leaders of brainstorming groups is to ask a group to produce a target number

of ideas. The leader might say: "Generate twenty more ideas". Then, once the group has done this, the leader might push the group to generate twenty more, and so on until the group runs out of ideas.

This particular method actually has been supported by some research. It seems setting realistic goals helps increase our motivation. By achieving a series of goals, we can produce more ideas than if we don't use any specific goal. The trick, however, is to set a realistic target number each time we generate ideas. If the number is too high, our motivation and our idea productivity are likely to decrease.

9. Establish a solution deadline

Give yourself a certain amount of time to produce some of your ideas. There are at least two different ways you can do this. At the beginning of the day, decide that you will produce a certain number of ideas by some specific time later on in the day. Or, you can sit down and begin generating ideas for a specified period of time, say thirty minutes to one hour. In either case, you will find that establishing a deadline works much better if you precede work with a period of incubation. Engage in some unrelated activity or relax before you start working toward your deadline.

10. Try problem-switching

Another way to take advantage of incubation is to switch from one problem to another. When you have been working on a problem for a while and begin to run out of ideas, put it aside. Switch to another problem and work on that until you begin to run out of ideas (or after a specified period of time). Then, return to your original problem and see how many new ideas you can think of.

11. Read any material that relates to the problem

This hint is one of the most basic and elementary of all hints for dealing with problems. Before you can expect to produce bright ideas, you should learn everything you can about your problem. Read everything that might have some bearing on your problem. Collect as many facts as you can and look for solutions that other people have tried.

When you read problem-related literature, however, read it with a somewhat critical eye. If possible, you should try to validate any factual claims made about possible solutions or about your problem in general. Determine how competent the author is and how accurate the information is. Many "facts" are only conjectures about what something is, given the current level of available knowledge. Facts about a problem can change over time and you should take this into account when evaluating the relevance of any information.

12. Read in other fields

The best creative problem-solvers are knowledgeable about a wide range of different subjects. If you want to widen your perspective, you also should read literature outside your field of interest. The more information you acquire, the more resources you can bring to bear on your problems. You learn to see with new eyes and apply your insight to your problems.

13. Withhold all judgement

The odds of producing bright ideas are diminished considerably when you judge every potential idea with a critical eye as soon as it is proposed. You should first produce as many ideas as you can and then evaluate them. In many instances, some ideas you are tempted to reject during this evaluation period can be modified to produce a bright idea.

The situation is somewhat analogous to planting flowers. If you throw away a seed because you don't like the way it looks, it will never have a chance to bloom into a thing of beauty.

14. Ask: "What is good about it?"

After you have generated all of the ideas you can, ask yourself what is good about each idea. Ignore every negative aspect that may be staring you in the face. Instead, try to find at least one positive thing about each idea. After you have done this for all your ideas, go back over them and see what modifications you can make using the positive feature you identified previously.

To illustrate this guideline, suppose you are tempted to discard an idea because it will be too expensive to implement. Ask yourself what is good about implementing an idea that costs a great deal. For example, examining the idea further may reveal a new source of funding that you had not considered before. In addition, you might learn more about funding procedures and how money is acquired and used to solve problems like your own.

Conducting a positive examination of your ideas, will obviously require more time and effort than rejecting them outright. However, the easiest course of action is not always the best. Remember, bright ideas do not usually present themselves to you. They have to be coaxed out.

15. Move beyond conventional ideas

When you are trying to develop unique solutions to a problem, it sometimes helps to get rid of all the obvious, conventional solutions that you think of first. Push yourself to think of every known and conventional idea. Generate as many as you can. Then, put them aside for later reference and start trying to develop bright ideas. As you do this, avoid using any of the conventional ideas. Shut them out of your mind and concentrate only on producing ideas that are original to yourself. When you have produced as many original ideas as you can, go back to the conventional ideas you discarded temporarily and examine each one to see how it might be altered to suggest a more unique solution.

Putting aside conventional ideas at the outset will make it easier to think of more unconventional ideas later on. By temporarily getting rid of tried-and-true problem solutions, you will remove some of the mental constraints that can inhibit generation of bright ideas. With your mind more open and receptive, unique ideas should flow out more freely.

16. Ask: "Why?"

This technique is a variation on the preceding one. The objective of this technique is to either broaden or narrow a problem statement to uncover information that will lead to a solution.

To use this technique, you first write down a statement of your problem. Ask why you want to solve the problem and use your answer to develop a problem restatement.

Using this restatement, repeat the process several times until the problem statements reach a level of abstraction that seems to make further questioning useless or impractical.

17. Work backwards

Who says you have to solve a problem by beginning with a logical starting point and working forward towards a solution? Working forward towards a solution can work very well for many types of problems. However, there are other problems (e.g. planning problems or ones requiring use of visual images) that can be solved best by working backwards from a solution.

This reverse logic makes sense when you place problems in their proper perspective. Most problems are part of larger situations that have no clearly defined beginning or end. Each component of such situations is linked together so that the end of one problem is also the beginning of another. Beginnings are ends and vice versa. Beginning and end are arbitrary designations that we place on certain points in time that are associated with a whole continuum of events. Thus, when you think you are working forward towards a solution to your problem, you may actually be working towards the beginning of someone else's problem. Conversely, when you work backward from your solution, you may be working towards someone else's problem. It's all relative.

To use the work-backwards technique, you must first identify the current and desired state of your problem. That is, what your problem is like now and what you would like it to be at some point in the future. Be as specific as you can in your descriptions. Next, ask yourself what action or behaviour will be required immediately prior to the solution (or desired state) in order to achieve it. What is the last thing that will be needed to be done to solve the problem? Then, determine what action or behaviour precedes that action or behaviour, and so forth until you have examined each preceding step back to your original starting point.

Once you have done this, you may be able to solve your problem in a relatively straightforward manner as the pieces of the required solution begin to fall into place. In effect, working backwards helps add structure to an ill-structured situation.

However, this technique may not work at all for some problems and only in combination with working forward for other problems. You will have to experiment to determine when this method is likely to help you.

18. Brainstorming

Some people call it brainstorming, others call it free association.

By connecting or associating one idea with another, we can produce an endless stream of ideas. The words used to describe these ideas are symbols devised to serve a specific purpose. And because of the way we order and process information, many of these symbols are linked together. For example, when I think of the word car, I associate it with windows, which I associate with house, which I associate with view and so on. One idea leads to another. It's a fairly natural way of thinking for most of us. Yet some of us fail to take advantage of it when we are trying to solve our problems.

Begin by selecting a word that seems to best represent the essence of your problem. It may be a word in your problem statement or some other word that comes to mind. Whatever word you choose, it must be related to your general problem situation in some way.

Write down this word, quickly look at it, and immediately write down the next word that comes to mind. Don't try to write down the right word. Just write down the word that pops into your consciousness. Then, use this word and write down a word you associate with it. Continue this process for several minutes. Establish a target number of words or a time deadline if you wish.

When you have completed your stream of associations, review the entire list of words. Examine each word and see what ideas it might suggest. Pick out four or five words that seem to imply possible solutions and try to modify and elaborate on them to produce bright ideas.

19. Ask a friend

Someone you know who doesn't have your problem may be able to provide a different perspective on it. So, try asking a friend to help you solve a problem. Give only enough information to give a basic understanding of exactly what the situation is. Leave out the boring details and don't try to give all the background if you want to remain friends.

Next, ask how he would solve the problem. Write down everything even if it becomes evident that your friend doesn't really understand what your problem is. Don't say: "I've already tried that", "That's stupid", or "It will never work". When you are alone, review all of the ideas and see if any might be directly applicable or capable of suggesting another idea.

20. Look in a catalogue

This is an extremely simple technique to use. All you have to do is find a catalogue, randomly flip through it, and see if any words might prompt new ideas or suggest modifications of old ones. You don't even have to limit yourself to publicatons that we most often refer to as catalogues. A thesaurus, dictionary, magazine, cookbook or newspaper will all do quite nicely. The nature of the publication is much less important than obtaining new sources of stimulation.

Just scan over the words while keeping your problem in mind and wait for a connection to be made between a random word and some aspect of your problem. Then, write down whatever new idea or modificaton might be suggested.

Match your image of yourself to how others see you. Keep in touch with their reality
- Michael Shea

For one who has no objective, nothing is relevant
- Confucius

HOW TO IMPROVE YOUR MEMORY

A good memory is one of the executive's most immediate needs, but it is vital for others as well – for anyone who meets people on business or social occasions.

Forgetfulness is an irritating and costly problem for a busy person. It produces stress and results in loss of valuable time. An unreliable memory also has a negative influence on self-confidence and peace of mind. Many people are afraid to give a speech because they may forget important points. They dodge others at parties and business meetings because they can't remember names.

Today, most people are required to remember considerably more information than they once did in order to conduct their every-day activities effectively. Just consider numbers, for example. We have to remember telepone numbers, addresses, post codes, ID numbers, bank account numbers and automatic teller machine codes.

Over and above numbers, we also have to be able to recollect names accurately: first names, surnames and titles – from secretaries and clerks to senior managers and executive officers.

Then there are all the lists that we have to keep in mind: shopping lists, jobs to do, meeting agendas, idea lists, even laws and regulations that affect one's business.

To what extent can you improve your memory?

According to Robert Montgomery, author of *Memory Made Easy*, an individual using simple memory techniques can, with practice, increase his ability to remember by a minimum of 300 percent.

Before this can happen, however, the person must be strongly motivated to increase his memory powers. He must concentrate on improving his memory, and he

must learn to care about people. These are prerequisites to remembering information about specific people. Police officers are a good example. They are trained to report their observations at the scene of a crime or an accident with great accuracy.

Techniques for memory improvement

The three key principles are to visualise, repeat and associate. According to the experts, 85 percent of what we learn and remember is related to sight, 11 percent to hearing and the balance to taste, touch and smell. It is therefore of great benefit to see something we want to remember in picture form or written down.

For example, when you meet someone for the first time, take a look at that person's business card.

First, learn the name and form a mental picture of the person. See it in your mind's eye. Second, repeat the things you want to remember again and again.

That's the idea behind rote learning in school – the way most people learned spelling and multiplication tables. And it is an important law of advertising. Radio and television commercials rely heavily on repetition to remind listeners about products.

Third – and most important – memory improvement depends on being able to make vivid associations. To recall a name, date or fact, what the brain needs is a cue – something that triggers a connection.

One effective method is to use a rhyme. The old spelling rhyme about "*i* before *e* except after *c* or when sounded like *a* as in *neighbour* and *weigh*" is one common example. Others can be: Mr Brown owns a gift shop: We browse in Mr Brown's gift shop. Or, Mr Bowles is a barrister: Mr Bowles bowls over the jury. The pictures may not be the ones you

would use, but they do demonstrate how to associate a business with a person's name.

Recollection of names

For names, it is useful to use the acronym ACE – this stands for action, colour and exaggeration. Whenever you make a new acquaintance, these three ideas should be built into the name association. The more ridiculous, the more ludicrous the mental picture, the better.

For example, you want to remember the name Donald Bacon. Think: Bacon and eggs at dawn. Or, Captain Andrew Bell. See: Andy Capp drinking Bell's whisky.

Before long, you'll find associations becoming almost automatic. The best association is usually the one you think of first.

The cocktail party situation

How does one handle the cocktail party situation, where meeting a succession of people for the first time involves trying to remember each one's name?

You need about 15 to 20 seconds of interaction with an individual before an association occurs.

You can't just concentrate on the name to the exclusion of the conversation. But if you can repeat the person's name once or twice, either silently or out loud, that helps. Questions about the origin of a name often help, too.

Let's say you are introduced to Colleen O'Flynn. You might say: Colleen O'Flynn – do you come from an Irish family? Delighted to meet you, Mrs O'Flynn.

List recollection

One of the most successful methods for list recall is the 'stack and link' method. This way of thinking links items on a list in a specific sequence, so that they can be recalled consecutively. The basic idea is that whatever you want to remember – a poem, a speech, a checklist, textbook material or a shopping list – can be stacked and linked mentally.

For example, to recall the particulars of an estate planning programme that offers several benefits: First, picture an office site with a combination lock. Then visualise the name "Total Safe Company" on the front of the safe. There's an axe jammed into the safe with a card attached to the handle of the axe. On the card is printed the word "special".

There is a woman dressed in black holding the handle of the axe. Hanging on the black dress of this women are two children – a girl and a boy. The little girl has her hair done up in curlers.

The little boy is holding a balloon. A man comes up to the boy and pulls the balloon down as he says, "Lower".

Now, all the ideas stacked and linked in that scene represent the benefits available to customers who allow a banker or insurance man to handle their estate planning. Here's what the objects represent:

First, a safe is a place where you can save things. The benefit of an estate plan is that it can save thousands of pounds. The name on the safe means you'll benefit from total estate planning.

Next, the axe suggests that the estate planner can cut Inheritance Tax, and the card marked "special" means that specialists – professionals – will be managing the investments.

The woman in black is the widow who will benefit through the plan, and the two children remind you that a trust is provided for survivors.

The girl's curlers, representing a perm, signify permanent financial security for the surviving children.

The man telling the boy to keep the balloon lower indicates the benefit of lower taxes on future settlements, such as might arise on the death of the mother.

Sales people can benefit greatly from this kind of technique because it builds associations on top of one another. A person can cover all the main points in a sales talk and slant or embellish them in the most effective way. You have to trust your creativity, sense of humour and experience to provide you with ideas for objects to picture.

Speech-making

The stack-and-link method works equally well for speechmaking. Mark Twain was a noted raconteur who used a version of the stack-and-link idea. He could get up in front of an audience night after night and talk for an hour or two without using any notes.

How did he do it? He used to walk through a park in the town he was visiting, before the time for his appearance on the platform, and he would attach ideas for his speech to items in the park – such as a bench here or a tree there, or a flower bed or water fountain or bandstand.

Then, when he got up for the speech, he would mentally walk through the park, linking key items in his talk to what he had seen. The associations would just flow out.

Don't memorise a speech. Rather, build your speech around a theme, and use key words to link different sections together. With practice, you will be able to give a speech without having to refer to notes or a written text.

General hints

- *Consistency*. Get into the habit of putting things, such as your car keys, back in the same place each time. Not only will you never forget where you've left them, but you won't waste time looking for them.

- *Checklists*. Before you have to be somewhere, make a list of everything you want to do. Include on the list everything you need to take with you.

- *Record*. Carry a notepad and pen with you for all those odds and ends you think of and want to remember.

- *Motivation*. Finally, if you consciously want to remember something, you will. Make an effort to improve your memory. As more than one memory expert has noted, the amazing thing is not that we forget, but that we remember so much.

COPING WITH EXECUTIVE STRESS

In the work system and particularly in our managerial population, it is almost taboo to admit that you are experiencing stress due to your job. Admitting to stress is a way of saying that you cannot cope with the job demands and the inference is that you are failing, not man enough for the job, not fit for further promotion. Consequently our reaction is to deny to ourselves and others that we are under stress, anxious and worried in certain work situations.

All executives experience stress, periodically, severe or mild – and while we don't admit to it openly, we show it in any case by drinking a little too much, by smoking a little too much – we become irritated or withdrawn, we develop an ulcer or suffer a heart attack. No matter what our specific reaction, our job performance suffers and we do in fact become less able to cope, unfit for our job or further promotion. Our various failings, however, are more often than not rather the result of maintaining secrecy about stress. This secrecy actually handicaps us in managing our stress effectively – you rarely do something to improve a situation when you deny its existence.

Understanding the concept of stress

Stress and stressor
The term "stress" is used in at least two contexts. In the first place it refers to the inner experience of:

- a feeling of being unable to cope with the demands of a particular situation
- anxiety, discomfort, apprehension because of the inability to cope

and the appearance of individual and characteristic patterns of physical and mental symptoms of stress and defensive behaviour.

Secondly, the term "stress" is used to denote the factors which cause the above reactions.

We shall use the term "stress" to denote the inner experiences and the term stressor/s to denote causes of stress.

Threat perception
Whether a situation becomes a stressor or not, depends on the individual in the situation and the meaning he attaches to that situation. If the individual perceives a threat to himself in one way or another, he will experience stress. If he perceives no threat in the situation he will not feel under stress.

Threat perception is personal and with a few exceptions different individuals will perceive the same situation differently.

Person A may perceive a speech-making situation as a threat – Person B not at all.

Threat perceptions are determined by factors such as:

- basic personality characteristics
- previous experiences
- expectations.

There are very few universal stressors as the following statements will indicate:

- almost everything in the work situation is at some time, or by someone, identified as a stressor
- frequently both a situation and its direct opposite can be a stressor, e.g., overwork or underwork, too many decisions to make or too few
- many stressors that have been identified, in certain studies, have in other studies been found to be sources of job satisfaction, e.g., a "poorly defined task", while causing anxiety, can also provide scope for initiative and satisfaction of a job well done.

Stress development and subsequent reactions
The experience of stress is followed by either adaptive or non-adaptive behaviour.

Adaptive behaviour deals directly with both the stress and the stressor by:

- admitting stress
- seeking and implementing solutions.

Adaptive behaviour not only does away with the current stressor, but also prepares the individual to deal with similar situations in future.

Non-adaptive behaviour, on the other hand, fails to deal directly with the stressor by:

- denying (or trying to) that stress is felt
- self-protecting reactions.

While non-adaptive behaviour may remove the stress and stressor, it is likely to do so only temporarily. It does not alleviate the anxiety and/or other symptoms and does not help the individual to cope with future similar situations.

For example:

A manager deals actively with the job environment by both receiving and making demands. Then a particular configuration of demands (a hazily worded request from his superior) coming in a particular situation (already very busy) is perceived by this particular individual (who detests being seen as incompetent) as a stressor.

His immediate defensive reaction might well be to accept the request without question (thus not admitting weakness), and put it aside for a day or two (to delay admitting the fact that he doesn't understand it).

An adaptive sequel to this would be for the manager to

return fairly soon to his superior, ask some considered and pertinent questions and arrive at an understanding of the request. By so doing, the manager will:

- know what is required

- have improved the relationship with his superior and, thus, have reduced the likelihood of similar incidents happening in the future

- not normally have damaged his reputation.

A non-adaptive alternative would be for the manager to pass the assignment straight on to a subordinate, avoiding the latter whenever he asks for clarification of the task for fear of exposing his own ignorance. The likely outcomes of this course of action are:

- the work is unlikely to be satisfactory, might well have to be redone and only by sheer luck will enhance his status as a manager

- relationships with his subordinate will have deteriorated rather than improved, and

- the manager will be in no better position to deal with such incidents in future; in fact, he may be worse off as the admission of a failure to understand will be even more difficult to make.

Managing stress

The management of stress is concerned with how the switch from non-adaptive to adaptive behaviour can be achieved. The onus is, therefore, on the individual - you, to take actions which will:

- solve the present problem

- allow you to grow in competence with the managing of future stressors.

There is no way in which you can escape the experience of executive stress - you can however, improve your ability to cope with your stressors more effectively.

It is best for many reasons that the initiative comes from the individual under stress because:

- the action is more immediate

- loss of self-esteem is actually less likely - particularly in the long run

- the situation is less likely to develop to an unmanageable stage.

Steps in solving stress situations

- identifying stressors in the job situation

- clarifying exactly why you perceive these situations as stressors

- identifying your habitual responses/reactions to these stressors and clarifying whether they are adaptive or non-adaptive

- considering alternative ways of coping with these stressors

- planning steps to be taken to manage the stressors in future.

Categories of stressors

Stressors intrinsic to the job:
Stress can be caused by too much or too little work, time pressures and deadlines, fatigue from physical or mental job demands, excessive travel, long hours, having to cope with changes at work and the consequences of making mistakes. Stressors intrinsic to a job are largely explained by the function the employee performs (i.e., whether he is an accountant, market researcher, salesman, production manager, etc.) and will very often be common to a function across companies (the stressors intrinsic to a job of production manager A in company A will more likely than not

be the same as for production manager B in company B).

Role in the organisation
Stress can be caused by factors such as:

- role ambiguity

- role conflict

- responsibility for people or things

- no participation in decision-making

- not enough authority - or too much

- lack of management support

- having to reach successively higher standards of performance

- being located at organisational boundaries (i.e. salesmen, research workers, PR staff).

The concepts of role ambiguity and role conflict are important. Role conflict can occur in various ways. Most important of these are situations in which the individual receives role messages from different role senders which are well understood but incompatible. (For example, the buyer in a company will be expected by the research and development division to purchase high quality components which will make goods in accordance with their design specifications; the company accountant, on the other hand, will expect the buyer to keep costs to the minimum. The buyer has a role conflict because the two sets of expectations are incompatible.) Role ambiguity occurs when the individual is uncertain of the expectations role senders have of him, what his responsibilities are, what authority he can exercise to achieve them, etc.

Relations within the organisation

Stressors in this category are:

- poor relations with boss
- poor relations with colleagues and subordinates
- not being able to call on others for help to solve problems
- difficulty in delegating responsibility
- lack of trust
- lack of support.

These stressors are likely to become even more severe as the insistence on participation and consultation becomes stronger and the competition for scarce resources becomes more intense.

Career development

In our ambitious and achievement oriented society, career development is a major concern. Some of the significant stressors are:

- over promotion
- under promotion
- lack of job security
- fear of redundancy or retirement
- fear of obsolescence
- frustrated ambitions
- loss of status
- feeling trapped.

These stressors are severely aggravated by the rapid development of both technology and management techniques which make old ways obsolete, bring in waves of freshly trained recruits with more appropriate skills which upset the age-ordered hierarchy and add to the stress of the "older" manager.

While career development and achievements have high value, managers often have limited ability to influence their career development. Often the rules of the game are ambiguous. Do you do your job and rely on results or should you rather use your energy

to be seen by "important people"?

Organisation – membership

The mere fact of being in an organisation can be restrictive in terms of behaviour and freedom of action. Stressors in this category are:

- budgets
- uncertainty about what is happening
- no sense of belonging
- loss of identity
- office politics
- existing organisational norms
- rules, regulations, channels and procedures.

The larger the organisation, the more likely that above stressors will operate and the more powerless the individual might feel to influence them. The very necessity for conformity in large organisations often threatens individual freedom, autonomy and sense of identity.

Organisational interface with outside

Stressors that have been identified in this category are:

- boundary positions where work contact is mainly with people outside the company and which may create divided loyalties, e.g. sales people
- situations where individual attitudes and values are in conflict with those of the company
- the conflict of company and family demands.

Characteristics of the person

The factors in this category are:

- basic personality in terms of the anxiety level, level of neuroticism, tolerance for ambiguity
- inability to cope with change

- lack of knowledge
- declining abilities
- lack of insight into own motivation and goals
- lack of skill in dealing with inter-personal problems.

The individual characteristics – i.e., the personality, knowledge, experience, skill, attitudes, etc., which the person brings to the job – play an important part in the complex interaction between job and employee. Very often these characteristics determine threat perception and dictate the coping style adopted.

HOW WELL CAN YOU HANDLE STRESS?
TEST YOURSELF

Doctors, psychologists, counsellors and others who deal in the field of human behaviour tell us that we are going through a time of stress. There are many things to worry about – drug abuse, disasters, wars in various parts of the world. The list goes on and on. For most of us, however, it is not the events themselves which affect us, but how well we can cope with the resulting stresses and strains. This quiz by Jane Sherrod Singer, M.A. Psychology and Education, will give you some hints about how to live happily, calmly, even to be stimulated in a positive manner by the daily happenings of modern life.

Please select the answer nearest to your own with complete honesty.

1. **My weight**
   (a) is about right for my age, height, and bone structure
   (b) at least a stone more than I should weigh
   (c) at least a stone less than I should weigh.

2. **I take medication to help me sleep**
   (a) only if the doctor prescribes it for me
   (b) most nights
   (c) on rare occasions when I am in pain or overwrought.

3. **When it comes to hobbies, I**
   (a) have one or more which I enjoy and do well
   (b) have one which frustrates me, but I refuse to give up on it
   (c) have more important things to do than to pursue a hobby.

4. **Each day, I**
   (a) leave time just for me
   (b) am so busy with daily chores that there is no time left
   (c) hurriedly snatch a few minutes for me when I can.

5. **I feel that those around me, my family, friends**
   (a) do not understand me very well
   (b) are helpful and considerate of my feelings and needs
   (c) fight my ideas, ideals, and aspirations.

6. **As I evaluate my meals, I find that**
   (a) my diet consists primarily of junk food – crisps, fizzy drinks and sweets, etc. – which I gulp down while on the run
   (b) I follow a balanced, well-rounded diet
   (c) I rely heavily on vitamin pills to supplement and/or replace food.

7. **During the week, I**
   (a) usually take at least 30 minutes of planned exercise
   (b) exercise at least 15 minutes each day on a regular basis
   (c) consider that my working activities make up for planned exercise.

8. **During my waking hours, I**
   (a) am dependent on sound – people to talk to, TV, or radio
   (b) take time off for silence at least three times a week, doing such things as yoga, meditation, or deep relaxation
   (c) keep my wheels turning in order to accomplish the many things that need to be done.

9. **My after-work hours are**
   (a) filled by more-of-the-same. (I bring my work home or I continue my house-work.)
   (b) a time to relax or at least a time to do something different

   (c) tense and unsatisfactory because I don't know what to do with myself.

10. **When I am on a vacation, I**
    (a) don't really enjoy it because I know things are piling up at home or at work
    (b) can put home and work in the background and enjoy the change of pace and location
    (c) at times miss my home and friends.

11. **In my daily life, I have established**
    (a) a satisfactory work pattern to accomplish those things that must be done
    (b) no pattern, but work according to impulse
    (c) a balance between work and relaxation.

12. **When I see a beautiful thing in nature — such as a flower, animal, a sunset or rainbow,**
    (a) I stop and admire it unless my presence creates a safety risk or inconvenience to others
    (b) I dash on because of time-pressure
    (c) I give it a fleeting glance and sometimes later regret my haste.

13. **I consider tears**
    (a) are a safety valve to be used by men, women, and children during times of stress or sadness
    (b) permissible for only women and children
    (c) to be a sign of weakness in any adult.

14. **I consider myself to be**
    (a) a practical materialist rather than spiritual person
    (b) a person with a high degree of spiritual awareness and sensitivity
    (c) a person who sympathises with the problems of others.

Developing personal skills

SCORING

1. a = 6   b = 2   c = 4

(Most doctors feel that being overweight is more dangerous than being underweight.)

2. a = 6	b = 2	c = 4
3. a = 6	b = 4	c = 2
4. a = 6	b = 2	c = 4
5. a = 4	b = 6	c = 2
6. a = 2	b = 6	c = 4
7. a = 4	b = 6	c = 2
8. a = 4	b = 6	c = 2
9. a = 2	b = 6	c = 2
10. a = 2	b = 6	c = 4
11. a = 6	b = 2	c = 6
12. a = 6	b = 2	c = 4
13. a = 6	b = 4	c = 2
14. a = 2	b = 6	c = 4

What your scoring may mean

70-84: Your answers on this quiz indicate that you can cope with stress well. You have a physical and emotional calm that helps you sort the important from the unimportant and to make the best moves during times of pressure. The *inability* to react coolly is only for the hazard spots during stress periods.

50-68: This is about a normal score. Each of us has his breaking point which can range from some such simple cause as a dog that barks all night to the tragedy of death. If you can locate the causes of your stress, you may be able to eliminate them. If that is not possible, then it is up to you to create internal calmness, mentally, emotionally, and spiritually. Look to silence as being a major solution. It perhaps will not be easy at first to cut out the sights and sounds of the busy world, but a vast number of medical professionals are now agreeing that meditation is a key to physical health, disease resistance, and the capacity to handle stress.

28-48: You are probably a "bundle of nerves". Every little thing upsets you and stress is your constant companion. As has been suggested elsewhere in this quiz, your approach must be tri-pronged: physical, mental, and spiritual. Decide where you are weakest and approach that first. Take some time for yourself, try to be good to yourself.

A TEN-POINT PLAN FOR DEALING WITH STRESS

1
Learn to recognise when problems are developing and what the early warning signs of stress are for you. Do you get a headache, have difficulty sleeping, feel irritable?

2
Be prepared to limit your exposure to stress. Cut back your commitments, reduce your workload, resign from a committee or two.

3
Remember that your life has four cornerstones - family, work, leisure, and friends. When planning changes to the structure of one, be careful not to make any changes to another area.

4
Learn to plan your life a little more efficiently. Make lists. Think of the things that annoy you most and try to work our how you can solve the problems before they develop.

5
Learn how to relax your body when you are under pressure. By learning to relax your muscles in private you'll be able to relax them in public when you're under pressure.

6
Learn how to relax your mind. Sit with your eyes closed and day-dream.

7
Keep yourself as physically fit as possible.

8
Take a break at least once a week, and take a weekend off every now and then. When you have a holiday, make sure it is a proper holiday.

9
Don't always hide your feelings. Frustration is a major cause of stress, so make your voice heard.

10
Remember that you need a little bit of stress in your life. Problems arise when the amount of stress in your life becomes excessive. Learn what your breaking point is and you will be able to cope better with stress, and enjoy life.

COPING WITH CRITICISM

We stop ourselves from saying what we want to, living as we wish to, even being who we want to be, simply to avoid criticism and disapproval. Why does criticism hit so hard? Often because we experienced it as rejection when we were children, and also because it is usually negative and unloving.

Giving and receiving criticism tends to be handled badly

The first step to dealing assertively with criticism is to distinguish between valid criticism, invalid criticism and criticism which is nothing but thinly veiled put-down.

If you view criticism as a misunderstanding or an unsolved problem instead of a personal attack, you will have the composure necessary to deal with the situation positively. You will be able to respond instead of react to angry clients or impatient colleagues.

Responding to criticism assertively can involve any or all of the following strategies:

- Agreement – accepting your mistakes and faults without guilt, hostility or excessive apology, and agreeing with criticism if it is true.

- Disagreement – stating your disagreement when the criticism is clearly invalid.

- Disarming – listening closely for a grain of truth and admitting to that truth or, when the criticism is vague, admitting there is some possibility of truth in the statement.

- Empathy – listening out for the critic's feeling and acknowledging that feeling or rephrasing the criticism.

- Inquiry – asking a question in order to discover more about what the critic thinks.

As with all skills, those listed above will take practice. A list follows of possible responses to criticism using each of the above-mentioned skills.

Skill	Criticism	Response
Agreement	You didn't produce those sales figures as I asked.	You're right. I haven't got the figures ready yet.
Agreement	You didn't include a summary with the sales report.	I'm sorry. I didn't include the summary. You're right.
Disagreement	You're too sensitive.	I don't agree. I simply care very much about this case.
Disagreement	You're getting pushy.	I don't accept that. I'm just stating my feelings. I care about your feelings too.
Disarming	You've been slipping lately. You missed the deadline on this report.	I did miss the deadline on this particular report.
Disarming	You don't look very organised.	Maybe I don't look organised to you.
Disarming	You're getting very aggressive.	I might seem aggressive to you.
Empathy	Who do you think you are? Asking all these questions.	I see you are angry. I'm sorry about that.
Empathy	What's the matter with this company anyway? Are you all stupid? Why can't I get my question answered?	I understand your feelings. I'd like to help you.
Inquiry	You're getting very aggressive.	It may seem like that. What am I doing that makes you say I'm aggressive?
Inquiry	You're not very organised lately.	Perhaps not. How would you like me to handle things differently?
Inquiry	You didn't do the proposal the way I wanted it.	What would you have liked me to do differently?

Developing personal skills

HOW TO BE ASSERTIVE WITHOUT BEING AGGRESSIVE

What is assertive behaviour?

Behaving assertively means putting oneself forward boldly, positively and insistently. To be assertive implies maintaining and defending one's rights in an affirmative way. Assertiveness should be distinguished from two other styles of behaviour: timidity and aggressiveness.

Managers who behave timidly tend to feel inhibited. Such behaviour is characterised by agreeing with others regardless of how one feels, not expressing one's opinions, walking and speaking somewhat hesitantly, maintaining a fearful type of expression and demeanour. Managers who behave in a timid way give the impression that they think poorly of themselves. They also communicate inadequacy and self-deprecation, thus drawing negative reactions from others which can result in actual feelings of inadequacy and hurt.

Managers who behave aggressively tend to act and feel hostile toward others. They characteristically speak loudly and abusively, vigorously and vehemently expressing their feelings and opinions, and accusing, blaming and demeaning others. Such managers communicate that they feel superior to others. By behaving aggressively, they give the impression that they think badly of others and have the right to hurt others to avoid hurting themselves. They also communicate an inadequacy that considers self-enhancement at the expense of others justified, and creates defensiveness on the part of those who are the objects of their aggression.

Managers who behave in an assertive way, on the other hand, tend to feel confident and positive toward others. Behaving assertively allows a manager to respond spontaneously, to use a conversational tone and moderate volume, to address the issue, and openly express feelings and opinions. Managers who behave assertively tend to communicate that they regard others as having equal value and are seeking to achieve goals without hurting others or themselves.

What does it do?

Assertiveness helps to increase a manager's sense of personal worth by avoiding both a self-demeaning and a hostile approach to others. Assertiveness allows managers to act in their own best interest, to stand up for themselves and to exercise their rights without denying the rights of others. Managers who can behave assertively will tend to reduce the anxiety usually associated with interacting in difficult situations and experience the pleasure of trusting themselves to express feelings and opinions honestly.

Behaving assertively increases self-confidence, self-acceptance, and self-reliance. By behaving assertively managers enhance their self-respect and earn the respect of others. Assertive behaviour encourages self-expression without hurting others.

Hints for assertive body lanaguage

A person's body language is often a reliable indicator of his behavioural attitude. Assertiveness, timidity and aggression are all expresssed through eye contact, posture, facial expressions, and vocal tone, inflection, volume and fluency. Here are some hints on the non-verbal behaviour associated with an assertive person:

- *Eye contact:* Making direct contact with the other person is an effective way of indicating that you are serious and sincere about what you are saying. A relaxed, steady gaze, coupled with occasional looking away, emphasises your intent. Let the other person know that you are asserting yourself by looking directly at him. Avoid looking out the window, or at the floor or ceiling. Talk and listen while maintaining relaxed, but direct, eye contact.

- *Posture:* Assertiveness is expressed through a person's posture. When you face the other, stand or sit at an appropriately close distance, lean forward to the other, and hold your head up. When you are attempting to be assertive, leaning toward the other person is stronger than leaning away, while an erect posture, rather than a slumping one, adds power to what you say.

- *Gestures:* A statement that is accentuated with appropriate gestures projects more assertiveness than stiff or folded arms. Relaxed hands and arms suggest a willingness to express oneself openly and with a sense of personal enthusiasm. Although overly enthusiastic gesturing can be distracting, purposeful gestures that are consistent with how you feel and what you are saying are helpful in projecting a calm but determined assertiveness.

- *Facial expressions:* Assertiveness requires facial expressions that support the point you are trying to make.

- *Vocal tones:* Assertiveness requires a level (although not monotonous), well-modulated vocal pattern. The inflections should emphasise and carry the meanings you intend to convey and attempt to communicate. Your voice should be loud enough to be heard easily. Your words should flow smoothly and at a rate that is neither very rapid or very slow. Fluency can be a genuine asset in being assertive.

Eight steps to being assertive

Behaving assertively is defined and analysed in terms of specific behaviours. Thus, the development of assertiveness skills involves a systematic step-by-step procedure for changing behaviours. The key to learning this technique is the practice of new ways of behaving. Here are eight steps to changing non-assertive behaviour and learning assertive behaviour:

Step one: Analyse your own assertive behaviour. Rate your ability and characteristic behaviour in dealing with your own and others' anger. Think about your reaction toward authoritarian behaviour and about the situations in which this tends to occur. How do you deal with situations where you have to decide whether to make or refuse requests? Are you able to initiate and sustain meaningful communication? How do you rate your performance on the various aspects of non-verbal assertive behaviour?

Step two: Imagine how you would handle a situation assertively. Reconstruct the details vividly, including things like what was said and how you felt. Write down the assertive behaviours (distinguishing them from timid or aggressive ones) that intuitively seemed to make the situation go better.

Step three: Observe an assertive model. This can be done by watching a friend or colleague who seems assertive and seeing how he implements the technique. The situation that you reviewed and imagined could be role played. You could observe someone else taking the assertive role, after which the verbal, non-verbal, and vocal behaviours should be discussed. Note the consequences of being assertive. Talk about how the incident could be handled differently. Talk about specific behaviours.

Step four: Imagine yourself dealing effectively with the situation. Visualise yourself being assertive, using the behaviours discussed earlier. Imagine different ways of handling the situation that you feel are consistent with your own self-concept. Attempt to arrive at a comfortable style.

Step five: Try being assertive. Begin slowly but decisively. Start with a role playing situation. You take the role of the assertive person. Select a situation with which you would like to experiment in real life. Act consistently with the style that you imagined earlier. Review how you handled the situation, with emphasis on the positive dimensions of your behaviour. Work to adopt more assertive behaviours.

Step six: Move to a real experience. Pick a time and place in which you will experiment with your new behaviours. The important thing is to be assertive. Get out and do your thing!

Step seven: Return to rehearsal. Evaluate the real experience and participate in some additional role-playing experiences. Practice until you respond more or less automatically.

Step eight: Go back to the arena. Continue the active practice of being assertive until it is a natural part of your life.

In the new corporation, creativity and individuality are organisational treasures
— *John Naisbitt*

To disregard what the world thinks of us is not only arrogant but utterly shameless
— *Cicero*

Want the job

The biggest part of turning an interview into a job is wanting the job in the first place. This is not as easy as it sounds, as it requires a knowledge of yourself and a knowledge of the company and the post for which you are applying. Sometimes it is not possible to find out as much as you would like about a job before you go to an interview. In that situation you should find out all you can while the interview progresses. If you do not first know yourself, however, you will not know whether or not you like what you are hearing about the job. You will not feel that interest and enthusiasm which could make you a special candidate in the eyes of the interviewer.

Something in reserve

Strangely enough, another factor in turning an interview into a job can be having the safety net of other interviews lined up or other applications in the pipeline. This may seem to contradict the requirement that you want the job. If you do want the job, why apply for others? The answer is, to give yourself some more power in the interview. It is probably better not to mention other applications, but they will give you the inner confidence of being a seller of sought-after services - your own. This confidence allows you to see the whole process objectively and makes less likely the absurdity of saying anything to get the job. This absurdity can creep up easily - even where the interview is revealing more and more clearly that the job is unsuitable - perhaps because we don't like to admit the error in putting in the application, or perhaps from a need to seek approval or avoid failure. Saying anything to get the job, however, often alienates the interviewer, or worse, brings you

a job that is entirely inappropriate.

Sometimes people are lucky - they 'know' they want a job, they make that single application, the interview confirms everything they thought, they get the job. More often it is better to feel that you can say no to the job without being right back where you started.

Knowing yourself

Getting to now yourself should take place before you even begin to look for a job, but it is never too late to start. The following three questions will help, whether you are in the planning stages of a job hunt or about to go to your first interview:

• Who am I?

• What are my skills?

• What are my achievements/ experience?

The first of these - who am I, or what is my personality - can be a complicated study, but for job-hunting purposes it is not necessary to probe all the subtleties and contradictions you may feel constitute yourself. Think of the ways in which you describe other people - is that person an introvert or an extrovert, excitable or quiet, anxious or calm? - and apply them to yourself. A book, such as Hans Eyseneck's *Know Your Own Personality* could be useful, and it is increasingly likely that your employer will be using a system of assessing your personality similar to Eyseneck's.

If you are thinking that these simple measures are unnecessary, and that you know yourself well enough without any investigation, remember that if you attend an executive recruitment agency you may well be asked to complete such a test.

You should arrive at a broad

description of yourself with which you and perhaps a few of your acquaintances are happy. It is essential to be realistic about yourself, otherwise you may find yourself applying for jobs for which you have the intellectual but not the emotional aptitude.

The second two questions - what are my skills? and what are my achievements/experience? - can be more easily answered. You should nevertheless sit down and list them along with your personality traits.

When you are considering your present and future career, consider them in the light of this list. Are you where you should be, or where you could be? When you are considering applying for a job, check the requirements against the list and when you are preparing for the interview, think about this list.

What to take to the interview

There is no harm in taking some copies of your CV to an interview. You may need to hand one to an unprepared interviewer or you may need to refer to it yourself to make sure of some dates. It is better not to refer to it, of course, but the worst thing is to make a mistake about your own past which the interviewer, a complete stranger, puts right for you. You should also take paper and a pen or pencil and a short list of questions to ask at the interview. The questions should be about the nature of the job itself. Did anybody do the job before? Why is it vacant? Who will you be working with? Make sure to modify this list as the interview goes along, otherwise at the end you may ask a question which has already been answered. Do not ask about holidays and fringe benefits. You can find out if these things are acceptable after you are offered the job. If neither party has mentioned the rate of pay, however, you should ask about it. Try to get the interviewer to mention a figure first. If it is high you are in luck. If it is lower than you expect you can try to raise it. If you mention a figure first you could immediately award yourself a pay cut. You should, however, have a fair rate in mind for the job, so that, if pressed, you do have an answer ready.

Appearance

Men should always wear a suit to an interview unless they know it will be inappropriate. Women should be smart but not sexy. Neither men nor women should wear noticeable scent.

When you arrive

Never arrive late or too early. If necessary, spend some time in the locality before attending the interview. Be polite to all staff before you meet the interviewer. When you meet him, shake hands, make eye contact and introduce yourself. Do not use his first name and do not sit until invited. Do not smoke, even if invited.

The interview

The interviewer wants to find out whether:

• You can do the job

• You will fit in

• You are affordable

To find answers to the first two questions will take up most of the interview. The interviewer has two basic methods of enquiry at his disposal. He can either ask questions which will elicit useful information (e.g. How do you cope in stressful situations?) or questions to see how you react (e.g. Don't you think this whole thing is a waste of time? – a question designed to provoke a stressful situation). Most interviewers use

both techniques with a strong bias towards the information-gathering type of question. The second technique may be rare, but you are almost certain to come across it, so be prepared.

Many interviewers will be using one of the assessment charts shown below, or something extremely similar. A mark out of five or ten will be given on each criterion.

Seven-point plan of the National Institute of Industrial Psychology:

• Physical make-up

• Attainments

• General intelligence

• Special aptitudes

• Interests

• Disposition

• Circumstances

Five-point grading devised by John Munro-Fraser:

• First impressions and physical make-up

• Qualifications

• Brains and abilities

• Motivation

• Adjustment

Each of these lists is an expansion of the first two points in the trio mentioned earlier – Can you do the job? Will you fit in? Are you affordable?

To mark you on these five or seven criteria, the interviewer may ask any number of questions of the type that seek information or of the type that create situations in which you can react. Some questions of course fulfil both functions – in particular the 'What is your biggest weakness?' question that everybody dreads. The question is itself stress-inducing and can reveal actual weaknesses.

Other difficult questions include:

• What are you most proud of?

• Why do you want to work for XYZ company?

• What did you dislike about your last job?*

• How long will you stay with XYZ company?

• Why are you earning so little?

• Why are you leaving your current job?*

• Where do you plan to be in five years' time?

*NB: Never speak ill of your former employer. Refer only to 'drawbacks' or possibly absence of opportunities.

If you have thought carefully about who you are, what your skills are and what you have achieved, compared the list with the job for which you are applying, and thought about it in relation to your present and future career, you will be able to find good answers to these questions. Whatever answer you give, always remember not to ramble. When you have said all you have to say, bring your answer to a close.

Getting the edge on your rivals

Knowing yourself will enable you to apply for the right jobs and to show the interviewer that the job suits you. Something that may give you the edge over your unseen rivals is to remember that your interviewer is probably part of a profit-making concern and that he needs an employee who will make or save money. At every opportunity find out how you can contribute to the profitability of the company and bring that to the attention of the interviewer. As in many situations, if you can show someone they have a need which you can address, the selling is almost done.

Are you affordable?

Usually both candidate and interviewer know the rate of pay for the job because it was advertised along with the job. Sometimes, however, the rate of pay is not mentioned, or the band within which the pay is to fall is very large, or the interview is for an unadvertised job. In such situations, the interviewer may be wondering what to offer if he wants you for the job. You, on the other hand, should not be wondering what you will accept, because, as we said earlier, you should already know. Have in mind a figure that you consider a fair rate for the job, a figure you consider to be the minimum rate for the job and one figure in between. This way, if you have to 'show' first, you will not be left floundering for something to say.

Ending

If your questions about the job have not already been answered, you should ask them now.

Before you leave you must find out what happens next, but parting shots about other interviews and applications are not advisable as they may be seen as empty threats. Your back-up applications are to give you confidence, not to put pressure on the interviewer. If you are actually holding other offers, however, or if you receive another offer after the interview, those offers can be used to speed up a decision, because they cannot be seen as empty threats.

As you leave the building be polite to everyone, as you were on the way in. Follow up the interview by a letter. A simple note thanking the interviewer for his time will keep your name in circulation without appearing pushy.

Summary

Know yourself, the company and the job and match your personality, skills and experience against the requirements of the job. If you do this and still really want the job, then you will be able to answer the most difficult questions an interviewer can put to you.

The best leaders are apt to be found among those executives who have a strong component of unorthodoxy in their character. Instead of resisting innovation, they symbolize it
– David Ogilvy

A corporation without a strategy is like an airplane weaving through stormy skies
– Alvin Toffler

HOW TO ASK FOR A PROMOTION OR A PAY RISE

At some stage in his professional career, each promising and developing manager has to face asking for a promotion or a pay rise. Although the nature, content and intention of this kind of interaction differ significantly from those of the employment seeking interview, one basic golden rule applies in all of these situations: Planning is of paramount importance!

One of the main differences, however, is that in asking for a promotion or a pay rise, the candidate is already a part of the organisation, and should take advantage of having a degree of intimate knowledge of the organisational context. From this viewpoint, the candidate is able to relate his professional and personal qualities to the requirements of the new position or the higher salary. In addition, the candidate will know the relevant superior and should therefore be able to make an effective approach to that person.

Here is a number of hints on how to prepare for asking for a promotion or a pay rise:

Review your suitability

Your endeavour to ask for a promotion or a pay rise will be successful when your superiors realise that there is a match between your personal and professional qualifications and the requirements of the higher position. The question *Is this person qualified?* will naturally be uppermost in the minds of these persons. Your goal is to show and confirm this match during the interview, to demonstrate that your qualities and the relevant requirements for promotion or higher pay fit together to make an acceptable picture.

Be able to argue and demonstrate your best qualities

Your qualifications for a promotion or a pay rise include not only your previous applicable work experience, education and social activities, but also any saleable personal characteristics you have. You should be able to justify clearly any claims you make about personal attributes which would enhance and support your request for a promotion or a pay rise. Remember that your superiors will be critical and are not interested in statements such as *I'm a self-starter* unless you can give evidence of your initiative. Be prepared to show and prove that you are dependable, adaptable, mature, and so on. Any activities that can provide the necessary evidence should be prepared and integrated into your arguments. In short, pick your major qualities, document them, review them, and be prepared to talk about them during the interview.

Be totally informed about the requirements

One factor that may hinder your chances of being granted a promotion or a pay rise is an apparent lack of knowledge about the requirements accompanying the position or the higher salary. This will undoubtedly be interpreted as a lack of interest, or even worse, selfish opportunism, on your part. As you will discover in the interview, your superiors will normally ask you why you consider yourself suitable for a promotion or a pay rise. Your knowledge about the requirements for higher honours will demonstrate your interest in the company and its objectives. Remember that your superiors will not only be primarily interested in you as an individual, but also in your ability to make a meaningful contribution to the overall goals of the organisation and of your particular division.

Prepare to ask sensible questions

Asking relevant and sensible questions about the responsibilities accompanying a promotion or a pay rise will help show the interviewer that you are interested and at the same time help you to learn more about your potential new status. Be sure to avoid questions that might create ego-threat or other negative feelings in your superiors.

Think through all the possible questions you may be asked

You can undoubtedly expect to be asked a number of questions when requesting a promotion or a pay rise. Many of these questions are typical of all similar situations, while others will be specifically relevant to the context of the position and the accompanying responsibilities. Perhaps the best way to think through these questions is to jot them down, and even rehearse your answers to them. Your superiors will undoubtedly be assessing your logic and oral communication skills, and you can enhance this assessment by responding immediately to the questions in a clear and concise way.

Consider your appearance

Don't let the simplicity of this suggestion mislead you. One survey of practising interviewers found that in a 20-minute interview the average interviewer had made a decision within the first four minutes of the interview. Some interviewers claim that they can decide whether a candidate is suitable for a position the very instant the applicant enters the room. Obviously, this will apply more to instances where persons from outside the organisation apply for a position. However, your appearance, posture and general non-verbal behaviour will contribute to the decision by your superiors whether to grant your request for a promotion or a pay rise.

Consider your approach

Remember that you will be initiating the interview to put across your request for a promotion or a pay rise. One of the crucial factors to consider is your timing of the interview. Do not schedule the meeting at a time which will not be conducive to your intentions.

You will have to decide whether to arrange the meeting for early in the day, before the hustle and bustle of work pressures, or even after normal working hours in a more relaxed atmosphere. Your decision will be determined by the specific persons involved, and your past experiences as well as your present relationships with them. Another question to consider is whether to give written notice of your intentions in advance of the actual interview. Here, once again, you should be guided by a careful assessment of the persons involved, and the relative advantages or disadvantages of putting pen to paper in preparation for the personal

interview.

Summary

Obviously, asking for a promotion or a pay rise calls for persuasion – you are trying to shape the decisions of your superiors. While there are no hard and fast rules for a successful request for a promotion, thorough preparation is undoubtedly the golden rule. Make use of your intimate knowledge of your own qualities and capabilities, the requirements and responsibilities of the position, the general objectives of the organisation and the specific division, and of the persons involved in the decision and the interview.

Am I qualified?

One of the most important questions to consider when asking for a promotion or a pay rise, is whether your own personal characteristics match the requirements of the position and the responsibilities which will be expected of you. Here is a list of qualities that your superiors may consider to be important. Check your suitability for a promotion or a pay rise by marking both your own performance on each attribute and the requirements of the position on the same attributes. In the interview, concentrate on those attributes in which you are particularly strong.

	Superior	Above ave	Average	Below ave	Poor
Leadership skills					
Initiative					
Decision-making					
Written communication					
Oral communication					
Adaptability					
Professional conduct					
Working with others					
Enthusiasm					
Dependability					
Self-confidence					
Maturity					

MANAGING
YOUR
TEAM

THE ART OF DELEGATION

What is delegation?

All managers face a paradox: they need to produce results beyond individual capabilities. The solution to this paradox is not to do more, but to delegate more.

Delegation is more than just assigning work to someone else. It always means making your subordinate accountable for results. It usually means giving that person the latitude to make decisions about the ways to reach those results. That is not to say that to delegate is to abdicate. You always monitor and control the tasks you delegate. This is necessary because you cannot shed the ultimate responsibility for their completion.

A delegated task is one for which you pass specific responsibility to a subordinate. Naturally, subordinates also complete the essentials of their own jobs without much contact with you. And you yourself have a number of duties that you must always handle personally. Delegation covers the large group of tasks between these two areas, those duties that you could handle yourself, but choose to pass on to subordinates.

Delegation is always a tool, never an end in itself. Your success in delegation will never be measured by how you go about delegating, to whom you delegate, or how often you delegate. Rather, you will always be judged according to the results you achieve through delegation.

Why delegate?

Practising delegation improves your ability to manage. Because delegation is an interpersonal process, the act of delegating enhances your ability to work with others. Telling someone to do something requires little skill. Delegating authority and responsibility to others requires adeptness in communication, a willingness to listen, an ability to motivate, convey trust and inspire loyalty.

You may now be asking: "Once I have delegated a substantial portion of my current work, what do I do with myself?" The answer:

- You *plan*. You set goals, consider contingencies, devise methods for achieving results. You look ahead.

- You *direct*. You guide subordinates towards effective efforts without making decisions for them. You check their work to keep them on track.

- You *organise*. You devise structure and policy that is best suited to maintaining efficiency within your sphere of control.

Delegation clears away time for all these important managerial tasks. It helps you to avoid crises and to cope with them when they come. It turns you from a "doer" into a true manager.

Tasks to delegate

The following guidelines can help you isolate tasks which are suitable for delegation. Naturally, you must evaluate each task on its own merits. However, those that fall into these categories are worth considering:

- Routine
- Trivia
- Special skills
- Chores
- Pet projects

Routine
When you do a task repeatedly, that spotlights it as one to delegate. Why? First, because a routine task is usually easy to pass on to a subordinate. You've done it yourself. You're aware of any problems that may come up. You approach it with tested methods.

Second, delegating routine pays big dividends. Once you've prepared the delegatee, set up controls, and passed on the task, you're a winner – you benefit each time the person performs it. The results you achieve from passing on routine tasks are greater than those that flow from a one-time delegation.

Trivia
It's easy for managers to become involved in many tasks that have very little impact on the results they are trying to achieve. You know the type of situation. Someone has to arrange for a service contract on the photocopy machine and nobody knows whose responsibility it is; you've been asked to make a decision about the layout of the reception room; a repairman turns up to work on the power cables and needs someone to explain the problem to him.

Tasks under the heading of trivia are prime targets for delegation. First, they take up your time – often a great deal of your time – without producing really important results. Second, they rarely require the skills of a manager. A subordinate can handle them adequately. Third, they are often easy to delegate. And finally, they give the delegatee a chance to exercise authority and decision-making in an activity where the consequences of poor handling are not devastating.

Special skills
The delegation of tasks that require special skills is often one of the easier and more natural forms of delegation. Say, for example, you have been given the task of implementing a new computerised inventory system. You are a production manager, but you're familiar with the basics of data processing. You come to a point, however, where you have to

choose from among various types of software for specific applications. You could research the options and make the decision yourself. Or you could delegate the task to the computer programmer who handles your department's current data processing needs.

This is a clear case for delegation. Let the subordinate apply his special knowledge to the task. Brief him on the criteria you require. Exercise control by making him report back to you before buying.

Chores
Chores may fall under the categories of routine or trivia. But one characteristic that always marks a chore is that you don't like doing it.

Anything can become a chore. Consider those long drawn-out meetings that eat up time and produce few results; reports you've completed many times before; complex scheduling; tedious research. With too much repetition, all these tasks can become dull and dreaded. The best way to rid yourself of them is to delegate.

Delegating a chore means an expanded view of the department's functioning, a new challenge, an escape from monotony, to the subordinate.

Another factor justifies delegation of chores. Because delegated tasks are new to your subordinates, they may bring to these tasks a new interest and enthusiasm that allow them to do the job better than you would have done. Delegation removes routine tasks that you approach half-heartedly.

Pet projects
It may seem paradoxical to delegate the aspects of your job that you most enjoy. Yet these are often the tasks that you hang on to even though they don't represent the best use of your time and energy. They may be related to your area of expertise or to earlier positions you've held with the company.

Naturally, this doesn't mean that you need to delegate every pleasant aspect of your job. Many true managerial tasks are enjoyable. The point made here is that you risk retaining tasks that are easy to delegate simply because they're your pet projects.

Tasks not to delegate

Tasks that generally should not be delegated include:

- Ritual
- Policy-making
- Specific personnel matters
- Crises
- Confidential matters

Ritual
Some duties depend more on your position than on your skills. While anyone could do them, only you can do them effectively because of who or what you are. Such tasks call for your position, your prestige, your title.

Policy-making
Policy sets the limits of decision-making. Managers can delegate tasks to be accomplished within established policies. They should not delegate responsibilities that require the delegatees to make decisions that actually determine policy.

Specific personnel matters
A large part of a manager's responsibility involves working with people. Every contact you have with one of your subordinates involves a human element, a crossflow of emotions and perceptions. Because these contacts involve evaluation, discipline, praise, resolution of disputes and handling of crises, you should as a rule not delegate specific staff-related matters.

Confidential matters
Maintaining the secrecy of confidential information is a vital responsibility for a manager. Clearly any form of delegation that requires you to reveal confidential information is inappropriate. Personnel data, customer information, salaries, trade secrets and security data are examples of information which often fall into the confidential category.

Selecting the delegatee

Ideally, the person you choose to do the work should have the knowledge, skills, motivation and time needed to get it done to your complete satisfaction. Frequently, however, you will have to use someone who has less than ideal experience, knowledge or skills. In these cases you should try to select an individual who has intelligence, natural aptitude and, above all, willingness to learn how to do the job with help and guidance. This is how people develop, and the development of your staff should be your conscious aim whenever you delegate.

You are looking for someone you can trust. You don't want to over-supervise, so you have to believe that the person you select will get on with it and have the sense to come to you if he is stuck or before he makes a bad mistake.

How do you know whom you can trust? The best way is to try people out first on smaller and less important tasks, increasingly giving them more scope so that they learn how far they can go and so that you can observe how they get on. If they get on well, their sense of responsibility and powers of judgement will increase and improve and you will be able to trust them with more demanding and responsible tasks.

The elements of delegation

When you delegate you should ensure that your subordinate understands:

- Why the work needs to be done

- What he is expected to do

- The date by which he is expected to do it

- The authority he has to make decisions

- The progress or completion reports he should submit

- How you propose to guide and monitor him

- The resources and help he will have to get the work done.

Your subordinate may need guidance on how the work should be done. The extent to which you spell it out will clearly depend on how much he already knows about how to do the work. You don't want to give directions in such laborious detail that you run the risk of stifling your subordinate's initiative. Follow Robert Heller's golden rule: "If you can't do something yourself, find someone who can – and then let him do it in his own sweet way".

Monitoring performance

At first you may have to monitor a subordinate's performance carefully. But the sooner you can relax and watch progress informally the better.

You will have set target dates, and you should keep a reminder of these in your diary so that you can ensure they are achieved. Don't allow your subordinates to become careless about meeting deadlines.

Without being oppressive, you should ensure that progress reports are made when required and that you discuss deviations from the original plan in good time. You will have clearly indicated to your subordinate the extent of his authority to act without further reference to yourself. He must therefore expect to be reprimanded if on any occasion he exceeds his brief or fails to keep you informed. You don't want any surprises and your subordinate must understand that you will not tolerate being kept in the dark.

Try to restrain yourself from undue interference with the way the work is being done. It is, after all, the results that count. Of course, you must step in if there is any danger of things going off the rails. Rash decisions, overexpenditure and ignoring defined and reasonable constraints and rules must be prevented.

There is a delicate balance to be achieved between hedging someone around with restrictions which may appear petty and allowing him licence to do what he likes. You must use your knowledge of the subordinate and the circumstances to decide where the balance should be struck. The best delegators are those who have a comprehensive understanding of the strengths and weaknesses of their staff and the situation in which they are working.

Every business has a belief system – and it is at least as important as its accountancy system or its authority system

– Alvin Toffler

It is surely a good thing to know how to command as well as how to obey

– Aristotle

HOW EFFECTIVELY DO YOU DELEGATE?

The effective manager is always the person who knows when and how to delegate work to subordinates. According to the managing director of one very large company: "The single most important criterion of managerial effectiveness is how efficiently authority is delegated". The do-it-yourself executive faces a limited field for growth within the company, while the thinker and planner gets the job done through others and has a bright future. Take a moment to check your approach by answering these questions:

	Yes	No
Do you have enough time during the course of each day for creative thinking and planning?	☐	☐
When subordinates come to you with problems, do you help them find solutions rather than solve the problems yourself?	☐	☐
Do you train your people to qualify for higher level assignments and tasks?	☐	☐
Do you generally have confidence and faith in most of the people who report to you?	☐	☐
In delegating, do you do your best to match the individual to the job at hand?	☐	☐
Do you seek out your subordinates' unused talents and skills?	☐	☐
When you delegate work and the authority that goes with it, do you give your people a chance to prove what they can do without your peering over their shoulders 20 times a day?	☐	☐
Do you set high standards of performance for every assignment, and monitor the work to make sure those standards are met?	☐	☐
Do you make it clear to your people that you are available for guidance any time it is needed?	☐	☐
Are you flexible enough to permit employees to do the best job they can in their own way?	☐	☐
Do you check employee attitudes and aspirations before delegating with the realisation that your most ambitious people are the best ones to delegate to?	☐	☐
Do you try to delegate to as many employees as possible?	☐	☐
Do you let your people know you're there to help in a crisis?	☐	☐
Do you establish realistic controls – and control points – to keep track of work progress?	☐	☐
Do you make a point of complimenting workers and expressing your appreciation when they do an outstanding job?	☐	☐

Total number of yes answers: _____

Your rating: A score of 14 or 15 yes's ranks you as outstanding. Any score under 9 indicates you're handling too much detail yourself.

MANAGING YOUR BOSS

Many managers take time and energy to develop good relationships with subordinates but ignore the importance of managing relationships with their superiors.

A good relationship with a boss revolves around mutual dependence and is an essential aspect of effective management.

This situation of mutual dependence requires that you:

• acquire a thorough knowledge of your boss and of yourself, paying particular attention to strengths, weaknesses, work styles, and needs

• use this knowledge to manage a compatible working relationship – one which suits both parties' work styles and is in line with mutual expectations.

Gaining an understanding of your boss means you need to be familiar with his goals and pressures, strengths, weaknesses and working style. Without this basic information, the manager can blunder into conflicts which could be avoided. Because priorities are constantly changing, managers need to seek out information about their bosses in an ongoing way, questioning them and watching for clues in their behaviour.

Being sensitive to a boss's style of working and making the necessary adaptations can go a long way to smoothing the relationship. For example, one boss may be formal and prefer rigidly structured meetings, another may be more informal.

You also need to know your own strengths, weaknesses, needs and working style. While you can't transform your own personality, or that of your boss, you can become aware of the factors that cause friction.

Although your relationship with your boss is one of mutual dependence, you are more dependent on the boss than the other way around. This dependence can result in subordinates feeling frustrated or angry because they can't always make their own decisions. Some managers may rebel against this, and may disagree with the boss just for the sake of it, viewing the boss as the enemy. On the other hand, there are some subordinates who are overdependent, and will agree with the boss even if they know the decision is a bad one. They tend to see the boss as infallible and all-knowing.

Both these points of view result in an unrealistic view of the boss. In most cases the boss is neither a hostile enemy, nor a perfect paragon of virtue, but human and fallible like anyone else.

While it is not easy to alter one's attitude to authority, it can be useful to be aware of this.

Once you have a clear picture of both yourself and your boss you can develop a working pattern that suits both, and that results in both becoming more effective and productive.

A good relationship with a boss will allow for differences in work style. A manager can adjust working methods – during meetings for example – to fit in with the boss's needs. Other adjustments can be made according to how much information the boss wants and how he wants it presented, how much he wants to delegate.

It is also important for boss and manager to be able to draw on each other's strengths and help out with weaknesses. It is up to you as manager to find out what the boss's expectations are. This could be done by drawing up a memo dealing with important issues, sending it to the boss for approval, and following up with discussions. Another boss may insist on a system of regular meetings at which objectives are reviewed.

The manager also needs to let the boss know what his own expectations are. This becomes particularly important if the boss sets unrealistic targets.

Managers need to find ways to keep the boss informed about what they are doing. This upward channelling of information can be difficult if the boss doesn't want to hear about problems. Be careful of underestimating what the boss needs to know, but on the other hand avoid using up his time over minor issues.

It is vital to a boss to be able to feel he can depend on and trust his subordinates. For this reason it is important for managers to meet deadlines very strictly and avoid making promises they can't keep.

By managing your relationship with your boss effectively you can streamline your job and iron out many potential problems. Also keep in mind that he's the person who decides whether – and how fast – you move up the ladder. He can make your life a misery if your relationship turns sour.

It's important to understand what sort of person your boss is, because:

• it will enable you to prevent friction and work more efficiently

• you will be a step ahead of colleagues who don't take mental notes about how the boss works

• knowing what makes a boss effective or otherwise will help you to hone your own management skills.

Notice how your boss

• schedules his day
• develops plans
• conducts a meeting
• delegates responsibility
• gives and takes criticism
• deals with complaints
• researches information or problems
• works under pressure
• acts when angry
• apologises

Most information can be picked up by observing his behaviour and being alert to letters, memos and conversations. Or simply ask.

GUIDELINES FOR WORKING WITH YOUR SECRETARY

Remember that your secretary looks to you for guidelines. Whether you are aware of it or not, your style of management is making an impact on her own development. There is no secretarial school that can prepare a secretary fully for her position. You, and the environment of work, are her main tutors. This is a responsible position.

If you had a very good secretary, and now have a secretary who is still learning to adapt to your style, don't make comparisons. Ask yourself whether **you** can take the credit for the previous secretary's performance. If you feel you can, why not develop your present secretary's abilities?

As the person who translates your ideas into a working reality, your secretary is certainly worth developing!

(As elsewhere in this book, the pronouns are chosen for convenience and because they reflect the usual situation. The editor does not imply that there are not or should not be female managers and male secretaries.)

The following are some guidelines to show what you can do to help her feel committed to her job.

Holding a daily briefing session

Whenever you choose to do this – first thing in the morning, at the end of the day, or whenever – share present and future activities. Briefing sessions help overcome time-management crises. A manager should know what the secretary's workload looks like, and should ensure that she is working **effectively**, i.e. according to his priorities. If the secretary keeps an activity planner, this session need not take much time.

Where a secretary has more than one manager, keeping an activity planner is absolutely essential. A secretary could have a serious priority conflict should

several managers make demands on her time. Only the managers can decide on her priorities. Obviously, the most senior ranking manager will have the ultimate say, but he too should consider the effectiveness of his subordinates. If the manager's objectives are being met through a team of people, everybody should be considered.

Keeping your secretary informed of your whereabouts

When a manager is "lost" somewhere in the building, his secretary is seen as ignorant. She needs to know, not only where he is going, but also for how long. Her professional image is at stake – and so is the manager's.

Giving a secretary feedback on performance

A secretary needs to know how she is doing. The manager doesn't have to constantly be saying "thank you", but an occasional word of encouragement, or a compliment – or simply pointing out areas for improvement – will add to her feeling of emotional security.

Highlighting and presenting incoming mail in order of importance and writing routine business letters

Your secretary can highlight your incoming mail to make it easier for you to get through the mound of paperwork on your desk, but she will need to know what your commitments and objectives are. This will also help her to sort out the most important mail. She can attach a draft reply for your approval or correction. This is a tremendous time saver. Even if you don't agree with her writing style, at least the key thoughts have been processed, and the

background information researched. Your editing will be quick. As you keep doing this your secretary starts getting a feeling of your style, and how you approach matters. Eventually, she will be able to write letters for your signature.

Screening your calls, and callers

Your secretary obviously needs to know who you would like to speak to; who always has access to you; who to reroute calls to; etc. If you expect your secretary to lie for you, then you should be just as complacent when she lies to you. There is no rule, however, that says you have to take all your calls. You're entitled to manage your contacts. Your secretary simply has to state that she will take a message; and if possible, will help, or reroute the caller.

Making your appointments

Let your secretary know what you intend to discuss and how much time you think you will need. She can prepare whatever paperwork you might need. She should also know if you need any other information, or preparation, prior to the appointment.

Co-ordinating your diaries

Your secretary must have access to a control diary. It's her job to check it daily for new appointments and to remind you of commitments. If she controls the diary, she can further assist you by typing out a note of your appointments for the next day. All appointments should have telephone numbers. This makes life easy if you're out of the office, and you need to phone to the place of your next appointment to say you're delayed. If telepone numbers are noted in the diary, your secretary can trace you more quickly.

Maintaining your confidential files

Obviously, both you and your secretary will have a key to the filing cabinet, as well as a list of the files in the cabinet. You should both agree on the filing system, as you may have to have access to information when she's not around to retrieve it. Review and update the system regularly.

Taking minutes at meetings

If you let your secretary sit in on short, informal meetings, it allows her to grow into the job, and she gets used to your pattern of thinking. If she has speedwriting skills, let her use them. She can type up brief minutes of these meetings. With your editing, she will know how to handle more important, larger meetings.

Serving refreshments to visitors at meetings

A secretary normally doesn't have any objection to pouring tea, provided she is seen as a valuable helper. However, delegates at meetings often ignore her efforts to serve them, and make it very difficult. Why not stop the meeting for those brief minutes, and clear the needed space. This will save her embarrassment, and actually reduce the interruption time. Delegates lose their concentration anyway, while someone is trying to make space to put down a cup.

Making travel arrangements

Communicate the purpose of your trip, and each meeting, so that your secretary can prepare the necessary paperwork, and think through the co-ordination

of all tasks. Let your secretary know what your personal and business priorities are while you're away.

Keeping your desk uncluttered

This doesn't mean that your secretary will be making a clean sweep of your desk each time she enters the office. This means using desk organiser files. If magazines are sitting on your desk for too long, she can photocopy the table of contents and keep the magazines circulating through the company.

Your secretary will also ensure that important paperwork is not being covered up by junk mail, or unimportant messages. You would need to agree on a system, so that when you get to your desk and she's already left, your important papers are noticeable.

Monitoring media for information relevant to your position/objectives

Once again, if your secretary knows your objectives, she can keep a watchful eye on the media for news on your clients, your competition, the industry in general, raw materials, etc. If a business colleague has excelled, or his company has performed well, she can alert you to this so that you can write a congratulatory note, or make a phone call. The more knowledge your secretary has, the more effectively she operates.

Controlling physical access to you

This includes terminating visits that are eating into your time. To be effective (and credible), your secretary will need your loyalty. If you have asked not to be dis-

turbed, and an employee ignores her, tell the intruder that you would like respect for the authority you have given her. Obviously you will have to do this tactfully.

Even if you have an open-door policy, it may still be necessary to close your door from time to time. This helps when staff members need to consult you. The closed door indicates that your time is currently in short supply. They usually get the point more quickly then. Help your secretary to see that she is part of the "office culture"; part of the company and its growth within the environment of business.

DECISION-MAKING AND PROBLEM-SOLVING

Probably the most important part of any manager's job is making sound, timely objective decisions. Sound decision-making depends, in the first place, on having a clear picture of what you are trying to achieve. You must understand what the problem really is. Secondly, decision-making involves choosing from a number of possible consequences. Thirdly, there is the crucial problem of selecting the optimum solution. In practice, decisions often have to be made quickly and you may have to make one which is satisfactory rather than ideal. A decision is normally better than none at all! Finally, since decision-making is wholly directed towards achieving action, decisions must clearly be communicated to those concerned.

We list here some simple, but practical problem-solving and decision-making principles.

Be systematic

- Make decision-making a habit. You may make a few bad choices at first, but decision-making, like most other things, improves with practice. Experience will improve your judgement to the point where you will be correct most of the time.

- Brainstorm as many alternatives as you can. Be adventurous in your thinking and create enough options for yourself. Seek the greatest number of ideas and do not criticise any ideas until you cannot create any more. We tend to kill our creativity by being too critical too soon.

- Write down the decision you have to make as clearly and simply as you can. Make yourself write it out fully. Do not let yourself off with a few snippets and the thought: "Yes, I know the rest of that". You may do, but by writing it down you force

yourself to clarify it, express it and make it precise.

- Use the balance sheet approach. List all the advantages of a solution on the left side of a sheet of paper and all the disadvantages on the right side. Compare the pluses and minuses and make your decision.

- Set a deadline for making the decision. Allocate enough time (based on the importance of the decision) for gathering and analysing information. Then make your choice by the deadline. This will keep you from falling into the trap of over-analysing, vacillating and procrastinating.

Respond to your instinct

After working it all through on paper, ask yourself: "Now does this decision feel right?". If it does, do it. If it doesn't, then you need to do some more work on it.

Most of us have at one time or another acted on a decision only to think afterwards: "That wasn't right and I knew it." Sometimes we act too quickly, and when we do, we do not give our instinct time to offer its advice.

The important aspect of working through a decision on paper is not what is on the paper, but the effect working it through has on your thinking. What you must aim for is to have your logical analysis match your intuitive judgement.

Seek alternative points of view

Consult other people, particularly those who will be affected by your decision. They will be more co-operative about implementing it if they have some input into it.

Don't defend your ideas and persist with them beyond good judgement. What is important is to get good results using the best

ideas, no matter who created them.

Use ideas to build relationships, not to destroy them. Ask people what they think, but do not become angry if they are critical. Accept their opinion and respect their right to hold it.

Ask questions

Obtain the best information you can within the time limits. If you wait for the perfect information you'll wait forever. Identify key assumptions and clarify alternatives. You can only do this by asking questions.

- Take nothing for granted. Don't assume what you think something means is what the other person meant.

- Ask basic questions. Why is it being done this way? Why do we think it will have this result? What assumptions have we made?

- Seek the negative as well as the positive. What could go wrong? Why can/can't it go wrong? How is it different from our competitors' approach?

- Retain a neutral tone. Use questions to establish facts and not as a form of attack.

- Endeavour to improve the plan. Are there any better ideas? Are we satisfied that this is the most effective approach?

- Define assumptions. What assumptions have we made? Why do we believe people will act in accordance with our assumptions?

There are always assumptions. There are always alternatives. You must sharpen your questioning technique until you can identify and clarify both.

Train your subordinates

Very often managers complain that they cannot rely on their staff, that they don't think, that they act impulsively, etc. This situation generally arises from not spending the time to train and develop their staff to be able to work independently.

It is important that you agree with your subordinates on what results you expect from them. Ensure that they understand their responsibilities. Offer training and expect them to make their own decisions.

Don't tolerate reverse decision-making. Don't give a staff member a problem to solve only to have him drop it back in your lap. Prepare responses that put the responsibility back on him. Ask for example:

- What would you recommend?

- What do you think should be done?

- Don't you think this is actually your responsibility?

Make some suggestions that put the ball back in the employee's court, e.g.:

- Let's make a list of possible courses of action.

- We did it this way last time. Do you think the same approach should be followed again? Why/ Why not?

Explain to your staff that when the task is their responsibility, you are interested, but do not expect to be involved. If the decision is near the limits of their responsibility, tell them you expect to be consulted. They must still make the decision, but you would like them to approach you, outline the problem and what they propose to do.

It is important for you to develop your people. Place the emphasis on managing rather than doing. Focus on training and coaching people and on encouraging or guiding them through decision-making. Don't offer a solution to every problem presented to you. Put pressure on people and make them think for themselves. In this way you'll ensure that you are not surrounded by a passive, uncreative team which can only act on detailed instruction.

Implementing your decision

What action is required to implement your decision? Consider the following points:

- What action must be taken, and when?

- How long should each stage take to complete?

- Who will implement the decision? How and when should they be informed?

- Who else should be informed of your decision?

- What effect will your decision have on others?

- Have you established a system of follow-through and control?

If you have made a bad decision ...

How can you cut your losses when you realise you have made a poor decision? Here are some suggestions:

- Don't try to cover up. If your main concern is covering up your original error, you're likely to find yourself compounding the problem by making **more** bad decisions.

- Remember your goal average. If most of your decisions have been good ones, it will be easier to acknowledge that you, too, can trip up once in a while.

- Get advice. Consult with the people who had a hand in the decision and thrash it out with them. Or seek out someone yourself who was not involved and who is not in the chain of command.

- Let your boss know. Once you feel confident about your new plan of action, clear it with your boss. Be ready to justify your position and don't be defensive.

- Don't try to shift the blame. Others were probably involved, but you were responsible.

- Try to estimate future implications. Are you setting a precedent? If so, spell it out.

- Prepare people for a change. Have a well-thought-out phase-out period planned and let your people contribute their ideas to it. Minimising losses is just as much, and just as important, a function of management as making the most of opportunity.

SOLID SOLUTIONS vs QUICK FIXES

Oren Arnold once described the prayer of the modern society as "Dear God, I pray for patience. And I want it right now!"

We live in an instant culture that prides itself on having an easy, quick fix for everything. And not surprisingly, this is reflected in our work. Too often we go for short-term, patchwork solutions that ultimately create more problems than they solve.

Solid solutions require time, foresight, patience, sacrifice and discipline, but they have long-term payoffs. The basic difference between solid solutions and quick fixes is the difference between investing in the future and mortgaging it.

Here are ten examples of each:

A solid solution is:	A quick fix is:
1. Making a commitment to a long-term plan and staying with it.	1. Achieving short-term goals at any cost.
2. Regularly investing in new and better ways to get things done.	2. Using old equipment until it falls apart because it is the cheapest way.
3. Treating employees the way you would like to be treated. Investing in the growth and development of a committed, well-trained team.	3. Hiring and firing employees as needed.
4. Commitment to the development of new and better products and services because innovation is any business's greatest capital asset.	4. Avoiding the development of new products and services unless the payoff is high and the risk is low.
5. Having customer service that generates repeat business.	5. Trying to make a large sum of money without taking follow-up business into account.
6. Maintaining fair and stable prices that generate customer trust and loyalty.	6. Raising and lowering prices to reach current profit goals.
7. Acquiring only those businesses the company has the skills to manage.	7. Venturing into a new industry because the financial gurus promise fast payoff with low risk.
8. Rewarding people, through an ongoing programme, for finding ways to work more efficiently.	8. Slashing expenses to the bone in a cost-cutting drive.
9. Emphasising quality as the key to improving productivity.	9. Delivering the goods on time at any cost.
10. Realising that the people closest to the job usually know most about it and tapping their brain power.	10. Letting managers make all the decisions because it is faster and they are paid to do so.

To encourage solid solutions and discourage quick fixes, a company or manager can do a number of things. For example:

1. Evaluate people over longer time periods. In addition to annual evaluations, give each employee a five-year review that looks at his performance over the entire period and give large rewards to the best performers.

2. Give long-term rewards. For example, part of a top manager's yearly bonus might be in share schemes that can be cashed in only at retirement or when he leaves the company. That way, his short-term performance will have a long-term impact on his own bank account.

3. *Identify the one or two key factors that are most important to the long-term success of your team and reward people for contributing to those factors.* If quality improvement is most important, reward those who provide the greatest improvements in quality. If teamwork is essential, reward those who help develop cohesion and build morale. If you are after a larger market share, reward those who expand the company's markets. And be sure to tell **everyone** at the outset what those one or two strategic factors are.

4. *Give bonuses and recognition to those who make intelligent, long-term decisions* instead of those who just look good today.

5. *Evaluate capital investment decisions in basic research, new products and new plant and equipment over longer time periods* instead of tying them into the quarterly budget.

6. *Make a substantial part of every employee's total remuneration dependent on company prosperity.* This gives everyone an incentive to be productive.

Of course, you can't ignore short-term action. Every manager's job includes finding the right trade-off between today's profits and tomorrow's growth. Both are essential. But solid solutions need more attention and greater reward because they are so much harder to come by. Long-term success in business – or anything – is rare because it is difficult.

Are you managing as if tomorrow mattered? Reward solid solutions. They're indispensable. And be wary of quick fixes. Those who dwell on the tricks of the trade never learn the trade.

New opinions are always suspected, and usually opposed, without any other reason but because they are not already common
– John Locke

The leader must have infectious optimism ... The final test of a leader is the feeling you have when you leave his presence after a conference. Have you a feeling of uplift and confidence?
– Field Marshall Bernard Montgomery

PERFORMANCE COACHING: TARGETS, GUIDANCE AND FEEDBACK

If employees are to perform successfully they need clear and relatively stable targets at which to direct their efforts. They also need guidance to direct them towards these targets and feedback to tell them whether they are succeeding in reaching them and, if not, how far off the mark they are.

Here is the challenge. You are an archer standing in a field. It is a foggy day. In the distance, there are targets of various sizes. Some sway in the breeze, some have fallen over, some seem to lack bull's eyes, and none is marked with point values. It is impossible to see all the targets at once, and every so often someone adds, moves, or removes a target. You have been given a bow and an unlimited number of arrows. You will have six minutes to accumulate as many points as possible. What are your chances of success? Not too good? Would you like some help?

So would your employees. The performance challenge facing them is quite similar. Your employees are motivated to do their best (they would be thrown out of the game otherwise), and they have the necessary education and experience for the job (they were hired for it). But in order to give their best performance, they need your help. They cannot aim their arrows for maximum points unless they can see the target clearly, know how they will be scored and receive coaching on their shooting.

Clarifying the target

To be successful then employees need clear targets. Performance standards that are part of their job descriptions should provide these targets. Job descriptions should be up-to-date and should include the major tasks, roles, and responsibilities of the job as well as the relative importance of the different tasks.

Of course, priorities constantly change. These changes should be communicated to employees on an ongoing basis. Too often an employee leaves his or her boss' office mystified and frustrated, after being told: "Why were you wasting your time on A? I am waiting for B!" "Why didn't someone tell me?" says the employee. Thus the more specific your communication with your employees, the better their chances of hitting the target.

Performance criteria

Guidance, coaching and performance feedback can improve the score on performance rating sheets.

Effective feedback does not mean once- or twice-a-year performance appraisals; it means ongoing coaching and review of progress.

Understanding and achieving standards of performance are easier for your employees if you provide them with feedback that is:

• *Honest and specific*
Too often, managers aren't totally honest when they give feedback. An employee should be told as clearly as possible why his performance was below par. If feedback is too general, subordinates will not understand how to correct their behaviour.

• *Behaviour-orientated*
It is easier for an employee to accept feedback when it describes specific behaviour than when it makes judgements about the employee as a person. Labelling another's behaviour does not encourage constructive communication. Telling a worker that he is "too aggressive", for instance, will only make him more so. Instead, the employee should be told when he was aggressive and why such behaviour is considered aggressive. One person's aggres-

sion is another's assertiveness. To be effective, feedback must describe specific behaviour and its consequencues.

• *Constructive*
Managers need to identify not only what is wrong, but how it can be corrected. It is not enough to tell someone where he rates on the scale of job performance. The manager should also offer constructive suggestions that the person can adopt to improve.

• *Balanced*
If your subordinates kept a record of the feedback that you gave them in a typical month, what would they find? Mostly positive comments, mostly negative ones, or none at all?

The experience of hundreds of companies shows that "none at all" would be the most likely response with "mostly negative" a distant second.

Too often managers have a "straw that broke the camel's back" approach to giving feedback. They avoid giving negative feedback either because it's not worth the effort, they don't have the time, or they hope that the performance will improve.

Meanwhile, dissatisfaction with the employee mounts. Finally, an incident, often relatively insignificant, triggers an angry outburst and a barrage of complaints. The employee finds himself or herself hit with weeks of stored negative feedback at once. This is too much for the individual to absorb, much less use.

Regular feedback of a positive nature is most effective in reinforcing what the employee does well. It is also far easier for an employee to receive suggestions for improvement without being defensive if he has been recognised as well for good performance. It is easier for employees to hit the bull's-eye if they know their strengths as well as the areas needing improvement.

• *Timely*

The closer to the event that feedback is given, the more effective. Also the more frequently it is given, the more effective feedback is.

In supervising employees, you should be realistic in your expectations. Usually people don't change overnight. An employee who is learning and growing will sometimes falter. When that happens you should provide encouragement and support. The challenge of supervision is helping employees hit the target.

How good a coach are you?

Many managers are able to use opportunities created by daily work as a practical training ground. The questions that follow help you to clarify how well you are taking advantage of opportunities to use actual work as a tool for training your subordinates.

For each of the following questions put a tick in the appropriate answer box.

Question	Answer	Score
Do you intentionally seek opportunities to coach your subordinates?	☐ Often	(2)
	☐ Sometimes	(1)
	☐ Never	(0)
Do you keep a written record of your coaching activities?	☐ Yes	(2)
	☐ No	(0)
Do you establish a time schedule for coaching activities?	☐ Always	(2)
	☐ Sometimes	(1)
	☐ Never	(0)
Do you allow time for counselling and review when coaching subordinates?	☐ Always	(2)
	☐ Sometimes	(1)
	☐ Never	(0)
Does your plan for developing your staff include coaching as a means of achieving personal growth?	☐ Yes	(2)
	☐ No	(0)
Do you ask other managers to help you identify opportunities and to give you feedback when coaching activities are completed?	☐ Sometimes	(2)
	☐ Never	(0)

Scoring
0-4:   You do not use coaching as a specific technique.
5-8:   Coaching is attempted, but could be developed better.
9-12:   You are unusually systematic and probably coach well.

If your score was below nine, you could benefit from adopting a more deliberate and systematic approach to coaching.

ATTRIBUTES OF A GOOD TRAINING PROGRAMME

cf BKis.

Measure your training programme against these 13 categories, then add up the points and compare the total to the scale below:

SCORE: **3** for Thoroughly **2** for Mostly **1** for Somewhat **0** for Not at all	Thoroughly	Mostly	Somewhat	Not at all
1. **Effective**. The programme makes it as easy as possible for participants to master their jobs by minimising the struggle to learn new skills and knowledge and change old work habits.				
2. **Lasting**. The programme anticipates and deals with the obstacles to long-term behavioural change.				
3. **Useful**. The programme content is true, usable, and valuable to the participant. The programme limits its content to what has been shown to help most on the job.				
4. **Persuasive**. The programme overcomes the participant's objections to the content or to using the skills taught. The participant is successfully motivated to drop old habits and to deal with the fear of negative peer pressure and the inclination to take the path of least resistance or of short-term rewards.				
5. **Appropriate**. The content and delivery are geared to the target population's entry level, desired final achievement level, educational level, and learning style and speed.				
6. **Practical**. The programme's development and delivery are efficient and stay within the constraints of time, money, logistics, publishability, and repeatability. The programme uses technology to enhance the training and avoids technology for its own sake.				
7. **Enjoyable**. The programme actively involves participants and preserves the excitement that comes from self-development.				
8. **Safe**. The programme avoids or minimises any real or perceived threats to the participant's physical, emotional, or professional well-being.				

SCORE: **3** for Thoroughly **2** for Mostly **1** for Somewhat **0** for Not at all	**Thoroughly**	**Mostly**	**Somewhat**	**Not at all**
9. Focused. The trainer clearly understands the concepts, behaviour, and attitudes to be acquired by the participant. The trainer and participants clearly understand the programme's objectives and methods.				
10. Honest. The various elements of the programme are in harmony with each other, and the content and delivery are not misleading. The programme and the trainer are candid about the programme's objectives, especially as they relate to the participant's values.				
11. Intriguing. The programme motivates the participant to continue the training, just as a good novel advances the story and makes the reader want to turn the page.				
12. Communal. When appropriate, the programme accommodates group dynamics and promotes a sense of group membership and shared purpose.				
13. Well-executed. The programme is skilfully written and interestingly presented to appeal to the participant accustomed to sophisticated print, radio, television, and movie production. The programme's delivery enhances the training without distracting the participant.				
SUBTOTALS				
TOTAL				

TOTAL: Add up the points you assigned each item, then compare your total with this scale:

0- 7 Not a training programme; you may have a perfectly good something else.
8-15 A weak training programme; you're asking a lot of your participants to go through this.
16-23 A fair training programme, but definitely needs more work.
24-31 A strong training programme. Think about ways to improve it further.
32-39 An excellent training programme.

MANAGING YOUR TIME

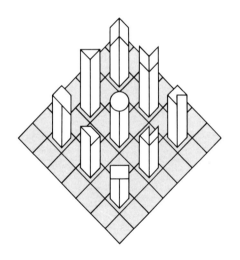

Some managers always seem pressed for time. They work through lunch and take home piles of paper. Others seem to have all the time in the world and still get the job done.

The ability to manage their time is often what separates the good managers from the poor ones. After all, before we can effectively organise other people, we have to be able to organise ourselves. Yet few of us manage time as well as we should. We tend to do the interesting jobs rather than the priority tasks we know we should be attending to first. We take on more work than we have time for. We spend time solving problems for other people, when they should really be thinking for themselves.

Here are some techniques to help you organise your day better.

Cut out unnecessary or routine work

One way of making better use of your time is to stop doing those jobs which can be delegated. Get rid of work that takes up your time, but that can be done just as well by one of your staff. You can cut out unnecessary or routine work by doing the following:

- Define your main goals and priorities

- Check in detail how you spend each working hour in an average week

- Spend your time managing, rather than doing

- Don't do work that should be delegated to others

- Don't do things that need not be done at all

- Spend your time on those things which only you can do

Eliminate time wasters

Here are some common time wasters and suggestions for preventing or minimising them.

- *Callers/Social chit-chat*

  - Use your secretary or assistant to keep unwanted visitors out

  - Say no more often

  - Make appointments and see that people keep to them

  - Arrange for some uninterrupted blocks of time when you have an important or difficult task to do

  - When you meet with someone, keep pleasantries to a minimum

  - Concentrate on keeping to the point in a discussion or conversation – it is too easy to be diverted

  - Encourage staff to think for themselves

- *Telephone interruptions*

  - Ask your secretary to deal with, and where appropriate, divert calls

  - Have a set time of day for making/receiving telephone calls

  - State firmly that you will call back when convenient

  - Be brisk and decisive when telephoning, stand rather than sit

- *Unproductive meetings*

  - Don't call a meeting if you can't state the purpose

  - Cancel any regular meeting if there is no business to discuss

  - If you call a meeting, set a time-limit and stick to it

  - Get taken off committees if your presence is not essential

  - Make your point succinctly. Avoid talking too much

- *Day-to-day tasks*
  - Delegate more

  - Do unpleasant tasks first. You'll feel better afterwards

  - Don't try to do too much at once. Learn to say no to yourself as well as to other people

  - Set yourself deadlines and stick to them

  - Be realistic in time estimates. Many people underestimate the time they need to complete a task

- *Paperwork*

  - Get off the circulation list of reading material you don't need

  - Learn to skim read. Study a text only if it is really relevant

  - Encourage your staff to write succinctly and clearly

  - Don't write when a telephone call will do

  - Write brief replies on memos you receive and return them to the sender. Avoid individually typed acknowledgements

  - Set aside some time each day to deal with urgent correspondence

  - Try to clear your pending tray daily

  - Set up a filing system with a place for everything and everything in its place

  - Handle each piece of paper once only. Act on it, file it, or throw it away

  - Tidy your desk before you go home at night

- *Travelling*

  - Write or telephone instead
  - Send someone else
  - Get other people to come to you

- If you have to travel, do it in the most cost-effective way

- Use travel time to read or study business and professional periodicals

Planning your time

You need to budget your time in the same way as you budget your money. Have a daily, weekly, monthly and quarterly plan. Although you may not be in a position to think too far ahead, you must begin each working day with clear intentions as to how you will spend it. Here are some ideas to help you plan your day.

- Keep a diary of appointments and meetings

- Design a workplan

- Keep your workplan where you can see it clearly

- Distinguish between things you have to do and those you can do if you have the time

- Take responsibility for your time and priorities. Communicate your priorities to those who need to know them

- Review your plan at the end of each day, noting what has been achieved and what must be carried forward.

Conclusion

When you establish high expectations for success and achievement you automatically act to fulfil your expectations. You begin to reap the benefits and rewards of time control, i.e.:

- Increased productivity

- Increased income resulting from higher productivity

- A greater enthusiasm for life and work

- Ability to tackle a long list of tasks without depression

- Ability to face problems without frustration

- Improved decision-making skills

- Adequate time for planning and organising

- Control and management of interruptions

- More time to control your life at work and at home.

Plans are nothing, planning is everything
– Dwight D. Eisenhower

The world stands aside for the person who knows where he or she is going
– John Crystal

Meetings come in for a lot of criticism in organisations. Many managers regard the meeting as a negative institution. They feel that meetings:

- are a waste of productive time
- slow down decision-making and discourage individual enterprise
- concentrate on trivialities and gloss over the real issues, etc.
- tend to be dominated by a few people with strong personalities.

There are many reasons why a meeting may flounder: it may, for example, be unnecessary, held at the wrong time or poorly controlled.

However, a well-organised meeting held at the right time for the right reasons can have a number of benefits. A meeting can:

- create group identity, defining the team or unit
- help to clarify thinking as the members have to justify their opinions before all present
- ensure that different viewpoints come to the fore
- save time by getting a number of people together
- create a commitment to the decisions reached and the aims pursued on the part of those present.

For a meeting to work three things must happen:

- it should have a purpose and be set up properly
- there should be a good chairman
- the members should participate effectively.

Purpose and planning

Every meeting should have a purpose. If you can't state the purpose of the meeting, don't have it. Too many meetings are held just because it is regular meeting time and not because there is anything to discuss.

Once you have decided to hold a meeting, and are clear about its purpose, it is time to draw up an agenda. A properly drawn-up agenda can speed up and clarify a meeting enormously.

Don't make the agenda too vague or too brief. Start off the agenda by stating the purpose of the agenda. Then give a short explanation of each item listed. This will enable those who will be attending the meeting to think about the items and it gives them an opportunity to look up the necessary facts and figures beforehand. It might also be useful to add 'for information', 'for discussion', 'for decision' next to each item.

The order of the items is important. Obviously those needing an immediate decision have to come first.

Here are some pointers to bear in mind when drawing up an agenda:

- The first part of a meeting is usually more lively than the end, so if a topic needs bright ideas, put it near the top of the agenda. Alternatively, it can be useful to put an attention-grabbing topic after a couple of other items, in order to avoid the attention lag that generally sets in after about 20 minutes.
- Some items unite the meeting while others divide it. In drawing up the agenda the leader should be aware of this, for such items can change the atmosphere of the meeting. It is a good idea to end on a united note.
- Often meetings dwell on trivial but immediate items, then run out of time to deal with important but long-term considera-

tions. This can be remedied by deciding on a time when the discussion will switch to long-term issues, and sticking to it.

- Meetings should not run on too long. Two hours should be about the limit. It is often a good idea to put the finishing as well as the starting time on the agenda. One way of setting a time limit is to start the meeting an hour and a half to two hours before lunch or the end of the working day.
- Although your agenda should be well organised, it must not leave the impresison that it is so cut and dried that it precludes member participation.

Chairmanship

The success or failure of a meeting largely depends on the chairman. The chairman's function is to help the group achieve the best decision. He is there to interpret and clarify, to move the discussion forward and to bring it to a resolution that everyone present understands and accepts as the majority decision of the meeting, even if each individual does not agree.

The chairman should:

- Start the meeting by clearly defining its objective.
- Go through each item on the agenda in turn, ensuring that a firm conclusion is reached and recorded.
- Not dominate the meeting but invite contributions from other members.
- Bring people back to order if they drift from the point.
- Encourage the expression of different points of view and not show resentment or subject anyone to harassment or ridicule.
- After each item on the agenda, summarise the discussion and

any decisions/conclusions that have been achieved and thank the people present.

- If a further meeting is needed, agree the purpose of the meeting, and what has to be done by those present before it takes place.

Members

Here are some guidelines worth thinking about when you are attending meetings called or chaired by someone else:

- Prepare thoroughly – have all the facts at your fingertips, with any supporting data you need.

- Arrive at the meeting on time.

- Make your points clearly, succinctly and positively. Avoid rambling and talking too much.

- If you have nothing to say, keep quiet, but show that you are actively listening.

- If the topic is unfamiliar to you, don't make statements or ask questions until you have heard what your more expert colleagues have had to say about it.

- Be open to incorporating other people's ideas into your proposal – aim for it to be seen as 'ours' rather than 'mine'.

- In questioning or criticising other people's proposals, be as courteous as you would wish them to be to you.

- If your proposal is rejected, accept your defeat gracefully.

The minutes of the meeting

The secretary or one of the members may take the minutes, but they remain the responsibility of the leader. The minutes can be brief, but should include the following:

- Time and date of meeting, where held, name of chairman or leader.

- Names of all present and apologies for absence.

- All items discussed and all decisions reached. If action was decided on, the name of the person taking responsibility should be recorded.

- Time at which meeting ended.

- Date, time and place of next meeting.

It is a mistake, in distributing copies of minutes, to neglect people who may not have been at the meeting, but who will be affected by action resulting from the meeting. Don't assume that the receipt of minutes will automatically remind people of assignments. Before every progress reporting date, or a follow-up meeting date, send a reminder note to people with assignments.

If we could know where we are and wither we are tending, we could better judge what to do and how to do it
– Abraham Lincoln

The better you think you are doing, the greater should be your cause for concern
– Mark McCormack

The leaders we most admire in business are those who have a sense of balance in their lives. They know when to close the door and go home. They do not exploit their families. They have real lives away from the office. In the end, these personal qualities count heavily when we assess those who present themselves as leaders in business, the political arena, or any other field. When we ask ourselves if someone is a balanced person, what comes to mind sooner or later is their ability to manage their time in such a way that it allows them to spend quality time away from work.

While it is difficult to tell managers exactly how to spend time with their families, it is possible to provide them with some guidelines on how to manage their time at work so that they will indeed have stress-free, quality time beyond the confines of their work environment.

The following are guidelines for effective working time management in order to make time for family and friends:

1. Prioritise

Although successful managers range widely in temperament, interest and ability, they seem to have one trait in common: a talent for getting the right things done. That means picking priorities - separating the wheat from the chaff and sending the chaff elsewhere. Time management means having the courage and foresight to concentrate on the critical tasks rather than trying to do it all.

2. Learn to do scheduling

Scheduling is something that managers find both difficult and important. In essence, it entails looking at your calendar for the coming year, month or week, and first filling in essential activities, such as board and executive meetings, and - very important - some vacation time. Pencil in other known activities, such as business trips and strategic exercises. Once all the known activities have been scheduled, the blocked-out calendar will give you the shape of the playing field of the year ahead and let you know where your discretionary time falls.

3. Leave room for the unexpected

Advance scheduling of known activities doesn't mean that the appointments are chiselled in stone. There will be a fair number of crises which will mean rescheduling from time to time. Wise managers in fact leave room on their daily calendars for the unexpected.

4. Leave a cushion between appointments

The hours at work should not be packed cheek by jowl with activities. Some managers even succeed in keeping 50% of their time free of appointments. It is especially important when going from meeting to meeting to leave plenty of time to shuffle papers, return calls and check messages. If this is not provided for, you may find yourself becoming nervous and tense, and in the end finding that you have to get to work early - to catch up on the paperwork - and stay late, to the detriment of your family and social life.

5. Leave time for thinking

Nothing can be worse than the manager lapsing into spells of deep thought about work when he is at home and needs rather to be fully aware of and give quality attention to his family. But finding time for deep thinking - the kind of strategic contemplation that helps define priorities - can be tough. Yet the best man-agers agree that it is one of the most important things to do. Most dig into the nooks and crannies of their schedules to find the time. Some discover time for contemplation in the morning while exercising, showering or driving to work. Others do a lot of deep thinking during local and overseas air travel. What is important, however, is that this should not deprive your family of your full attention when they need it.

6. Be selective on community activities

As a manager moves up in the company, community activities often take more of his time. This can cause problems, considering how inefficient some public organisations can be. Managers can grow irritated with outside activities that dawdle along beyond their control. However, smart managers learn to limit their outside commitments. This may even mean strict control of friends visiting your home over weekends with all kinds of requests.

7. Watch out for meetings

For many managers, the largest consumer of corporate time is meetings. A lot of executives hate them, some - believe it or not - love them, but they all emphasise the importance of managing them. The only thing that stands between dismal meetings and productive ones is discipline. It is a good idea to have regular scheduled meetings with key subordinates. That way they'll save their routine questions and comments for the weekly sessions. The basic principle, however, is to institute effective measures to ensure that meetings do not constitute hours of time which could have been spent much more productively in other ways.

8. Make proper use of electronic communication media

The telephone is a blessing, but most managers probably curse it at least once a day. However, the best managers make this and more modern technology into tools and not burdens. Fax machines are essential these days, but the junk fax phenomenon has taught managers that fax messages must be screened like any other mail. The bottom line is that these electronic aids should save time rather than waste it.

9. Get a top-class secretary

The most effective managers seem to agree that all the electronic mod cons in the world cannot compare with the skills of a talented executive secretary who screens calls, diverts mail, and steers visitors in and out. Years of working together produces the telepathic effect that many managers have come to appreciate and rely on. A good secretary can prevent a working day having to be four to six hours longer than is necessary.

10. Learn to say no

Perhaps the ultimate time-saving technique is simply to say no. As Peter Drucker writes in *The Effective Executive*: "If the pressures, rather than the executive, are allowed to make the decision, the important tasks will predictably be sacrificed." Saying no to that which is not a priority is the real key to time management. Some executives are more likely to say that it is half the key, with the other half being to set priorities. Setting priorities requires forgoing activities that probably seem important in favour of others that you hope are more important. Saying no requires displeasing people regularly. But until science figures out a way to add an hour to the day, setting priorities and saying no are probably the best time management techniques any manager has.

Dost thou love life? Then do not squander time, for that's the stuff life is made of
— *Benjamin Franklin*

Good order is the foundation of all good things
— *Edmund Burke*

ARE YOU WASTING TIME?

Whatever your job or field, whether you're young or old, prosperous or poor, time is the most valuable asset you will ever have. Money and material possessions can be replaced. But once your time is lost, stolen, or wasted, it's gone forever.

A manager's effectiveness and productivity - and this applies as much to the managing director as it does to the junior supervisor - will rise or fall in direct proportion to the way he uses time.

How effectively do you manage your time and the time of the people you supervise? Do you waste it or do you use those precious moments wisely and carefully?

Perhaps the best way to find out is to take the time to answer these questions honestly.

	Yes	No
1. Do you periodically analyse the way you spend your time?	☐	☐
2. Before tackling a project or assignment, do you plan how you will do it?	☐	☐
3. Before spending time on a project, do you evaluate its importance so that you won't spend too much time on jobs that don't warrant it?	☐	☐
4. Can you honestly say that you delegate effectively?	☐	☐
5. In assigning tasks to others, and in tackling jobs yourself, do you always take priorities into consideration?	☐	☐
6. Do you encourage your staff to come up with suggestions to perform their jobs faster and more efficiently?	☐	☐
7. Do you take a tough, no-nonsense approach toward employees who waste time chatting to each other on the telephone?	☐	☐
8. Do you keep careful tabs on your staff to make sure they are working when they're supposed to be?	☐	☐
9. Do you employ work measurement techniques in your department to determine if employees are taking excessive time on tasks and duties assigned to them?	☐	☐
10. Do you allow yourself sufficient time for the creative aspects of supervision such as planning, problem-solving, and generation of ideas?	☐	☐
11. Do you review work procedures periodically to determine if some steps can be liminated or done more efficiently?	☐	☐
12. Do you keep reminder lists of things to do?	☐	☐
13. Do you compare manual operations in your department with possible automation?	☐	☐

Total Number of Yes Answers _____

How you rate: If you scored 11 or more, you're using your time wisely.   Nine or ten is well above average, seven to eight mediocre to fair.   Any score under seven means you'd better change in order to manage your time properly.

THE ART
OF
COMMUNICATING

The way we speak affects the image we project more than any other single factor. You may be bright and competent, but if your speech and manner don't project those qualities, you sell yourself short. Many people simply don't know how to present themselves and their ideas to others so that they seem important and worthy of attention.

It is particularly helpful for women to learn to make the most of their voices, since they often feel at a disadvantage when talking to men. Research studies have found that men interrupt women far more often than they interrupt other men.

The way many people speak puts them at a disadvantage in conversation. Some people's language has characteristics that make the speaker appear weak and unsure. For example, they often:

- Use indefinite modifiers such as "sort of" and "I think", which indicate lack of confidence in the answer.

- Ramble and repeat at great length – a habit that is distracting as well as a sign of lack of authority.

- Trail off without finishing sentences.

If you find that some people don't take you seriously – that they often interrupt or ignore your conversations – perhaps your speech is at fault. But don't despair. You can sound more important and talk in a way that others will enjoy by applying the following techniques and suggestions.

Role models

You can begin to improve your speech by observing others. Make a list of people you have heard – in person, on the radio or on television – whose style and voice

say: "I'm important, listen to me." Try to pinpoint the qualities that help these people come across so well. The people on your list probably have energy, enthusiasm, conviction, animation, clarity, expression, confidence and ease. What they do **not** have are irritating speech sounds, habits and mannerisms. You don't hear the best speakers er-ing, umm-ing or mumbling. While you work to improve your own presentation, it helps to keep the sound and qualities of good speakers in your ear as role models.

Analyse your voice

Once you become aware of the positive qualities of others, you need to sharpen your awareness of yourself. The best way to do this is with a tape recorder. Keep it near your phone and record yourself in several conversations. Play back the tape and listen to it as though you were listening to a stranger. Take note of your good points, but also listen to your deficiencies. As you listen, consider these questions:

1. Do you talk too much or too little?

2. Do you sound tentative, sing-song and questioning?

3. Do you sound nasal, whiny or negative like an unhappy child?

4. Do you sound apathetic, monotonous, aloof? (Your voice should reflect enthusiasm and conviction about what you're saying.)

5. Do you hear any speech tics – those annoying habits such as "uh", "um", "you know", "well", "like", "OK"? Do you repeatedly clear your throat?

6. Are you a fast or slow talker? (You shouldn't sprint through conversation, nor should you dawdle. A good rate is 170 words a minute. Time yourself

to find out how many words you speak in a minute.)

Correcting your speech

Speech habits
Annoying speech habits, such as you know, can be eliminated fairly quickly through a simple trick. Print your problem words on a number of small stickers. Then put them in obvious spots like the middle of your watch, on your telephone, your briefcase, mirror, or on anything else you look at repeatedly throughout the day.

This battery of visual reminders will constantly catch your eye and remind you to avoid those annoying habits.

Pacing
To conquer a speedtalking problem, read aloud at your normal pace, from a magazine for one minute and time the number of words you read in that time. To slow yourself down to a pleasanter speed, read the same passage again and again, more slowly each time. Put a slash mark at the word you were speaking when the one minute was up, then count the number of words you have read. Speak fewer and fewer words each time until you have slowed down to about 160 words per minute. This is a good technique for putting a brake on your speaking speed and for giving you an idea of how well-paced speech sounds.

Inflection
The sound of authority goes down in pitch at the end of sentences, like this:
"Yes, I'll be
    very
        glad
           to."
Practise this inflection by visualising sentences going down a stairway as you speak.

Projecting
Quiet, whispering voices, some-

times considered soothing, are actually a strain for the listener and make the speaker sound helpless, apathetic and dull. To correct this, train yourself to use your abdominal muscles to control your breath and support your voice in this way: With the palms of your hands together in a steeple position at chest level, elbows straight out to the side, take a normal breath and hold it. Then press your palms together as hard as you can, while pulling the stomach muscles back toward your spine. Let out your breath in a long sh-h-h sound, making it last as long as you can. The muscles act like bellows, sending the air up with pressure to make the vocal cords vibrate and give you a more vital sound. Now relax your hands and arms and practise the same sound.

Posture is important to voice projection. Hold your body upright when you speak and notice how much more alive and important you sound. If your body sags, your voice sags. The best posture for producing a stronger, more energetic voice is head and rib cage held high, stomach in.

To strengthen your stomach muscles and your voice, try this exercise: Standing erectly, clench one hand into a fist. Pretend it's an empty balloon. Hold it tightly against your mouth and blow until the make-believe balloon is inflated. While blowing, keep the other hand on your abdominal muscles at the bottom of the rib cage. Pull those muscles back as you exhale. This is the posture you should assume when speaking to project your voice with energy and enthusiasm. Do this exercise several times a day until the muscles are strong. Also try it before making an important phone call or speech; it will not only give energy and enthusiasm to your voice, but will also help you relax. (Tenseness can make you sound strident.)

Presentation
In any speaking situation, eye contact is essential. Looking directly at the person you're talking to adds enormous belief, excitement or concern to what you're saying, whether you're in front of a group, around a coffee table or lunching with a friend. The eyes should be in action almost constantly, but the tongue should not. In conversation, non-stop talking can overwhelm, irritate and make others want to escape from you. If you talk too much or repeat yourself, you lose your sound of importance. Don't be afraid of a few seconds of silence when you collect your thoughts and edit what you're going to say next. A pause – especially when giving a talk – is not only refreshing to the ear, it also adds emphasis to what you've just said. And it can help introduce a new thought.

By following these guidelines and practising these exercises, you can dramatically improve your style of speaking. You can become a persuasive speaker with the sound of authority and confidence, whether you're talking to your spouse across the dinner table or addressing a group of five hundred in the town hall.

The best way to improve an after-dinner speech is to shorten it
                              – Mark Twain

Language is the dress of thought
                              – Samuel Johnson

A BRIEF GUIDE TO SPEECH-MAKING

The formal or prepared speech

When preparing a speech, one of the first things to establish is how long it should be. Never exceed this time limit.

The first sentence should get the attention of the audience. A good way to do this is by telling a story. The next step is to build a bridge to the listeners' interests. Show the audience how the opening remarks tie in with their interests.

In the body of the talk, use examples, anecdotes, charts, slides, diagrams, etc. to convince the audience that the information is based on knowledge and that they will benefit by listening to you.

The conclusion should demand some specific action from the audience, e.g. join, vote, investigate, buy, etc. If the talk ends without such a request it has not achieved anything. A Chinese proverb puts it in a nutshell: "To talk much and arrive nowhere is the same as climbing a tree to catch a fish."

The impromptu speech

A successful unprepared speech depends on the ability to organise your thoughts quickly. Here are some tips for effective on-the-spur-of-the-moment speeches:

- Choose your opening remarks carefully, taking your cue from what someone else has said, then move to your own ideas and a few points to support your main theme.

- Try to marshall your thoughts in a logical sequence.

- Focus on points of controversy or doubt, and try to clarify them.

- Relate your ideas to the experience of your audience.

- Note the reaction of your au-dience and respond accordingly.

- As soon as you've said everything you wanted to say, stop speaking. Some experts put a time limit of three minutes on an impromptu speech.

- An impromptu speaker is not expected to cover all aspects of a topic – rather be simple and direct, avoiding jargon.

- Never apologise for not being prepared or bemoan the fact that you weren't expecting to speak.

- Don't feel obliged to be witty or humorous, don't repeat yourself, and don't ramble from the point.

The speech of introduction

When introducing a guest speaker you need to know something about his background. If you've been given prior notice, you can phone and ask for a *curriculum vitae*. If the task has been sprung upon you unexpectedly at the function itself, you'll simply have to make inquiries on the spot.

Some hints for a good speech of introduction:

- Avoid clichés and laboured phrases.

- Be brief – 90 seconds maximum, say experts.

- Don't exaggerate the speaker's achievements, and don't feel you have to discuss his entire career history.

- Whatever you do, don't get the speaker's name wrong.

When introducing a speaker there are four questions that you need to answer for the audience.

- What is the subject?

- Why this subject for this audience at this time?

- Why this speaker?

- What is the speaker's name?

If you answer these questions skilfully, the short prelude of your introduction will create a pleasant harmony between subject, audience, occasion and speaker.

The speech of thanks

The person delegated to thank the main speaker seldom gets much warning, but if you follow a few simple rules, there should be no reason to panic:

- Speak for 60 to 90 seconds.

- It is important to show the speaker you have been following the speech carefully and appreciate the time given up to be there.

- In your opening remarks, single out something you like about the speaker followed by something you like about the speech.

- Conclude by thanking him formally, turning towards the speaker leading the applause.

The speech of welcome

In many organisations, as well as in associations or societies, a speaker is delegated to welcome honoured guests or new members. If the main purpose of the meeting is to welcome new members, make your speech as early on in the proceedings as possible. Be sincere, and avoid stale jokes.

Be warm and friendly, remembering your purpose is to make the new members feel part of the organisation. In your speech, all you need to do is state the goals of the organisation, recall your own feelings on joining it, inspire new members to contribute, and formally welcome them.

In the case of a guest, you would state the goals, describe how the guest contributes to those goals, give a summary of his career, and state the guest's name. The speech should be about three minutes long.

The farewell speech

When a member of a company or association is leaving, a function is usually arranged at which a gift is presented and a short speech made. Again, the operative word is "short". Avoid a dull recitation of the person's life history. Get the speech over as early as possible as well – guests are usually standing. Include the audience in your talk, using "we" instead of "I", so they feel they are also saying goodbye.

Your main purpose is to make the person who is leaving feel that he was valued as a member and will be missed. Open by saying you are honoured to be chosen to make the speech (if this is not so,

refuse to do the speech). Express appreciation for his contribution, relate one or two anecdotes concerning the person's contribution, say how sorry you are he is leaving and say goodbye. The farewell speech should not be longer than 60-90 seconds.

The presentation speech

If you are asked to present a gift or award to someone for a specific achievement, keep in mind that the audience is in the mood for celebrating, so don't become too heavy.

Your purpose is to express recognition to someone for his performance, and it is important to be sincere. Start by expressing pleasure at being invited to present the award. State why it is being presented, summarise the

achievements of the winner, explain what the gift or award is and what it represents, and hand over the award. This type of speech should be about three minutes.

The speech of acceptance

If you are presented with a gift or award it becomes necessary to make a short speech expressing your appreciation. Start by showing the award or gift to the audience, then say how much you appreciate it, reply to remarks made in the presentation if necessary. Say something about the gift. Thank anyone who has contributed to your success, in the case of an award. Formally thank the gathering. (Time: about one minute).

The gods gave us two ears, but only one mouth. Does this mean that we should listen twice as much as we talk?
– Attributed to Socrates

The attraction of an authoritarian management style is almost irresistible – and wrong
– John Naisbitt

The following is a short quiz where a number of propositions are made about public speaking techniques. Mark each statement as true or false, then look at the answers and comments that follow.

True or False?

T   F

1. It is advisable to hold onto something when speaking in public.

2. Speeches should be written out word for word.

3. A speaker should avoid being dramatic or emotional.

4. It is not really necessary to know your subject to give an effective talk.

5. Always mention the speaker's name at the beginning of an introduction.

6. Don't worry about the content, just make sure the delivery is right.

7. Illustrations and examples are boring.

8. Avoid mentioning the names of some people in the audience.

9. Always begin your talk with a joke.

10. To give a good talk it is not necessary to feel excited about the subject.

11. When addressing an audience, use "you" not "we".

12. Make sure apologies are made for any of the speakers' shortcomings.

Effective speaking is one of the most important "weapons" in any executive's arsenal. The man or woman who can communicate his or her ideas or proposals with wit, enthusiasm and clarity, stands at an immense advantage over the individual who is unable to do so.

Every statement in this quiz is false. Here's why:

1. If our hands are free when we're talking, we would tend to feel more relaxed and our words and ideas would flow more easily. Holding onto an object when talking before a group makes the audience focus on the object – and not what we're saying. It's the ultimate distraction that can ruin even the best of talks.

2. Talks written out in full tie the speaker to his own words, and prevent him from tuning in to the audience's needs. The speech becomes a monologue and not a shared experience. Brief points made on a small sheet of paper are a much more effective cue, as they allow the speaker to adapt the prepared material to the situation.

3. The dramatic or emotional impact of a talk is often remembered long after other aspects are forgotten. As long as the impact is tasteful and relates to the objective of the talk, it is a powerful way in which to touch your listeners.

4. It is vital that we never speak to a group unless we know forty times more than we'll share in the talk. This knowledge is what gives us the authority and the confidence to do a successful job.

5. In introducing a speaker, a useful technique is to leave his name to the end. It heightens the dramatic effect, and causes the listeners to sit forward in eager anticipation of the climax. The device allows the speaker to start on a higher note because that is where the introducer left the audience – at the peak of anticipation.

6. A speaker's vocabulary, diction, voice and delivery may be exceptional, but nothing will save a speaker if he is not excited about his subject and eager to share the content of his talk.

7. We do not think in concepts, but in pictures. Thus the best way to affect an audience positively is by using an abundance of examples to make every point clearer.

8. Mentioning the names of peo-

ple in the audience causes them to become involved in the talk. It also causes the speaker to wrap his subject around the needs of his audience both in the specific and the general sense.

9. Unless you are completely familiar with a story and have practised it many times, do not start a talk with a joke. It may backfire and handicap you seriously for the rest of your talk. However, a humorous story highlighting a point within the talk does not need to be laughed at to be effective. Therefore, if no laugh is evoked, just continue, your point will have been made.

10. Excitement does not mean hysteria. However, an excited speaker deeply involved in his subject, will always outshine an intellectually perfect speaker.

11. Saying "we" instead of "you" makes the audience feel that the speaker is "one of us" rather than an outsider whose job it is to pass on information to them.

12. The rule is "never apologise" because the audience is probably unaware of the problem. Calling attention to something that the audience would not know about otherwise, can only detract from the main objective.

Talking and eloquence are not the same: to speak and to speak well, are two things. A fool may talk, but a wise man speaks

– Ben Jonson

The telephone is on every desk, in every home and in many cars and briefcases, but if we stopped to consider it, we would realise it is a strange means of communication. Though we tend to think of the telephone conversation as akin to a face-to-face encounter, it is in fact far removed from that. The telephone is a very artificial medium and that is why thought should be applied to both making and receiving calls. The telephone can be used for many purposes, but the points made here should be observed whether you are selling, negotiating, or dealing in some other way with clients, suppliers, advisers, the press or interested members of the public.

When to call

This question can be split into two. When should you call to fit in with your schedule or mood and when should you call to fit in with the schedule and mood of the person you are trying to contact? The first question is entirely up to you, but you might consider the following points. If you group all your calls together you will know how long they are taking. Putting in the odd call around your other work may disguise too many unproductive minutes on the phone. Furthermore, you could find yourself trying to squeeze a ten-minute call into a five-minute space before an important meeting. Mood can also be a major consideration. If you are reluctant to use the telephone, you may find that you have reached the end of the day without making an essential call. This could not happen if you set aside a particular time of day for making calls.

Fitting in with someone else's schedule or mood is more tricky. If you know, or can make an intelligent guess, about someone else's busy times, then don't call

at these times. For instance, if you have urgent news to communicate to a journalist on a daily paper, it would be best not to call from mid-afternoon onwards. Mood is also more difficult when considering the recipient of your call. Some people say you should avoid ringing on Monday mornings or Friday afternoons, (or any afternoon according to others). If you know the person you are calling, it is worth considering whether they will be more or less receptive to what you are going to say at different times of day. Get into the habit of giving a moment's thought to the 'social' aspects of a call, such as the mood of the person you are calling. Even if you decide you do not know that mood, thinking about it will make you more likely to pick up on it when you get through – and that can lead to a more successful call.

In the UK, it is cheaper to call in the afternoon, so the timing of calls may be influenced by economic considerations. Another highly practical point is the time differences between the UK and other countries. When making international calls stop to consider that it may be a different time in the country you are trying to reach.

Preparation

This follows on from the last point. It is important to prepare for a phone call in a social as well as an intellectual sense. Your intellectual preparations should include listing in advance any arguments you wish to put, questions you wish to ask or facts that must be mentioned. It can also be a good idea to write down the main objective of your call. Social preparation is of a different nature. You should put yourself in a frame of mind to meet someone. If you go to see a colleague in another part of the building there

is a whole range of actions and protocols to be observed before you get down to business. The encounter starts with you walking to the office of the other person, during which time you will probably think about what will be said in a few minutes' time. This walk is followed by knocking on the door and various other preparatory gestures and words. Telephone calls will benefit from the equivalent of a walk to someone's office. It is a good idea to continue the illusion of social interaction while you are speaking. Using the gestures and expressions you would use when meeting someone is an easy way to enliven your telephone delivery. Remember though that while a word can be reinforced by a gesture, a gesture alone will be useless. Nodding your head while saying yes to someone will give the correct emphasis to your words, but nodding alone will mean nothing to the other party. If agreeing or disagreeing, the two responses most frequently made without sounds, you must remember to add noises or words to your actions when on the telephone.

If you have not spoken for some hours it might be an idea to clear your throat before you call and try out your vocal chords – strange sounds can result if you don't.

Always have a pen and paper ready and any documents you may want to refer to close at hand.

Getting through

If you know who you want, then trying to get through is no problem. Just ask for them by name, remembering to be polite to anyone you speak to before you reach the person you want to call. While trying to get through is easy, actually getting through can be more difficult. You may be mistaken for a salesman and put off by a secretary. (Incidentally, if you are a salesman, it may be best to try not to reveal the fact before you are speaking to your target.) If you cannot speak to the person you want, and only he will do, then arrange a specific time to ring back 'to see if Mr Smith can speak to me then'. This marginally raises the chances of Mr Smith coming to the phone when you call at the specified time. In this situation remember to leave your name and your company name and telephone number and take the name of the person you have spoken to. Your name will then probably reach the desk of the person you wish to speak to, though he may not actually ring you. Knowing the name of Mr Smith's secretary or colleague will be useful when you call back. People like to be remembered.

Never assume that the woman who tells you Mr Smith is at lunch is his secretary. She may be his boss and be highly offended.

If you do not know who you want to speak to by name, then be as helpful as possible to the switchboard operator in giving details of the department you want. Different companies have different names for departments, functions and roles, so more than one explanation may be needed.

The conversation

The quality of your call will depend on the quality of your preparation. If you have prepared intellectually by marshalling your facts and arguments and listing questions to which you need answers, you will have a successful phone call. If you have also put thought into the 'social' aspects of the 'meeting' you will have an excellent phone call.

On the 'intellectual' side, if you are ringing to gather information or to make appointments you should remember the difference between open and closed ques-

tions, for example: 'Do you publish Calculus and Business Maths?' (closed) or 'What do you publish on business mathematics?' (open). If you are not really interested in a specific thing it can be more helpful to ask an open question. Other aspects of intellectual preparation cannot be described here, as they will vary according to the kind of call you are making.

Perhaps the most important 'social' nicety is being aware that you have certainly interrupted the person you are calling. He was without doubt doing something when you called, even if it was only clearing away one piece of work and taking out another. You must be alert to the fact that the person you are calling may not want to speak to you when you call, either because an important meeting is minutes away, or simply because they do not want to speak to you in the presence of other people with them.

If you sense that you have rung at an inconvenient time from the person's tone of voice (and there is no other way to sense it unless they tell you) then offer to call back, suggesting alternative times for ringing (two times are better than one).

If you know that what you are going to say will take more than a minute or two, and the person you are calling was not expecting your call, it may be best to establish exactly whether or not the person has X minutes to speak to you. Make sure that X is a realistic number! Again, if it is inconvenient to continue the call, suggest alternative times for ringing back.

Remember too that the amount of acceptable social chat will vary according to the convenience of your call. No matter how well you know someone, it is not appropriate to ask after their family or how they are going to spend the week-end if you sense that they are busy and want you off the line. You can alway ask next time you

ring, or when you meet them face-to-face.

Making notes and conversation summary

When you are making a call that will result in action on your part or the other person's part, it is vital to summarise the call at the end. It is easier to mishear or misunderstand on the telephone than face-to-face. As you are speaking, write down important points so that you will remember them when it comes to the summary at the end of the call. It can also be a good idea to file your notes, just as you would a letter, if there is a possibility that you will need a written record of what was said.

Leaving messages

If you cannot reach the person you want and you have something urgent and important to communicate you may be forced to leave a message – but do not assume it will be delivered. The best course is to find out when the person you want will be available and say that you will call at that time, leaving your name, company name and telephone number in case he wishes to ring you. Only agree to wait for a return call if you are really not concerned whether the person calls back.

Receiving calls

There is less to consider here than in making calls, but most managers will need to develop some policies on receiving calls.

Screening

It is best to block all calls for certain periods of time if you wish to have some quiet time. Your secretary could take the calls or, if you don't have one, you could divert calls to a co-operative colleague. This is better than letting your secretary veto your calls all day or conducting whispered conversations on whether to receive each call that comes in. Remember that after a period of blocked calls you may have some urgent return calls to make. So that returning calls is easy, make sure that you have a commonly-known procedure for noting phone calls in your office – who called, from what company, what telephone number, for what purpose, who is to call whom at what time.

How to answer and phone etiquette

The phone should not be left to ring more than a few times and, when you pick it up, give your company name and your name. When you cannot help a caller, but someone else in the organisa-tion probably can, transfer the call (and tell the caller what you are doing). Remember that as far as the caller is concerned, you are the organisation at that point in time so always be helpful and polite. If you are taking a message for someone else (or yourself!) make sure you follow the procedure for noting calls mentioned above.

When you have no time or it is inconvenient

If you take a call when you have no time or it is inconvenient, do not hesitate to put the caller off and promise to call back later (if the caller does not first undertake to call you again). If you are busy or in a meeting it might be best to divert calls during that time. Interrupting a meeting with a long phone call is rude to your visitor or visitors.

When you are leaving the office

When you are walking out of the office, going home or going to an important meeting, it is best not to answer the phone unless you are really prepared to delay what you are doing. It is better to be 'out of the office' than hold a hurried conversation with an important client, for example, who expects more attention than you can give.

The telephone can be used to create business and continue business. Handled incorrectly it is an easy way to lose business. Much can be achieved by simply thinking of the other person and his situation before you dial.

You should think of your customers as partners, or better still, family
– Victor Kiam

The consumer isn't a moron; she is your wife
– David Ogilvy

The ability to listen and understand is one of the most important attributes of an effective manager. The majority of managers devote more than 60% of their total working hours to communicating, and much of this time is spent listening to people talk.

Some managers believe they have a poor memory, but poor listening skills are often the root of their absentmindedness. They may hear what is going on, but never fully absorb the nature of the situation. Failure to listen is partly to blame for differences which occur between management and staff, for example.

Poor listening habits also result in poor relationships and in unnecessary work being done. Listening should not be confused with hearing. Hearing is simply a physical experience, whereas listening is a complicated process of absorbing, judging and acting on what you hear.

The guidelines that follow will help you achieve better results by fine-tuning your listening skills.

Poor listening habits

Poor listening habits include the following:

- We tend not to listen when we have no interest in a particular subject, or when we believe a subject is too complex for us to understand.

- Our reaction, whether positive or negative, to a particular speaker, can also influence the degree to which we listen.

- When listening only for facts, we may miss other factors such as voice inflections or facial expressions used by the speaker. The latter factors can influence the real meaning of what is being said.

- Sometimes we fake attention. We manage to nod at appropriate times or interject with a non-committal phrase such as "how interesting", without hearing a word.

- We tolerate or create distractions. By so doing we openly announce that we are not interested in what the person is saying.

- We tend to be so busy planning what we are going to say in response, that we do not pay attention to the speaker.

Having listed some of the main problems in listening, let's look at how we can overcome them.

Guidelines for effective listening

Establish a good rapport

Make others comfortable and establish a good rapport. When people are relaxed, they absorb and retain more than twice as much as when they are under stress.

Use empathy

The key to effective listening is empathy – the ability to see an idea or concept from another person's point of view. Empathy is understanding and doesn't necessarily involve agreement. Try to have enough confidence in your own beliefs and attitudes so that you can reduce any defensiveness. Make an attempt to understand new information, even if it conflicts with your own beliefs.

Recognise prejudices

Prejudice is a major barrier to good listening. Ideally, your listening should be totally free of prejudice. Since this is practically impossible, the best thing is to recognise your prejudices and make a conscious effort to discount them.

Ask questions

Seek information through a variety of questioning techniques. Open and closed questions must be worded carefully so as not to reveal your personal opinion or to manipulate the discussion. Hold your comments until the other person has expressed his thoughts fully.

Verify facts

Verify facts and ideas by asking questions such as: "Is this what you mean?" Repeating what was said or deduced leads to better understanding.

Learn to concentrate

An important contributing factor to careless listening is lack of incentive. In order to listen effectively you need to feel convinced that what you are about to hear is relevant to you personally. Adopt a "What's in it for me?" attitude to everything you hear. Then when something worthwhile is being said, you won't miss it.

Be patient

Many people with whom we deal are slow in speaking or cannot express themselves well. Give them the opportunity to formulate and express their thoughts.

Also, you can think faster than someone else can speak. Rather than become impatient, use the time to review the information you have gained and fix it in your mind. The speaker will be gratified at your grasp of the new subject, and you might come away with some useful information.

Keep your temper

The easiest thing to do when someone angers us is to lash out ith an emotional tirade. We may say this aloud or simply stop listening and mull it over in our minds. Either way we lose a great deal in the communication process.

Be alert and attentive
Unless you are a good actor, the speaker will detect if you are feigning attention, and annoyance and confusion will further damage the delivery.

Be a critical listener

As you listen, weigh what the speaker is saying and the conclusions he is drawing. If you notice any weaknesses in his argument, bear them in mind when the time comes for discussion.

Managers need superior listening skills to deal effectively with situations they meet daily. All people, including customers and employees, benefit when a manager actively listens to them. People can accept an idea and become committed to it only if they listen. The best way for a manager to get people to listen to him, is to listen to them.

Silence and modesty are very valuable qualities in the art of conversation
                                            - Montaigne

A man who has committed a mistake and does not correct it is committing another mistake
                                            - Confucius

It has become apparent over the course of the years that a dictation system stands or falls, not only on the quality and ease of operation of the equipment used, but on the quality of the dictation which is put into it. It has also emerged that the standard of dictation in the average office is, regrettably, not always all that it should be.

This explains why, in some offices, the standard of copy resulting from dictation falls below the acceptable level.

This applies whether we are dealing with the simple system of a pair of machines in a small office or the sophisticated centralised dictation installations in larger companies.

In the majority of cases, shortcomings in dictation stem from ignorance of a few very simple rules.

What, then, are these simple rules which we must follow?

They may be summarised roughly as follows:

Handling the machine

If you are using a dictation machine for the first time, practise a little before starting to dictate in earnest. Read a few passages from a book or newspaper into the microphone. This releases you from the task of composition, and lets you concentrate on the controls.

After a few minutes, use of the controls on the microphone will become automatic.

Practise recording, playing back, and correcting by over-recording, then play back your dictation, and compare it with the original. If possible, have it typed out, and compare the result with the printed page. If it differs in any way, listen again to the tape, and analyse the reasons why it differs.

Your secretary will appreciate this effort on your part, and will usually be only too pleased to co-operate.

Think ahead

Try to remember that your secretary can only type **what** she hears, **when** she hears it. Form a mental picture of the letter, memorandum, report or whatever, and after identifying yourself, dictate references, salutations, headings, etc. in the order in which they are to appear.

Assemble your facts before you start, and don't be afraid of making a few rough notes to help you to put them in logical order.

Give warning in advance of tabulations, inset paragraphs or any deviations from the usual house style, and remember to state clearly **at the beginning** how many copies will be required, even if a distribution list is to be typed at the end.

Dictation manners

Think of your microphone as a telephone - imagine the typist listening at the other end, and talk to her as if she were really there. A pleasant "Good morning" before you start dictating never did any harm.

Speak clearly and distinctly, in a normal conversational tone, and at about conversation speed. If you are unsure about the speed, err rather on the side of too fast than too slow - she can always stop the machine by simply lifting her foot, but she cannot speed up too-slow dictation. Nothing is more frustrating to a fast typist than having to wait for the dictation to catch her up.

If you need to stop dictating in order to collect your thoughts or look up a reference, stop the machine. This avoids her having to listen through long periods of silence. Similarly, if you need to cough - nothing is more explosive than a well-directed cough when heard through headphones!

Punctuation

Your typist's punctuation may well be just as good as yours: she certainly will not expect you to dictate every comma, though she would like to hear the full stop. However, you have the advantage over her in that you know what is coming next - she doesn't, so help her as much as you can.

Dictate punctuation if there is any doubt, particularly the less common marks such as colons, semi-colons, quotation marks, question marks, etc.

Always tell her when you wish her to start a new paragraph, as there is no other way in which she can know this.

For normal 'running' punctuation, the typist will rely largely on the inflections in your voice.

Give special instructions (i.e. 'Open brackets ... close brackets') in a slightly different tone to your normal dictation voice, so that they may be immediately recognised as instructions and not typed by mistake.

Spelling

Not all typists who can't spell admit or recognise the fact.

... So, to be on the safe side, spell out any difficult or unfamiliar words. Names of people or places should always be spelt unless you know that the typist is familiar with them through usage or local knowledge.

Words which sound the same, but have different spellings and meanings (talk/torque, plane/plain, phial/file) should be either spelt out or avoided, and don't use obscure words that you can't spell in the hope that she can!

Phonetic alphabet

When dictating strings of apparently unrelated capital letters, such as occur in vehicle licence numbers, part numbers, etc., it may be advisable to use the Phonetic Alphabet.

Below is the official Phonetic Alphabet as used by NATO, police forces and international air traffic control:

A	Alpha	L	Lima
*B	Bravo	*M	Mike
*C	Charlie	*N	November
*D	Delta	O	Oscar
E	Echo	*P	Papa
*F	Foxtrot	Q	Quebec
*G	Golf	R	Romeo
H	Hotel	S	Sierra
I	India	*T	Tango
J	Juliet	U	Uniform
K	Kilo	*V	Victor
W	Whisky	Y	Yankee
X	X-Ray	Z	Zulu

This may also be used with discretion when spelling out words containing the letters marked thus *, which are the ones most frequently confused with others.

Corrections and instructions

Whenever possible, correct immediately by 'over-recording'. This automatically erases the mistake and substitutes the correct matter; the typist is unaware that a mistake has been made at all.

When this is impracticable, or you wish to change something which may be some way back in your dictation, mark the index slip with an instruction mark. Then dictate your instruction; i.e. 'Mary, will you please change the delivery date in the letter to Jones & Co. to September'. Your typist is trained to 'read' all instructions before beginning to type.

The stamp of a perfect dictator is the absence of 'instruction marks' on the index slip – but let's face it, few of us are perfect.

It is always easier to talk about change than to make it

– Alvin Toffler

Without the past the pursued future has no meaning

– Loren Eisley

CLEAR RULES FOR EFFECTIVE WRITTEN COMMUNICATION

When we write poorly, it is usually because our thoughts are muddled. Our writing tends to be poorly constructed, obscure in its reasoning and too long. If we use imprecise words, faulty reasoning, padding or jargon we cannot hope to get our message across. To communicate effectively we need to show both clarity of thought and clarity of expression.

Clear thinking

Language is the primary means of communication between human beings, so any exercise in clear writing is an exercise in the use of clear thought.

Clear thinking is hard work, but loose thinking is bound to produce loose writing. Clear thinking is required for both written and oral work. A knowledge of the common pitfalls will help you to argue logically, both when speaking and writing.

There are several obstacles to clear thinking and if you can identify them you may be able to avoid them. Here are some of the barriers and a few simple rules.

Language
People only speak the same language if they use the same words with the same meaning. Concrete terms such as 'table', 'book' or 'dog' are easy to use. Though we cannot communicate without them, there are dangers in the use of abstract terms which may mean different things to different people.

Habit
We all have habits of thought. These are beliefs that we originally accepted without question and that we have continued to hold ever since. We often call them our own 'convictions', but other people's 'prejudices'. Prejudices create obstacles in our minds and limit our thinking process. Although they are often strongly held, these beliefs generally collapse when subjected to logical reasoning.

Emotion
Many words appeal so strongly to the emotions that their basic meanings are obscured. Emotional words prejudice us in advance and prevent us from reaching impartial conclusions, e.g.:

We say:	They say:
inexperienced	incompetent
damaged	wrecked
enterprising	overambitious
adviser	meddler

Suggestion
Everyone is responsive to suggestion. For example, we tend to believe a statement that is repeated a great number of times – we don't take the trouble to check its accuracy. Suggestion can therefore be an insidious and formidable barrier to clear thought.

Generalisation
Many people are guilty of using the sweeping statement in an argument. Often the sweeping statement is untrue or is based on prejudice. To avoid the pitfall of generalisation, insert such words as 'all', 'some', 'most', 'sometimes', whenever it is necessary to make the meaning of an argument or statement more precise.

The principles of effective writing

There are two reasons why it is important to write effective English:

1. The aim of all writing is to communicate ideas. If there are no ideas, or these are misunderstood, then what is written serves no purpose.

2. What we write reflects our thoughts at the time of writing, and so our thoughts will be judged by the words we have written.

Here are a few stylistic guidelines to keep in mind.

Keep sentences short
When sentences average more than twenty words they are usually difficult to understand. An overuse of long sentences and long words, forces your reader to spend more time than he should in understanding your message.

Many overlong sentences can be shortened by adhering to the definition of a sentence. Webster defines a sentence as a "group of words expressing *one* completed step in a course of thinking." Often long sentences violate this definition. Here is an example:

The credit account you requested is now open and although no extra charge is made for this added convenience, we request that you send us your prompt remittance when you receive your statement on the 10th of every month.

This sentence expresses three thoughts. If the reader is a skilful writer, he will get the impression that you are not. This impression may adversely affect his reaction to your letter. Keeping the definition of a sentence in mind, it would be better to say:

The credit account you requested is now open. No extra charge is made for this convenience. Our statements go out on the 10th of every month and your prompt remittance is requested.

You can also keep sentences short by making sure that each word in every sentence carries its weight. Remove unnecessary words, and where one word will do the work of two, use it.

Not all sentences should be

short. Sentences must vary in length and in structure if the reader is to be saved from boredom. Ideally, you should maintain a balance between long and short sentences.

Paragraph length
The principle of keeping sentences short applies equally well to paragraphs. A paragraph should be a unit of thought and not of length. Every paragraph must be homogeneous in subject matter, and sequential in the treatment of it. In addition, short paragraphs improve the layout and general appearance of a letter or a report.

Prefer the simple to the complex
Be direct, simple, brief, forceful and lucid. This general principle means:

- Use the familiar word rather than the obscure, e.g. 'mean' not 'parsimonious'

- Use the concrete word rather than the abstract, e.g. 'letter' not 'communication'

- Use the single word rather than the circumlocution, e.g. 'scarce' not 'in short supply'.

- Use the short word rather than the long, e.g. 'go' not 'proceed'.

Although simplicity is stressed throughout this guide, this does not mean that you must limit yourself to words of one or two syllables. If you use less familiar words when you need impact, you can be sure that they will carry their weight.

Avoid unnecessary words
Many writers add unnecessary words to their phrases because of an erroneous idea that the padding gives emphasis or rounds off a sentence. Superfluous words waste your time, tire your reader and obscure meaning.

If, for example, we say: "the facts are these", we shall come under suspicion that on other occasions we have not given the facts. Never say 'true facts' – facts are, by definition, true.

Use adjectives to denote kind rather than degree. By all means say 'an economic crisis' or 'a military disaster', but don't use 'an acute crisis' or 'a terrible disaster'.

The list below further illustrates the points made.

The words and phrases in the left column below have shorter or simpler substitutes that are given in the right-hand column. These are only a few examples, but the principles involved can be applied to other useless words and phrases.

Wordy	Concise
A cheque in the amount of	A cheque for
During the year of 1992	During 1992
Owing to the fact that	Because
At the present time	Now
Until such time as you can	Until you can
Would you be good enough	Would you please
Beyond a shadow of doubt	Undoubtedly
Despite the fact that	Although
During the time that	While
Exhibits a tendency to	Tends to
Few in number	Few
Given encouragement to	Encouraged
He is of the opinion	He thinks

Wordy	Concise
Make an adjustment in	Adjust
In the event that	If
Past history	History
Of a confidential nature	Confidential
Preparatory to	Before
Orange in colour	Orange
The undersigned	I
With this in mind, it is clear that	Therefore
We deem it advisable	We suggest
In the vicinity of	About
In the majority of instances	Often
Present a conclusion	Conclude
Made the announcement that	Announced
Depreciates in value	Depreciates
The sum of ten pounds or £10	Ten pounds or £10
During the course of the campaign	During the campaign
For your information, the meeting will be held on Friday	The meeting will be on Friday
For the period of a year	For a year
As per your instructions	As you instructed
In compliance with your request	As requested

Wordy	Concise
Attached herewith is	Attached is
In order to arrive at a decision as to whether or not	To decide whether
It is our opinion	We think
In the city of Bristol	In Bristol
Your co-operation in letting us hear from you by the end of the week will be appreciated	Please advise us by the end of the week

Punctuation

Correct punctuation plays an important role in business letters. It can turn good copy into better copy and in the absence of punctuation it is sometimes difficult to follow the meaning of what has been written.

The object of punctuation is to help the reader grasp the meaning of what the writer is trying to convey. There are no hard-and-fast rules, but it is usually better to underpunctuate.

The full stop and the comma (.,)
The full stop is used at the end of a sentence that is not a question or an exclamation. It marks the end of a sentence. It is also used after abbreviations such as J.A. Smith, but not after contractions such as the 1st, 2nd, 3rd, etc. Modern practice does not require a full stop if the first and last letters are included in abbreviations such as Dr, Mr and Sgt.

- A comma is used to separate words, phrases or clauses within a sentence.

- Use a comma to mark off an expression that explains or gives additional information about a preceding expression.
The chairman of our company, Mr Bell, is in Australia.
Do not, however, separate two nouns, one which identifies the other.
The ballerina Dawn Weller is feeling ill.

- Separate the independent clauses of a compound sentence by a comma, unless the thought requires more emphatic separation than a comma. The comma precedes the conjunction.
We appreciate your letters of last month, but we are unable to comply with your request.

- The comma may be omitted before **and** if the clauses are short and closely connected in thought.
They left today and their family will leave tomorrow.

- Use a comma to indicate that one or more words easily understood, have been omitted.
She bought a dress, her friend, three.
Use a comma to separate an introductory word from the rest of the sentence.
Yes, we will be attending class.

- Do not separate words that belong together such as a verb from its subject or object, or a limiting clause from its antecedent.
She ordered paper, envelopes, pen and ink. (Pen and ink are closely connected in meaning and do not need a comma.)

- Do not use a comma between a name and **of** indicating place or position.
Mr Jones of Bristol.

- Use a comma after closing brackets if the construction of the sentence requires a comma.

Never use a comma before a bracket or an expression enclosed in brackets.
You need tea, a slice of lemon, sugar (preferably lump), cream and assorted biscuits.

- Place the comma on the inside of quotation marks. *When he spoke of "overtime," I thought he meant 40 hours.*

- Mark off direct quotations with a comma. *"I am interested," he said, "in anything you have to say." His reply was, "I do not really want to know."*
But if a question mark is needed at the end of a quotation, do not use a comma.
"Have you seen the new film?" he asked.

The question mark (?)

The question mark is used instead of the full stop at the end of a sentence that contains a direct question: *"Would you like me to make enquiries?"*

It is not used after an indirect question: *I asked him whether he would like to buy a new car.* It is unnecessary to use a question mark where a command has been expressed in the form of a question: *"Will you call me later."* When, however, a question demands a reply, the question mark is used: *"Can you call me later?"* Question marks are not common in letters, as questions are usually phrased as polite requests beginning with words such as "may we ..." Such sentences are statements and must end with a full stop.

The exclamation mark (!)

This is used instead of a full stop after words, phrases and sentences that express pleasure, surprise, indignation, or any strong emotion: *Help! Hello! How could you do that!*
These are seldom necessary in

business letters or reports, where the aim is to convey facts, not emotions. A possible exception is a sales letter, where exclamation marks can sometimes be used effectively.

The semicolon (;)

The semicolon is used instead of a full stop when several complete statements, which are closely connected in thought, are joined together in one sentence, either with or without the word "and" or "but":

The secretary should know how to put clients at their ease; she should converse comfortably with strangers and be able to keep a conversation flowing; she should avoid any tricky subjects; and, above all, she must show a genuine interest in the people who call.

(It is a common error to link such statements with a comma; this should be avoided.)

The semicolon is also used to separate phrases or items forming a series: *The case, when opened, was found to contain a quantity of jewellery, some of it extremely valuable; a few furs; half a dozen exquisite ornaments; and a bundle of old letters, now quite faded.*

Capitalisation

In keeping with the modern trend, it is better to capitalise as little as possible. With this in mind, it is easier to know what should be capped:

- Proper nouns should continue to be capped wherever used.

These include all names of people and places, titles of books, plays, films, etc.

- Where two words of different meaning but the same spelling exist, a capital letter may sometimes help to clarify which meaning is intended:

state	–	state of mind (l/c) State, as in country (u/c)
minister	–	of religion (l/c) of State (u/c)
press	–	verb (l/c) noun (u/c)
bill	–	capped as a Parliamentary Bill, ditto Act.

- For ranks and titles of important people such as Prime Minister.

It is not always necessary to capitalise titles within a company (except on door signs, etc.) such as managing director, manager, chairman. Company policy on this point should, however, be checked.

Numbers as words and figures

Whether to write numbers as words or figures can be confusing. To ensure consistency, it is better to make a decision and stick to it. Your company may have a policy already. If so, find it out and use it. If not, the following may be a useful guideline.

For all numbers up to and including nine, spell the word out. Exceptions may be when the number is used in dates, weights, prices or distances, e.g. 6 June,

8 kg, £2, 9 km. Use your discretion in other similar instances.

Numbers from 10 upwards should be written as figures. When referring to numbers in millions it is, however, more concise to use a combination of figures and words: £10-million.

Style

Where many writers experience most difficulty, and where many papers break down, is not in the structure of the paper, but in the style. Style is not some kind of garnish added afterwards to the first draft to make it attractive to the reader. It is something much more fundamental. It is the application of the principles of effective writing and a correct use of the rules of grammar and punctuation.

Conclusion

In your writing you should aim to be clear and logical because the hallmarks of all good writing are clarity, accuracy and effectiveness. You should also try to be as brief as you can without sacrificing these other characteristics.

But no marks are awarded for monotony. It is always helpful to introduce some variety both in the choice of words and in the balance and contrast of sentence structure. Sentences should run smoothly and the line of thought be clearly traceable from one sentence – and one paragraph – to the next. Above all, remember that it is not enough to write so that you will be understood: write so that you cannot be misunderstood.

The wise learn many things from their foes
– Aristophanes

Getting off to a good start

Writing business letters that are clear, concise and simple seems to be an art that eludes many businessmen and women. The skill is to keep it short and simple – this makes it easy for the reader to understand and respond.

General guidelines

- Stay on the topic. Don't digress or ramble.

- Use plain language, simple words and short sentences.

- When writing long letters, memos or reports, use headings and sub-headings. These give direction and tie thoughts together.

- Tone is important. A cordial tone will have a positive effect. An antagonistic tone will "turn off" the reader. A reader who is offended by the tone of the letter may become agitated and unco-operative.

- When replying to a letter, restate the subject of the original letter in your opening sentence. Use as few words as possible.

- Restating is done because the writer of the original letter may have written several letters on the same date. Your restatement of the subject will help refresh your reader's memory. In addition, restating the subject helps preserve the history and continuity of the communication.

- Put what the reader needs to know at the beginning of the letter.

- Do not argue. Just supply the information necessary to clarify points that are confusing or that might be misunderstood.

- When an apology is called for, make it.

- Avoid when possible, the use of the passive voice, e.g. "It was decided by the committee ..." Rather say "The committee decided ..." It is far more forceful.

- Edit continually. It is often difficult to say exactly what you mean the first time. So do not be afraid to rewrite and eliminate words, phrases and even paragraphs that are superfluous.

- Check the typed copy for errors. Your secretary may be an excellent typist but check for copy errors before you sign it. An incorrect word can sometimes change the entire meaning of a sentence.

Examples of business letters

Clearly you will determine your own letter style. The following letters are provided to show the type of information each should include.

1. Letter of invitation

Letters of invitation should be easy enough to write, for they carry no bad news, do not risk hurting or offending, and usually announce a pleasant event.

Invitations should never fail to specify the date, the time and place of the event in question. The reason for the event should also be specified. Try to add a note of warmth and welcome to your invitation letters. Enthusiasm is catchy and engenders good will.

(i) Informal lunch or dinner invitation

Dear Peter

I have just heard from my marketing manager that you are planning to be in Sussex next week. We are having our senior management lunch on the 13th and we'd like you to join us. In addition, I feel that it would be of mutual benefit if you would join the discussion which takes place afterwards.

We'll be meeting at High Gate place at 12:30.

Will you be able to come?

Regards

(ii) Formal dinner invitation

The formal third person invitation is usually engraved on a card, the guest's name being written in by hand.

Mr and Mrs George Banks
request the pleasure of
the company of
Mr and Mrs Barry Thring
at dinner on
Friday, 12 March
at eight o'clock

RSVP
27 Lawley Street
Moreton   Black tie

(iii) Invitation to make a speech or give a talk

Dear Mr Sweeney

The next meeting of the association to be held on 3 May at the Grange Hotel, Oxford, will be devoted to new developments in the field of Industrial Productivity.

We are anxious to secure a speaker of your distinction for the occasion, and I am writing to ask whether you would consider addressing the Association members for 30 to 45 minutes on that date.

The meeting starts at 8:30 pm and I would be honoured if you would be my guest at dinner beforehand. It has to be a rather rushed affair under the circumstances, but if we meet at 7:00 pm, it would still allow us a little time to talk.

Your sincerely

2. Letters of acceptance

Letters accepting an invitation to

an event which requires preparation should be sent within two days of receiving the invitation. It is often a good idea to reiterate the time, place and date of the meeting, to ensure that there will be no misunderstanding.

(i) Acceptance of informal lunch or dinner invitation

Dear Jack

I am delighted to accept your kind invitation to your senior management lunch on 13 October at Highgate Place. I shall be there at 12:30 as you suggest, and look forward to a very interesting afternoon.

Regards

(ii) Acceptance of formal dinner invitation

Mr and Mrs Barry Thring
have much pleasure in accepting
the kind invitation of
Mr and Mrs George Banks
to dinner
on Friday, 12 March
at eight o'clock

(iii) Acceptance of invitation to make a speech or give a talk

Dear Mr Whitelaw

Thank you for asking me to address your conference on May 3.

Unless you feel otherwise, I would like to discuss industrial accidents. The subject is quite topical and I think it will be of some value to your members. I'll limit my talk to 30 minutes, plus 10-15 minutes for questions.

I look forward to the occasion and hope there will be a good number attending. I'll be there at 7:00 pm, so that we can have a quick dinner and chat as you suggest.

Yours sincerely

3. Refusal letters

So as not to offend, letters of refusal must be both tactful and friendly. They should leave the recipient with the impression that his invitation is turned down with genuine regret.

(i) Refusal of informal lunch or dinner invitation

Dear Harry

Thank you for your friendly letter asking me to have lunch with you during my fleeting visit to London next week.

There is nothing I would have enjoyed more, but I'm afraid we shall have to postpone it. I shall be attending meetings all day long and lunch, will, no doubt, consist of a sandwich and a cup of tea in the conference room.

I hope you understand the situation. I look forward to seeing you either on my next visit or when you come to Dublin.

Regards

(ii) Refusal of formal invitation to dinner

Mr and Mrs Barry Thring
regret that a previous
engagement
prevents them from accepting
the kind
invitation to dinner on
Friday, 12 March
at the home of
Mr and Mrs George Banks

(iii) Refusal of invitation to join professional association

Dear Mr Stead

Many thanks for your letter of 3 September. I am highly honoured by your invitation to me to join the committee of the Board of Directors.

I wish I could undertake the task, but unfortunately my crowded schedule would not ena-

ble me to give the undertaking the time and attention it deserves. I must therefore ask you to excuse me.

I hope you understand, and do please thank the other members for their confidence in me.

Yours sincerely

(iv) Refusal of contributions, support of charities, etc.

Dear Mr Grey

I have carefully considered your request for our company to support your special "Cancer Week" appeal.

Unfortunately, however, the funds the company have set aside for charitable purposes have all been allocated already and I am therefore unable to respond this time.

I do, nonetheless, wish you the very greatest success in your wonderful work.

Yours sincerely

4. Letters of congratulations and good wishes

Everyone likes to be congratulated on his achievements and is pleased when the milestones in his life are recognised by friends and associates. Do respond to your associates' and friends' achievements with a short note of congratulations.

(i) A new business or professional appointment

Dear Dr Ballantine

I was delighted to learn you have been appointed Chief Administrative Officer of Hospital Services.

I know you will make a resounding success of it, as you have of all your undertakings. We, as a company, look forward to cooperating with you in any way we can.

Meanwhile, please accept my

congratulations and good wishes.

Yours sincerely

*(ii) A business anniversary/
business achievement*

Dear Mr Drake

Please accept my warmest congratulations on this twenty-fifth anniversary of the founding of your business. Your record in that time is one you may well be proud of. Your reputation and standing in the community are second to none.

Long may your success and prosperity continue.

Yours sincerely

(iii) A birth

Dear Fred and Paula

News has just reached me that the little stranger has arrived and that she is a beautiful girl. Congratulations to you both. With parents like you she is bound to make a splendid start in life.

My very best wishes to the three of you!

Yours sincerely

(iv) Wedding

Dear Tim

It's excellent news.

Congratulations and our very best wishes to you and Susan.

We know you will have a wonderful life together, certainly if all our good wishes for you come true.

Yours sincerely

(v) For outstanding work

Dear Tim

This is just a note to tell you how much I appreciated the outstanding effort which your whole department put into getting the direct mail brochures printed and distributed on time.

Without everyone's wholehearted effort it could not have been done and I want you to convey my sincere thanks to every one of your staff. It was a splendid effort.

Regards

(vi) Promotion of staff member

Dear Charles

Congratulations on you promotion to Technical Director. As you know, this gesture is in recognition of your conscientious and efficient work as production manager during the past four years.

My best wishes for your continued success.

Regards

5. Thank you letters

For a thank you letter to be effective, it should be written at once, for nothing creates a worse impression than a "thank you" letter which begins with an apology.

In these days of constant haste, few people send a note of thanks for a gift or a favour received, or a pleasant evening. Yet, this type of letter gives great pleasure to the recipient and contributes much to a friendship or association.

*(i) Appreciation for a business
gift*

Dear David

I was absolutely delighted to receive such an elegant gift. The decanter is so lovely that it far surpasses what is in my drinks cabinet. It was kind of you to reward me in this way for the slight help I gave you in editing some chapters of your book.

Congratulations on a splendid job, best wishes for its success, and thanks again for such an exquisite gift.

Yours sincerely

*(ii) For a special courtesy or
service*

Dear Jack

I wish to thank you most sincerely for the many courtesies extended to me during my brief visit to Chicago.

Your kindness and wholehearted co-operation, not to mention your true American hospitality, made my trip not only a most successful, but also an extremely pleasant one.

Please let me know if there is anything I can do for you here, either personal or otherwise.

Yours sincerely

(iii) For a donation

Dear Mr Simpson

Please accept my warmest thanks for your very generous donation to our Association. Ours is a cause which is so often neglected because other claims seem more urgent. Nonetheless we are doing vital work and need funds very badly if we are to succeed. You quite obviously realise this and we greatly appreciate your support.

Yours sincerely

*(iv) For making a speech/giving
a talk*

Dear Mr Sweeney

Your talk to our members last night was one of the most outstanding we have heard at the Association for a long time. The orginality of your approach to industrial accidents will give our members much food for thought.

Thank you for sharing with us your unique experiences in the field of accident prevention. I am sure that many of our members will adopt some of your methods in their own factories.

Regards

(v) For loyal service

Dear Fred

Twenty-five years with one company is a long time and a rare achievement these days. When this quarter of a century has been devoted consistently to hard work, cheerful co-operation and unstinting loyalty, then it is a record anyone may be proud of. And this is just what you have done.

I know you heard all these things last night at the Celebration Dinner, but I very much wanted to tell you in my own words just how proud of you I am and how much I have appreciated your loyalty throughout the years.

My heartfelt personal thanks go with you as you begin you 26th year with the firm.

Yours sincerely

(vi) For message of condolence or sympathy

Dear Craig

Thank you for your kind words of sympathy. At a time of great personal sorrow such as this, there is no greater solace than the knowledge that our friends are there and feel with us.

Thank you again.

Yours sincerely

Dear Mr Wells

Your kind words of sympathy on the death of our Managing Director, Dr Ross MacDonald, were deeply appreciated.

His sudden loss has been a great shock to us and his absence will be keenly felt by all at *Cleaver's*.

At a time such as this your

friendship and kindness are a great comfort to us all.

Yours sincerely

6. Letters of seasonal greetings

Letters of seasonal greetings can do a lot to cultivate and maintain a happy business relationship and to keep a contact alive.

Dear Paul

As the bells ring out the Old Year, we would be ungrateful if we failed to turn our thoughts back to the year that has gone by and to the valued support you have given us during that time.

We sincerely appreciate your loyalty and feel this is the time of year to express our thanks and send you our very best wishes for the coming year. May it be a happy and prosperous one.

Yours sincerely

7. Letters of apology

It sometimes happens that we or one of our staff members are negligent in some way or another. A prompt and sincere apology is the only way out at such times.

If you do have a convincing explanation for your lapse, then by all means give it, otherwise, an honest admission of your error will often work wonders to restore you to the good graces of your correspondent.

(i) Dear Mr Sloan

We are very sorry to learn that the chair you purchased from us seems to be of inferior quality, and we have notified the manufacturer of your dissatisfaction.

We certainly want you to be happy with any purchase you make from *ABC Furnishers*.

Will you kindly telephone Mr Brooks, our departmental manager, and advise him of the time and date when it will be convenient to have the chair picked up. Would

you also let us know whether you wish to choose a replacement, or if you would prefer to have the £150 credited to your account.

We do apologise for the inconvenience caused and we thank you for calling the matter to our attention.

Yours sincerely

(ii) Dear Mr Preston

Please accept my apologies for what happened yesterday. I fully expected to be back at the office by the time you arrived, but an appointment kept me tied up until 2:30 and the exasperatingly slow-moving traffic delayed me still further.

Do please give me an opportunity to make amends next time you come to London.

Yours sincerely

8. Letters of condolence and sympathy

A letter of sympathy or condolence is perhaps the most difficult to write. It is the kind of letter we all keep on postponing, making our task harder the longer we leave it.

The best procedure is to write the message right away and to tailor it according to the degree of friendship between writer and recipient, and the known feelings of the recipient towards the deceased.

(i) Family bereavement, colleagues and business associates

Dear Sally

I was most distressed to hear you had lost your mother. Words are such poor comforters at a time such as this, yet it can be of some solace to know that our friends are close to us and feel with us in our grief.

Do be assured that I am at

hand and if there is anything at all I can do, please let me know.

Yours sincerely

Dear Mr Baker

It is with deep regret that we have just heard of the death of your wife.

We are aware of the scant solace which words can bring at such a time, but all of us here at *Plantpack* want you to know you have our deepest sympathy.

Yours sincerely

(ii) On the death of a company executive

Dear Sirs

The entire *Plantpack* organisation joins me in expressing our deepest sympathy in the loss of your Managing Director, Dr Ross MacDonald.

His sterling qualities earned him and your company numerous friends in the profession and he will be mourned and missed by many.

Yours faithfully

9. Letters of appointment

The standard letter of appointment sets out the terms and conditions of employment – and is always formal.

Most firms have draft forms. The letter should stipulate the terms and conditions of employment and should in addition include:

- the employee's full name and status (Mr/Mrs, etc.)

- the date he or she starts employment

- the agreed salary and salary review dates

- the exact amount of leave granted annually (e.g. 20 working days)

- information regarding pension and insurance schemes

- motor car policy, if applicable

- notice of termination of services.

All letters of appointment are made out in duplicate – and signed in duplicate – one each for the employer and employee. The employee's signature signifies his acceptance of the terms and conditions of employment.

10. Letter of resignation

Dear Sir/Madam

Resignation: J Sharpe

In accordance with the conditions of my letter of appointment of 3 January 19__, I wish to give you three months' notice of my resignation on 30 December 19__.

I have recently been offered a position with a higher salary and with good prospects for promotion which I have decided to accept.

I would like to thank you sincerely for your help and support in the past.

Yours faithfully

Their hindsight was better than their foresight
– Henry Ward Beecher

SHARPEN YOUR REPORT-WRITING TECHNIQUES

There are naturally as many different types of reports as there are companies, management styles, personal differences and philosophies in business and life.

Some reports are standard and better handled by a computer if available. Others represent the crux of an organisation's decision-making process. These require the crisp, clear presentation of well-ordered facts and figures often leading to the clarification of a crucial problem.

Reporting techniques

Preparation, research, organisation, writing, revision and presentation – these six are necessary to produce a solid business report. It is a step-by-step process.

Each step depends on the step before it. You can't research effectively unless you have done adequate preparation; you can't organise well unless you have done the research; you can't write effectively unless the organisation is solid; you can't revise successfully unless you have made a good attempt at writing the first draft; you can't finalise the details of the presentation until you have revised successfully.

Preparation

A manager must first identify the specific purpose of the particular report and also who it is aimed at. Asking questions can be helpful in establishing the purpose and target audience of a report. The following are some questions to ask:

- to whom are you addressing this report? Who else may read it?

- if the report was requested by the readers, have they told you specifically what they want? Should you ask for clarification? Are there any unstated purposes your readers probably want the report to serve – purposes they are not likely to tell you about? If others may read the report, what purposes will they expect it to serve?

- if you are writing not in response to a request but on your own initiative, do you know exactly what you are trying to accomplish? What do you want the reader to do, say, believe?

- are you trying to persuade your reader? Are you attempting to change or strengthen their convictions, or are they undecided? Are you sure what their convictions are? Do you know why they hold them?

- how important will your report be to your readers? Will they be impatient with a long, detailed discussion? Will they think you have done a careless, skimpy job if you are brief?

Research

Although the information needed in a report will vary from one situation to another, the problems with establishing whether the required information exists and where to find it are common. Research basically concerns itself with the gathering, interpretation and analysis of available data. The objective should be to obtain accurate, comprehensive and practical information.

Valuable information sources include *inter alia*:

- company files, records, reports
- business publications
- libraries
- government departments
- statistical publications

Organisation

Another important factor is to ensure that every report is a simple and concise statement of only the pertinent facts. The recipient can then learn what he needs to know without having significant information obscured by excessive detail. More specifically, here are things that report writers can do to avoid the type of reports that discourage their use by management:

- make sure that the amount of detail is limited to that which is necessary. For example, reports for sales supervisors may not need to show the same detail as reports required by head office executives.

- eliminate all calculated figures that may have been necessary to build up a schedule but are not needed to understand the end result.

- report only actual performance and variance from plans. Including unnecessary material in the report serves only to complicate it and divert attention from the important facts.

- eliminate pence and round off large figures to the nearest thousand or million pounds to make the figures easier to grasp.

Report writing

A report writing tip that many specialists recommend is: Once you start, keep going. Don't get caught up in style, word choice or missing facts. If you feel you need to impart more information in a certain place, leave some space and carry on. Once you have completed a first draft you can always go back and fill in the gaps. The important thing is to make a first attempt at giving your report shape and direction. Ensure that you use language and terminology that your readers will understand.

Revision

It is often said that good reports are not written, they are rewritten. A first draft is very seldom perfect. Revision is an important step because it allows you to rethink certain thoughts and to streamline and put finishing touches to your whole effort. This is the time to make sure that report titles, tabular column headings and item/product names or descriptions are so clear that no one could misunderstand them.

Presentation

Use presentation techniques that highlight significant developments or out-of-line performance. The basic objective here should be to focus the readers' attention on matters requiring decision, action, or further investigation. This can be done by helping them grasp the significant facts and relationships quickly without first having to dig for meaning. This can be accomplished in several ways, the most common of which are the following:

- calculate and show deviations from the plan so the reader does not have to make the calculations mentally.

- if the significance of the data will not be readily apparent to the users of the report, then call their attention to the important facts or interpret the report for them. That is, if the report is not clearly self-explanatory, distil its significance. One method of doing this is to circle the important variances. This is satisfactory where no further explanation is needed to make the report meaningful. Another technique is to provide a narrative interpretation, either in footnotes or in a supplementary report.

Visual aids should be used wherever feasible - not only to reveal trends, but also to make the entire report easier to understand. Mere charting, however, does not by itself ensure clarity. A table, chart or graph that attempts to give too much information can be more confusing than helpful.

Conclusion

The aim in reporting should be to cut out unnecessary information and to make important facts clear. By using aids to understanding and assimilation such as those mentioned, top management will find reports more meaningful and not, "a do-it-yourself kit without the instructions to put it together".

The whole of science is nothing more than a refinement of everyday thinking
– Albert Einstein

HOW TO WRITE CONCISE AND ACCURATE MINUTES

Basic functions

Essentially minutes are kept of meetings for the following two reasons:

- Once approved and signed, minutes become the authoritative record of the proceedings.

- At the meeting something has been decided, and these decisions must be implemented. The minutes thus become the blueprint and authority for action.

To meet these requirements minutes must:

- provide a true and balanced account of the proceedings

- be written in clear, concise and unambiguous language

- be brief and to the point

- be presented in a way which makes it easy to assimilate the contents

- include the time and date of meeting where held, name of chairman, people present, etc.

It is thus apparent that in minute writing there is a perpetual conflict between accuracy, brevity and clarity.

Accuracy

To ensure accuracy, it is essential that adequate notes are taken. When taking the minutes of a meeting, keep the following in mind:

- Notes must be highly selective. Do not try to take a verbatim record. Learn to distinguish between the significant and the irrelevant. Taking minutes regularly will soon sharpen your judgement.

- Record the names of the main contributors. You may not include them all in the minutes, but it is helpful in case a query does arise after the meeting.

- Boldly indicate each topic with a clear heading. Allow plenty of space between different topics.

Draft the minutes as soon as possible after the meeting while the meeting is still fresh in your mind and obtain the chairman's approval of the draft before finally typing it for circulation to the members.

If you are new to minute-taking, a tape recorder is a particularly useful aid. It will enable you to go back to any part of the proceedings with accuracy. After some practice in note-taking, you will find the need for verification from the tape will rapidly diminish.

Contents

The contents must:

- put the proceedings into their logical sequence

- prune the irrelevant

- give a balanced emphasis to the views which shaped the final decision.

The hallmark of good minuting is the ability to give a comprehensive and meaningful account of the meeting – not only to those who were present, but also to those who were not. When minuting a discussion which was based on a background paper, it is helpful to append the paper to the minutes, as some readers may not have had access to the original paper.

Presentation

Attendance record
The names of the members who had been invited to attend the meeting must be recorded. The usual practice is simply to list the names under "present" and "apologies for absence".

Style
Remember that you are writing a document with a strictly limited objective. **Its sole purpose is to provide a factual record of the meeting**.

It follows therefore that your sentences should be short; your words simple; your expressions direct and to the point; and your meaning clear and capable of only one interpretation. Use indirect speech.

Layout

- Use headings and sub-headings. They make quick identification easier.

- Number paragraphs, sections and sub-sections. This makes for easy reference.

- Do not hesitate to use graphs, tables or illustrations. Often they are more effective than words.

Follow-up action

When sending out the minutes, add a note to those members who are required to take some action or highlight the relevant sections for their special attention. If a report is required, inform members by what date it should reach you for circulation to the committee, to allow them time to peruse it prior to the next meeting.

AN EDITING CHECKLIST

In the transmitting of business information, accuracy is of the greatest importance. The problems created by errors that are released into the channels of information and communication are not only time consuming to correct, but can also result in losses to the organisation. All written communication must therefore be checked carefully. Ensure that every detail is correct and that each item is complete.

A proofreading checklist

Following are a few guidelines that should be observed when checking any typewritten work.

1. Proofread the copy for meaning. Check for typographical, spelling and punctuation errors.

2. Read the copy a second time, scanning it for figures, such as dates and amounts of money, and check their accuracy.

3. Use a calculator to check typed figures that have been totalled.

4. When a long series appears in a paragraph, count the items and compare the numbers with the list in the original. Also count the items included in a tabulation.

5. When proofreading is so critical that you ask someone to read to you, ask the person to read from the rough copy.

6. Do not have material retyped to make a copy. Use a copier to eliminate any chance of error and the necessity for re-proofreading.

An editing checklist

Use the following editing checklist both **before** and **after** having long and complicated reports typed. The benefits of checking through a report **before** having it typed is that you are able to work out a layout and pinpoint possible problem areas and inaccuracies. In the long run this will save a lot of time and frustration.

Checking through the report after it has been completed gives you an opportunity to ensure that no mistakes have inadvertently slipped through.

Titles and headings

- Is the title of the publication correct?

- Has the same format been used throughout for
  - chapter titles
  - section titles
  - headings
  - sub-headings?

Text

- Does the text read smoothly and meaningfully?

- Are all sentences, paragraphs, sections and chapters complete?

- Check the copy for punctuation and spelling errors.

- Are all footnotes complete?

- Do the footnote numbers correspond with the numbers used in the copy?

- Are the names of persons, titles and organisations correct?

Visual aids

- Have all the figures and tables which are referred to in the text, been included?

- Have all figures and tables been numbered correctly?

- Are all the captions correct?

- Has the same format been used throughout for figure and table numbers and captions?

- Do the visual aids relate to the text?

- Are tables ruled correctly?

- Is any aid too cluttered, so it loses meaning?

Quoted material

- Are all quotations correct?

- Has credit been given to quotation sources?

- Where necessary, has copyright permission been obtained?

Figures and statistics

- Are all statistics accurate?

- Do all sub-totals and totals balance?

- Where applicable, has credit been given to the source of the information?

Contents pages

- Is the table of contents complete?

- Are the page numbers correct?

End matter

- Have all the necessary appendices been included?

- Is the bibliography adequate?

- Does the bibliography adhere to a standard format?

- Is the index adequate and accurate?

STANDARD CORRECTION MARKS FOR PROOFREADING

If you are required to correct the proofs of reports, circulars, memos, forms, etc., use these standard correction marks to indicate any changes that should be made before final printing.

Instruction to printer	Textual mark (example)	Marginal mark
Delete	point sizes	ℐ
Delete and close up	point speize	ℐ /
Delete and leave space	point/size	#
Leave as printed	point size	stet
Insert new matter	⋏ size	point ⋏
Change to capital letters	point size	CAPS
Change to small capitals	point size	S.C.
Change to lower case	(POINT)size	lc
Change to bold	point size	bold
Change to italics	point size	italics
Underline	point size	insert rule
Change to roman	(point size)	rom
(Wrong fount) replace by character of correct fount	poin(t)size	w.f.
Invert type	po(u) size	⊙
Replace damaged type	poin(s)ze	×
Close up	point siz e	⌒
Insert space	point size	#
Make space equal	point/sizes / used	eq #
Space between lines	POINT / SIZE ←	2 pt #
Reduce space	point ∠ size	less #
Transpose	used sizes point	trs
Move to right (left)	point size	⌐
Indent 1 em (2 em)	point size	▫⋏

Instruction to printer	Textual mark (example)	Marginal mark
Take words (or letters) to beginning of following line	The Phoenix and the Turtle	take over
Take words (or letters) to end of preceding line	The Phoenix and the Turtle	take back
Raise (or lower line)	point size	↓
Correct vertical alignment	‖ point ‖ size	‖
Figure (or abbreviation) to be spelt out in full	(12)point twelve(pt.)	spell out
Substitute separate letters	phœnix	oe /
Use diphthong (or ligature)	manoeuvre	œ
No fresh paragraph	point of the pen. The hair line of the	run on
Begin new paragraph	point of the pen. The hair line of the early	n.p.
Insert punctuation mark indicated	point size /	⸴⋏
Substitute punctuation mark indicated	point size /	⊙ /
Insert em (en) rule	point/size	⊢em⊣ ⋏
Insert parentheses or square brackets	/ point size /	( )
Insert hyphen	point/size	/-/
Insert single quotes (double quotes, apostrophe)	/ Phototypesetting /	⸲ ⸴⸴
Refer to appropriate authority	(15)point Helvetica	(?)
Substitute superior character	boys girl-friends	⸲⋏
Substitute inferior character	boys girl-friends	⸲⋏

GUIDE TO WRITING A CURRICULUM VITAE

In an era of take-overs, restructurings and mergers, virtually no professional can totally ignore the job market. Being prepared for the possibility of an abrupt change in your career path can be invaluable. One of the first steps in any job search is preparing the *curriculum vitae* (CV).

That most job seekers have little or no conception of what an employer wants to see in a CV, can be confirmed by even the most junior member of any company's personnel department.

CVs appear daily in these departments and they vary from the scant one-page listing of past employers and employment dates to the verbose book-length offerings detailing the applicant's entire work history!

It is thus important that we ask ourselves what the purpose of a CV is. First and foremost, the CV is a marketing tool, an advertisement. Its chief purpose is to "get a foot in the door", in other words to obtain a job interview.

Remember that for many advertised jobs there are hundreds of applicants. Reviewing all the CVs that arrive can be a daunting task. The applicant with the clear, concise CV which contains pertinent information and is readable, and scannable, has the advantage. The last factor is the most important. The most vital points must be easily visible to someone scanning the document for only a few moments.

Although a good CV will not necessarily get you the job, the poor CV will lose that all-important interview. The professionally prepared CV separates you from the masses and secures the interview.

Steps in writing a *curriculum vitae*

Heading and personal information

Give the first page the heading "Curriculum Vitae" followed by your name, address and telephone number.

Statement of career objective

A clear, concise statement of purpose should attract the reader's attention. Focus on your main skills and strengths relating to the job you're applying for. You might wish to express your job objective in terms of job functions rather than job titles.

Justify the career objective

This is a short summary of your main experiences and accomplishments and should back up your job objective. You can provide it either in narrative style or in point form. The information should prove that your job objective is realistic. Relate your achievements to your objectives.

Summarise your career experience

This section details your career history. Start with the most recent job relevant to your job objective and list job title, employer/company, a short description of the main duties, and the years you worked there. Concentrate on duties and responsibilties which relate to the job you are applying for.

Summarise your education and training

List your highest degree first, adding non-academic training if it relates to your job objective. If you feel your training and experience are equivalent to academic qualifications, list these as well.

Summarise other supporting data

Include society memberships, awards, interests, published work, etc. only if they are relevant to the job objective.

List personal data such as age, marital status, children.

The inclusion of references in a CV is generally premature. However, if the advertisement specifically asks for references then list the name, job title, business address and phone number of each one.

Proofread carefully

Check all the information to ensure it supports your career objective. Your CV should be as brief as possible, while containing all the details necessary to help you land the job.

Further tips

- Pay attention to style and format. Arrange the information so that your strongest and most impressive accomplishments appear first.

- Use spacing, capital letters and underlining for visual impact.

- A CV should present an accurate and positive picture of your qualifications and experience. But remember that the past is relevant only to show your potential to develop in the future.

- Use clear, concise language that is easy to read and understand.

- Include only information which is strictly relevant to the job you are applying for. Omit any information which could be interpreted in a negative way.

- Type your CV and covering letter on good-quality paper. Most guides recommend plain white standard-size stationery. This serves to enhance the business nature of the communication.

- Make sure that your CV and covering letter are perfect in terms of spelling, punctuation and grammar. If necessary ask

The art of communicating

an expert to check it for you. Typing errors and messy corrections will create a bad impression.

• It isn't necessary to mention the salary you want – you might get a better offer.

The covering letter

The covering letter's purpose is to introduce you to the prospective employer. The letter shares the CV's purpose of landing the interview. To that end, the covering letter must be brief, clear and concise. The CV itself will, if it has been properly prepared, contain all the necessary background information. Do type an original letter for each CV you send out.

Letters fall into two broad categories: those being sent in response to an advertised position and the unsolicited, exploratory letter. A recruitment advertisement will specify how the responses should be addressed, but the unsolicited letter must always be addressed to a specific person and use that person's correct title.

The letter should conclude on a confident note by proposing a meeting or by stating that you will follow up by telephone to arrange a meeting. When suggesting a follow-up phone call, to avoid sounding overly aggressive, include an explanation such as: "As it is difficult to reach me during the day, I will call towards the end of next week ..."

The professionally prepared CV and the targeted, well-written covering letter provide a winning "one-two" combination that makes you stand out in the battle for today's career opportunities.

The bitter taste of poor quality remains long after the sweet taste of low price is forgotten
 – *John David Stanhope*

Man's mind is his basic means of survival – his only means of gaining knowledge
 – *Ayn Rand*

GUIDELINES FOR EFFECTIVE GRAPHIC AND TABULAR COMMUNICATION

Faced with a mass of data it is not always easy to make sense of them or to grasp what they are trying to tell us. The average person has trouble to remember more than about ten digits in a row. The more numbers there are, the more incomprehensible they become.

In order to understand and remember them, summarise and reduce them, make them more compact and present them in different ways. If data is to be of any real value, clear presentation is essential. Following simple rules, understandable tabulation can be made easy.

Tables, diagrams, charts and graphs are used increasingly and the particular form the illustration takes will depend on the nature of the data, who is going to use it and the purpose for which it is going to be used.

The higher you go in the hierarchy of decision-making, the more reduced and summarised the statistical presentation will become. The chief executive will not usually be concerned with the details but rather with the overall picture and main points.

On the other hand, where critical decisions have to be made using special, as well as routine data analysis, the detail to be scrutinised will become greater.

Good charts and tables convey information in concise and readily comprehensible form. Inundated as we are by an ever-increasing outflow of data and information in almost every field of endeavour, we value the individual who can convey the relevant facts, concepts and ideas in comprehensive and readily acceptable form.

While in some instances charts are concocted deliberately to deceive, or to confuse an issue, the predominant reason for which charts are prepared is the opposite. The desire is to highlight the findings and ease the reader's task, all to the end of getting the message across and gaining ac-

ceptance of the author's ideas.

Constructing a table

When compiling a table you should pay attention to the following:

• Give every table a clear title.

• Arrange the columns and rows of a table according to the same measure of magnitude (e.g. size, frequency, rank order). Insert columns and row totals and the average where these will aid comparisons.

• Remember that it is easier for people to add columns than rows running across a page. Faced with a sheet of numbers our eyes seem to be much happier to go up and down than across. Space constraints in relation to the number of columns will often dictate the shape of the table. No one table should exceed eight columns.

• If there are too many figures in the table, break them down into two or three smaller tables. Other things being equal, e.g. eyesight, legibility and layout – the smaller the table size, the more the eye can take in at a glance.

• Try several different arrangements of the data in order to lift out the pattern and salient features more strongly and to show exceptions at a glance.

• At the end of the table always put a note indicating the source of the data.

• Keep footnotes brief.

Simple tabulation is the key to good data presentation. It can tell you whether the data is useful or worthless for the purposes intended.

Graphs

Graphs report the same type of data as tables do. However, they do so using lines, bars and circles.

When constructing a graph careful attention should be paid to the following aspects:

• Number graphs with arabic numerals (1,2) consecutively throughout the report. Number graphs and tables separately. Both graphs and tables may use arabic numbering in the same report.

• Use concise, but descriptive titles and sub-titles. The title should not leave the reader with any questions as to the purpose of the graph.

• Within the narrative, introduce the graph or chart by number and title. Insert it as soon as is possible and do not separate it from the text with which it is connected if at all possible.

• Make graphic presentations clear, concise, complete, accurate and attractive. Introduce colour when appropriate.

(a) Line graphs

When constructing a line graph you must pay attention to the following:

• Use appropriate scales to make the graphs approximately square. Do so by establishing the scale on the horizontal X-axis first. Then calculate the vertical Y-axis scale to make the height approximately the same as the width. If one dimension must exceed the other, make the height the greater of the two.

• The Y-axis should begin at zero. If the path of the data is far above zero, a break can be made in the Y-axis.

- Marks indicating the intervals on the Y-axis and the X-axis must be very clear. Do not use grid lines, as too many lines give a graph a cluttered appearance.

- Make all values on the Y-axis an equal distance arithmetically. For example, use values such as 20, 40, 60, 80 and 100 rather than 22, 31, 53 and 80.

(b) Bar graphs

While line graphs are useful for analytical purposes, bar charts are usually used for simple comparison. Bar charts should therefore be kept simple, and should communicate their message as clearly and unambiguously as possible.

When constructing bar graphs you should keep the following principles in mind:

- Keep the width of all bars equal. If one bar is both longer and wider than another, then the difference between the two bars will be exaggerated.

- Keep the space between all the bars the same. This space is usually one-half to one-third of the width of the bars themselves. In multiple bar charts, there is no space between the group of bars shown at each time point. Between each time point, however, there must be a space to help the reader distinguish between the several groups of bars.

- Label the bars and the value of the bars clearly.

- Begin the Y-axis at zero. If the bars are too high to show numbers continually from zero, show a break in the axis.

- Use crosshatching or colour to illustrate contrast among bars. This makes differentiation easier for the reader.

By studying bar graphs in annual reports, newspapers and business and other magazines you will increase your awareness of their use. At the same time you will also become aware of new techniques and adaptations you can use in your own reports.

(c) Pie charts

Pie charts or circle graphs are used to represent 100 percent. For example, sales or expenses during a certain period of time can be shown in a pie chart. The subdivisions of the graph would then be shown by several slices in the circle.

The use of pie charts is rather limited when compared to line or bar charts, in that it cannot illustrate more than one whole and it also cannot show change over a period of time. Nevertheless, because the pie chart is so simple and straightforward, its impact can be significant.

To make your pie charts consistent with accepted standards, the following principles should be adhered to:

- The first slice in the circle should be drawn at the 12 o'clock position. The segments of the chart should be arranged in descending order, going clockwise around the circle. If one of the segments is labelled "other" or "miscellaneous", it must appear immediately to the left of the 12 o'clock position, even if it is not the smallest segment.

- You can emphasise segments by colouring or crosshatching them, or by partially removing a certain segment from the rest of the circle.

- Clearly identify each segment of the chart. Identifying words can be typed inside each segment, or immediately outside with a line connecting them to the appropriate segment.

Interpretation and evaluation

Above, all, you must realise the importance of interpreting charts. Both graphs and tables are rather cold presentations of facts and figures. For example, they might say that sales for the past six months were £21,401.26. What you want to get across to the reader, however, is whether the figures are good, poor or average. Thus, you must give meaning to your tables and graphs by interpretation and evaluation. Only then can they serve their function as a report aid.

Flowcharts — the business map

Charts that describe work processes have been around since the pyramids were constructed. Various types of systems and procedures exist today; many of these are complex while others are quite simple. Their purpose is to provide a step-by-step image of some type of work.

Such charts are used for training, presentations, reports and many other activities. Charts are often constructed and used by groups of employees to document and analyse present methods so they may look for improvement opportunities. Often such charts are the heart of work simplification or quality circle efforts.

In any event, charts do have some very distinct advantages over other means of documentation:

- Charts are easy to construct and do not contain unnecessary verbiage.

- Charts are organised in a logical, step-by-step sequence and therefore facilitate analysis.

- Charts are easy to explain. They represent facts that illustrate a procedure from beginning to end graphically.

How to create workable charts

The following guidelines will help you create workable charts:

1. Limit the chart to a defined area. Don't try to cover too much in one chart. Stay primarily with the main flow. Additional charts can be developed for side flows if they are complicated.

2. Observe the actual job method. Very often what actually takes place is different from what is supposed to take place or what is described in the procedures manual.

3. Record the facts concerning the present method. Although not all the facts will be useful, it is better to know too much than too little. Account for exceptions even though they may not occur every day.

4. Resist the temptation to analyse as you chart or attempt to develop improvements. Wait until you have finished charting.

5. Collect samples of all records. It is better to have samples of completed documents and forms than to try to visualise them.

6. Make sure that the chart is accurate. Mistakes can lead to serious errors later in making improvements or changes.

7. Be as neat as possible. This will not only save time but makes the chart easier to read and explain to others.

The skeleton flow process or vertical chart is one of the easiest charts to learn to draw and to use. Like several other charting techniques, this approach centres around the five charting symbols.

CHARTING SYMBOLS

OPERATION
This indicates the main steps in a process or procedure. It usually indicates that the document or material is being handled or changed. This could include typing, sorting, entering data, collating, etc.

TRANSPORTATION
This symbol indicates the movement of the document or material form one place to another. It is a physical move from one work area to another.

INSPECTION
This indicates activities which mean examination. This includes checking or verifying for quality or quantity. The symbol usually signifies a decision resulting in more than one path on the chart.

DELAY
This is a temporary storage or delay. It is planned and controllable and would include work placed in an out tray or materials temporarily set aside.

STORAGE
This symbol represents formal storage. An example would be a document protected from unauthorised removal and kept in a filing system, whether hard copy or electronic.

COMBINED ACTIVITY
Once in a while two activities are performed at the same time. This example is a combination of inspection and operation.

Consult the dead upon things that were, but the living only on things that are
— Henry Wadsworth Longfellow

GETTING THE MESSAGE ACROSS WITH VISUALS AIDS

When making a speech, you need a way to capture your audience's attention, to hold it, and to convince them. You want your audience to do more than listen to you; you want them to think about what you have to say, because that is the only way they are going to accept your ideas, remember them, and act on them.

Visuals can help. We are well into an era of visual images in communication. Audiences expect visuals. For example, virtually every story on television news programmes includes on-scene reporting. Visual images by their very nature make communication easier and faster.

An effective way to lead your audience into active participation is to use visuals. People usually remember more of a message when they see it as well as hear it. Good visuals can carry a message; or support it by emphasising and illustrating the words, by providing the audience with more to retain and by stimulating them to think.

Script and slides should work together. Don't read everything parrot fashion from your slides, but use your script to complement them and *vice versa*. For instance, don't read: "This is how the gold price rose in 1990" when you can say: "Here's how gold looked" and let the slide say the rest. A script and slide that work together have more chance of getting the audience on your side.

Objectives

- Have **one**. Make your primary objective the focus of the message for the audience.

- What is the purpose of your speech? To inform? To entertain? To motivate? If you can finish the sentence: "The audience will ..." in less than 15 words, you will have a workable objective.

- Secondary objectives must be used to support your message and not to reduce its impact.

- There must also be the same single discernible objective for the visuals, e.g.: "The visuals will show that my company's financial holdings are well managed".

- The visuals must **support** the speech and not detract from it.

Audience

- Never underestimate the intelligence of your audience, and never overestimate their interest in your speech.

- Consider your audience first and your speech second. Whatever you say must first relate to the needs, desires and interests of your audience.

- Be as concrete and specific as possible. For example, a speech on economics must be written and visualised differently for an audience of financial analysts than for an audience of retailers. While the essence of your message may be the same, the delivery might well be quite different. For example one speech might use bar graphs to illustrate relative values of currency on an international scale; another might use shopping trolleys of food to show differences in buying power.

- With visuals you can lead your audience to participate actively. You can help them think about what you are saying – by providing them with examples and illustrations of your message. Pictures help you present your examples in concrete and stimulating ways. They help present your ideas from a particular perspective – yours.

Communications with visuals

Give scope to your visual imagination. Be just as productive in your visual thinking and illustration as you are in your verbal thinking and writing.

Charts and Graphs

Use them wisely. They can be deadly. Avoid using them as an easy way out; consider first whether a picture will make the point just as well or better.

Here are some rules to follow:

- Decide what information is absolutely essential, and show only that.

- Don't use copies from books or blueprints. Illustrations that look good on the printed page (which you hold about 30 cm from your eyes) can be far too confusing on a screen.

- Redraw them if you need to show the information.

- Keep everything simple, bold and graphic. Where you can, use symbols that will speak directly to your audience.

- Dark backgrounds with white or colourful lines work the best.

Laundry lists

Putting a list of words up on the screen can offend an audience, most of whom will wonder why you did not just distribute handouts.

Certainly, word slides can be used, but they are most effective when used judiciously – to introduce a topic, to label a machine part or feature, or to help review a complex subject.

Artwork

Some subjects, such as conceptual or abstract ideas, cannot be photographed easily. Artwork (as differentiated from photographs), can help you get your ideas across to your audience when nothing else quite suits the occasion, For example:

- Graphic artwork can give an immediate impression of size, value, direction or organisation.

- A cartoon approach is often chosen to simplify the subject matter and to add humour to the statement. At the same time cartoons are relatively inexpensive and easy to produce.

- Fine illustration on the other hand, impresses the audience because we all tend to respond positively when great care has been taken to provide us with excellent quality in image as with any product or service.

The most common use of artwork, however, is to title the speech and to highlight major points.

In any case, the most suitable choice is the one that supports your speech without overpowering your message.

Visual media

Before you can determine which visual medium to use you need to set your objectives, analyse your audience and you also need to know how much time, talent and money you have for production. With these considerations in mind you can begin to choose your media and equipment. The chart at the end of this article gives a list of the most common visual aids, together with notes on their different characteristics.

Visual writing

Doing it yourself

Illustrated speeches require the writer to think in terms of sequences - units of words and pictures that flow as a single stream of thought. To achieve this you must:

- Research your subject. What do you know about the subject? And what facts, figures and examples back up your knowledge, opinions and conclusions?

- Make only one point at a time. Use one or more visuals to support each thought.

- Write in a logical fashion. Each point:
  - should lead directly to the next, without diversion.
  - If you must digress - to provide additional background or explanation - structure your speech so that the audience understands why and when you will do so.

Using a freelance writer

Not everyone can write a presentation script. Some people lack the time, others lack the talent. The solution to this problem is to hire a freelance writer. When you look for a writer to help you with your script, consider these points:

- The writer should have experience writing material that's meant to be spoken. Look for someone who has written successful presentations. You want to sound like a speaker, not like someone reading from a press release.

- If you plan to use visuals, you should also look for a writer who has had experience of thinking visually. You want someone who knows how to convey thought through visuals.

- When you give a presentation, you want logic and continuity to further your ideas. That's why you should look for a writer with experience in developing visual sequences.

How do you prepare your visuals?

Unless you are an expert photo-grapher, use a production house to produce your slides. This caution also applies to creating your own artwork. Illustrations, charts, graphs and typography to be used in a slide presentation must be created within a very definite framework. If this framework is ignored, you will end up with slide images that bleed into the slide mounts or slides with images so small that legibility is affected.

The best approach when you need art slides is to find a producer who is familiar with the requirements of slide photography.

Before committing yourself to any specific production house, the following are useful questions to ask the producer:

- What are your qualifications?

- Show some examples of previous work done by you?

- Do you understand what I need?

- How much will it cost to meet the need as I outlined it?

- What are the tasks to be done and at what points can I make changes?

- What else must I do?

- When will it be ready for my review?

Computer graphics

Computer-generated graphics is the latest technique in the production of quality slides. When operating the system the artist works on the design tablet as if he were drawing on a sketchpad. Standardised shapes are first called up, different size options chosen and modifications made directly onto the design on screen.

Visuals can be altered at any stage or stored for future merging with other graphics. Chart design is virtually limitless and for text work there is a choice of typefaces which can be expanded or condensed vertically or horizontally.

Rehearsals

Practice not only makes perfect, it also makes for comfort. There are four major reasons for rehearsing a presentation, i.e.:

- It gives you a chance to refine your narrative and visual materials.

- It gives people who will be operating projectors and other equipment a chance to become familiar with their functions.

- It enables you and your presentation crew to combine your efforts, giving the presentation polish.

- Rehearsals also give you a psychological boost.

After you've made your presentation a number of times – even though it's to an empty room – you begin to feel comfortable in the role of presenter.

When something goes wrong

Presenters are frequently faced with one or more of the following catastrophies, e.g.:

- As the presentation begins, every visual that appears on the screen is upside down.

- Three minutes into the presentation the projector lamp burns out.

- As they begin to state their conclusion ... etc., etc.

When these mistakes and malfunctions occur they don't have to be catastrophes. All you have to do is to be prepared. That means that while you don't expect things to go wrong, you acknowledge that every once in a while something will.

Don't panic and lose control when they do. This will leave the audience feeling that you are a presenter at your wits end. They are likely to lose confidence in you and your message.

When something goes wrong, just stop your presentation and tell your audience what's happened and about how long it will take to clear up the problem. They will appreciate your straightforwardness, and all but the time-pressed will probably stay.

Summary

The visual is simple, straightforward, obvious. It is also powerful, emphatic and memorable.

A comparison matrix of audio-visual formats follows on the next two pages.

A straight path never leads anywhere except to the objective
                                – André Gide

You can never plan the future by the past
                                – Edmund Burke

Audio-visual formats: A comparison matrix

	Type of audio-visual aid						
Criteria	Flipcharts, other writing surfaces — usually presenter made	Transparencies for overhead projector	35 mm/6 x 6 slides	Films	Videotape	Models and mock-ups	Computer visuals or audio-visuals
Clarity, Resolution	Poor – dependent upon presenter's graphic skills. Crude lettering	Very good – if images are prepared. Can be shown without darkening room	Excellent – but requires that room be darkened for best clarity	Excellent – but requires that room be darkened for projection	Very good – can be viewed in a lighted room	Very good – also offer the dimension of depth and the sensation of touch	Very good
Adaptability to audience size	Poor – limited to small groups	Excellent – can be used with large audiences	Excellent – can be used with large audiences	Excellent – even for very large audiences	Moderate – restricted to small groups. Larger groups require the use of multiple monitors or special wide-screen projection	Poor – limited to small groups	Good – projections onto large screens are possible
Flexibility, Presenter control	Excellent – can easily be modified by presenter, on the spot	Good – very adaptable. Presenter can mark on visuals during presentation	Fair – if presenter narrates live. Poor – if prepared audiotape is used	Poor – although presenter can stop the projection in order to comment	Poor – although presenter can stop the projection in order to comment	Excellent – presenter can use as he desires	Depends on sophistication of software
Suitability for repeated use	Poor – susceptible to tears, smudges, etc.	Fair – susceptible to wear and tear	Excellent – but it is important to keep slides in proper order	Excellent – if heavy use is intended extra prints are advisable to ensure availability	Excellent – if heavy use is intended, extra prints are advisable to ensure availability	Excellent – but large models may be untidy?	Excellent – individual graphics or sequences of graphics can be stored on disk
Ease of updating	Not applicable – usually created fresh for each presentation	Excellent – transparencies are easily replaced	Excellent – slides can be replaced selectively, and tapes can be dubbed	Poor – editing, splicing, shooting new footage is complicated and costly	Poor – editing, splicing, shooting new footage is complicated and costly	Poor – completed working models are not easily updated	Excellent – individual graphics or sequences of graphics can be changed on screen
Duplication capability	Poor – not well-suited for duplication	Excellent – extra transparencies can be made from same original	Excellent – slides are easily duplicated; tapes easily copied	Excellent – extra prints are easily made from master	Excellent – extra prints are easily made from master	Fair – complex models may be costly to duplicate	Excellent – just copy the files

Audio-visual formats: A comparison matrix (continued)

	Type of audio-visual aid						
Criteria	Flipcharts, other writing surfaces — usually presenter made	Transparencies for overhead projector	35 mm/6 x 6 slides	Films	Videotape	Models and mock-ups	Computer visuals or audio-visuals
Realism, image sophistication	Low - usually images are crude and very simple	Good - when made by graphics specialists, but usually poor when made by amateurs	Excellent - high quality and sophisticated, but no motion capability	Excellent - the most realistic audio-visual medium	Excellent - a high degree of sophistication is possible	Good - some models are virtual replicas of the real thing	Excellent - motion video sequences can be projected or just text
Consistency (across repeated use)	Relatively poor - requires much narration which may vary between presentations	Relatively poor - requires much narration which may vary between presentations	Excellent - if an audiotape is used with slides	Excellent - presentations are always the same	Excellent - presentations are always the same	Relatively poor - narration will vary across presentations	Excellent - presentations without narration by the operator can be designed
Production effort	Low - can be produced even during presentations	Fairly low - can be pre-prepared by presenter or by graphics specialist	Moderate - artwork and photography must be well planned and executed	High - requires professional help, and special equipment. Time consuming	High - requires professional help, and special equipment. Time consuming	High - working models especially require time and expertise	High - requires special equipment and software. More sophisticated uses will require professional help
Dependency upon equipment	Low - requires only stand for pad. A pointer may be desirable	Moderate - requires overhead projector, screen and electrical source	Moderate - requires slide projector, screen and electrical source	Moderate - requires projector and screen plus electrical source	Moderate - requires projector (receiver), and recorder/player for videotape or cassette	Low - most models need no other equipment	High - nothing can be achieved if the electronic equipment fails
Production cost	Low - usually requires only flipchart pad and dark markers	Fairly low - most of cost is associated with artwork and lettering	Moderate - unless extensive location photography is required	High - quality films (sound/colour) are very expensive to produce	High - quality video shows are very expensive to produce	Fairly high - except for the most simple models	Moderate to high - initial expense on equipment is high. Subsequent use is expensive only if complex graphics are needed which call for professional help
Ease of use (presentation)	Moderate - uncomplicated but requires high input of presenter's energy	Moderate - uncomplicated but requires high input of presenter's energy	Easy - if slides are automatically advanced via tape with advance pulses or by remote control handset. Moderate - if slides must be manually advanced	Moderate - threading film can sometimes be complicated. Older projectors subject to malfunction	Easy - if video cassettes are used. Moderate - if videotape is used	Moderate - many models require manipulation by the presenter	Moderate - certain level of familiarity with computers required.

ALL THE BASICS FOR A SUCCESSFUL CONFERENCE

When you have to mastermind the planning of an important conference remember to allow yourself enough time and to be very well organised.

Here is a checklist that you can consult as a mind-jogger. Since no two conferences are identical, the checklist is general rather than specific.

Checklist for conference organisers — points to consider

Selecting the date

- Possible dates should be checked for clashes with other events, public holidays, peak work-load periods, availability of key speakers, etc.
- It is usual to plan about a year ahead, although international events may be planned up to two or three years in advance.

Choosing the venue

- Is the venue large enough to cope with the number of delegates expected?
- Does the venue offer accommodation for out-of-town delegates? If not, is it easily accessible from the hotel(s) where the delegates are staying?
- Is the venue quiet: free from traffic noise, not too near a school playground or building site?
- Does the venue offer the necessary air-conditioning, sound-proofing, lighting and sound amplification?
- Are there enough power points and are they conveniently situated?
- Can the room be darkened to allow for audio-visual presentations?
- Can a speaker's platform and/or audio-visual screen be accommodated?
- Is a suitable coffee/catering service available?
- Are there adequate cloak rooms?

- Is there adequate space either in the meeting room or in the foyer where tea and coffee may be served?
- Are the premises licensed or must a special licence be obtained?

Accommodation

- What type and standard of accommodation is needed? E.g., executive suites/single/double rooms, private bath or shower, television, air-conditioning, valet service, parking.
- Book early to secure required accommodation.
- What deposit does the hotel require?
- What accommodation discounts are offered for group bookings?
- Make arrangements for the settling of accounts, in order that no misunderstandings or disagreements may occur when delegates check out.
- Obtain accommodation and room lists well before the date of the conference.

Guest speakers

- Are guest speakers to be invited?
- Which of the following are the conference organisers going to provide?
    travel to and from the conference
    accommodation
    meals
    entertainment
    any other items.
- Ensure that speakers have received full briefings regarding the contribution they are expected to make.
- Ascertain whether copies of speeches can be obtained in advance for press release purposes.
- Will the speaker arrange for his paper to be printed and distributed to delegates subsequent to delivering his talk at the conference?

- Confirm all details to guest speakers in writing.

Conference programme

- Will the printed programme clearly define each day's events, giving details of the time, place, name and title of the speaker, the topic, tea and lunch breaks, evening entertainments?
- Has sufficient time been allowed for speakers to cover their subject?
- Has sufficient time and opportunity been allowed for discussion of papers?
- Has a balance been maintained between business and relaxation, formal and informal discussions?

Particular attention should be paid to the detail of:

- Sufficient time at the start for delegates to assemble, meet their friends and get their bearings, but not so much that they disperse or the momentum of the event is lost.
- A top quality opening (or 'keynote') speaker, to interest and excite delegates
- A logical sequence of following speakers, which maintains steady interest
- Sufficient (but not over-generous) time at coffee, tea and meal breaks.
- Careful planning of sessions immediately after lunch, during which most delegates will, if allowed, prefer to sleep. This may be used for a controversial debate, seminar or sessions requiring audience participation.
- Top-flight speakers for the last session each day and the final conference session. This will ensure not only that delegates leave full of enthusiasm, but that as many as possible stay until the end.
- The timetable should be neither too loose, which loses the momentum and interest of delegates, nor too tight, which tires

and confuses them. There should also be contingency arrangements, so that, as far as possible, over-running of one session does not throw the whole day into confusion. A clock at the back of the hall will help control timing.

- Special programmes for wives.

Social programme

- Will this offset the demands of the working sessions?
- Has sufficient variety been allowed to cater for different tastes?
- Does the social programme allow for the involvement of all the delegates?
- Social occasions should also allow for opportunity for informal discussions which might not have been possible during the conference.
- Have you arranged special day excursions for wives and friends? Will a colleague accompany them?

Equipment and special items

- Check that the meeting room has:
    water flasks and glasses
    easel, whiteboard or blackboard and writing materials
    flipchart holder
    rostrum for speaker
    adjustable microphone
    audio-visual equipment
    pointer
    large lettered name cards for speakers and delegates
- Have you appointed someone to control the lighting?
- Have handy the name of a technician in case of equipment failing during a session.
- Do you need flower arrangements? In what quantity and when must they be delivered?
- Are sufficient car parking facilities available?
- If press coverage is planned, will there be a press desk equipped with the conference pro-

gramme, copies of papers, press releases? Has a person been appointed to look after the press?
- Will a secretarial service be required?
- Ensure that the conference area is clearly signposted throughout the duration of the conference.

Catering

- Arrange times when morning and afternoon tea/coffee is to be served.
- Arrange times when lunch is to be served and whether it is a working buffet or semi-formal.
- Arrange dinner, whether it is à la carte, buffet, or a banquet at a location away from the conference centre.
- For a formal dinner a seating plan and place cards will be required.
- Take into consideration religious eating habits, e.g. Jewish, Moslem, etc.

Travel arrangements

- Will it be necessary to collect delegates from the airport and drive them to the hotel?
- Will transport be necessary from hotel to conference venue and back?
- Will car or bus hire be necessary? How many vehicles will be required, for how long?
- Check on transport requirements for technical and sightseeing tours.

Registration of delegates

- Arrange that delegates receive a "conference kit", which should include the following items on arrival:
    document folders
    name tag
    conference programme – business and social
    names and places of origin of all delegates

information sheet explaining what costs the registration fee covers and what costs are for their own account.
- Arrange for meeting of participants at registration area and for making introductions.

Costs

When drawing up the conference budget the following items should be taken into account:

- Venue
    conference room
    accommodation at venue
    decoration
    lighting
    signposting
- Equipment
- Printing
    conference programmes
    circulars
    name tags
    participants' list
    invitation
    certificates
    document folders
- Stationery
- Material for delegates
- Tea and light refreshments during sessions
- Guest speakers
- Social programme
    opening ceremony
    evening entertainment
    luncheons
    dinners
    ladies' programme
    banquet
    other special functions
- Photographer's fee
- Transport
- Insurance
- Miscellaneous
- Reserve
    It is essential to budget for a reserve for contingencies.

After the conference

- Attend to letters of thanks

Now think again ... what have you overlooked?

Conference room layout plan

The size of the room and the layout chosen will depend on the number of delegates, the types of presentations and the general mood required.

- a large room or auditorium with an auditorium layout is suitable for a conference with many delegates, where not much participation is expected

- a medium-sized room with furniture in a U-shaped layout is ideal for presentations where delegates are expected to make contributions

- a small room (for under 10 people) with a centre table surrounded by chairs is the kind of set-up necessary for a working-session with direct contributions from all delegates. (See the seating plan choices provided below.) For details to check on lighting and sound equipment, see the checklist.

U-shape or horseshoe

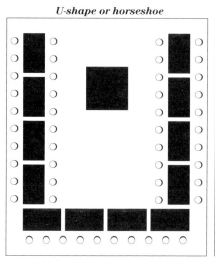

Hollow oval

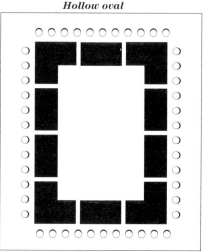

Tiered U-shaped

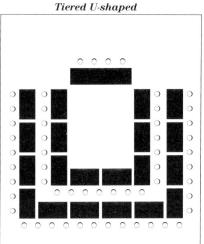

Theatre style

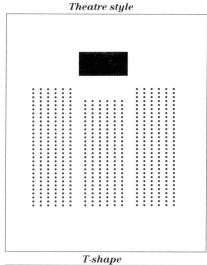

Discussion groups

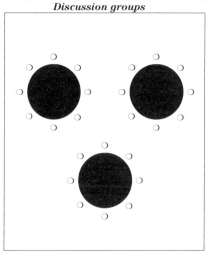

T-shape

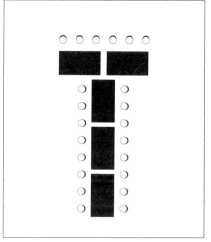

The art of communicating

One of the continuing problems facing the spokesman of any organisation in times of stress or major change is how to tell his company's story to a newspaper, radio or television reporter. The dilemma is that while the official wants to get the company's views or policy across, he is fearful of blundering by saying the wrong thing. He knows he is at a disadvantage in talking to a reporter who is skilled at asking provocative questions in order to get provocative, interesting and controversial answers.

There are, however, certain guidelines that you can learn and remember, which will enable you to communicate effectively and truthfully with the press.

1. Always prepare carefully

It's always wise to prepare carefully for a press interview. Never walk into a meeting with the press, planning to play it by ear. Preparation is essential. The best preparation consists of anticipating the most likely questions, attempting to research the facts, and structuring effective answers to be held ready for use. Probably it is unwise to carry such notes into the interview. It would be better instead to have the answers well in mind, although not literally memorised.

2. Talk from the viewpoint of the public's interest, not the company's

For example, often during negotiations for a new union contract, corporate spokesmen will tell the press, in effect: "We can't afford the increase the union is asking." That may be true, but why should the public be concerned with the company's financial problems? Employees often respond with hostility and resentment It is much better to say: "We'd like to give our employees the increase

they seek. But if our costs and prices go up too much, our customers won't buy. That will hurt us, and in the end, it will endanger our employees' jobs."

Every industry has its own language, its own terminology. When a corporate spokesman uses company lingo, he knows exactly what he means. But the public generally does not. So speak in terms the ordinary citizen can understand.

Instead of saying: "Our management is considering whether to issue equity or debt," it might be better to say: "We are considering whether to sell more shares in our company, or to try to borrow money by issuing bonds."

3. If you don't want a statement quoted, don't make it

Avoid "off-the-record" statements. There is no such thing as "off-the-record." If you tell a reporter something off the record, it may not be used with your name attached. But it may well turn up in the same published article, minus your name, and with the qualifying phrase added: "Meanwhile, it has been learned from other sources that ..." The damage is done.

The same off-the-record rule applies to telephone conversations with the media: whether or not you hear a beep, your words may be recorded. A recording makes it impossible for you to deny later what the reporter has taped in your own voice.

4. State the most important fact at the beginning

If an executive is asked what he is planning to do about the development of a new product, he will frequently respond along these lines: "We are facing shortages of plastics. And their cost is rising so fast I don't think we can price the product at an attractive level.

Moreover, we have a labour shortage in the plant. So I recommend we don't take any action now to develop the product."

The executive's format lists the facts that lead to his final conclusion and recommendation. But such organisation of his material will fail when it is used in talking with the news media. There are both psychological and technical reasons why.

Psychologically, we tend to remember most clearly the first thing that is said, not the last. So when you speak to a reporter, you should turn your statement around to begin with the conclusion. For example: "We don't plan to develop the product. We are facing material shortages. Our costs are going up, and we also have a shortage of skilled labour." In such a reverse format, the most important statement is likely to be best remembered: "We don't plan to develop the new product."

Technical considerations in printing and production are also an important reason for giving your conclusion first. The newspaper reporter who writes the story seldom knows in advance how much space will be available for its publication. So he has been trained to put the most important fact at the beginning, using subsequent paragraphs to report items of declining importance. If the most important fact is buried at the bottom of the story, it may simply be chopped off in the composing room to fit the available space.

On television, time pressures and broadcast deadlines often make it impossible to screen all filmed material. Frequently, programme producers or news editors are compelled to select segments from the beginning of a film. So, again, the most important fact should be stated first. Afterwards, it can be explained at whatever length is necessary, but even if the full explanation is cut, the initial statement will survive.

5. Don't argue with the reporter

Understand that the newsman seeks an interesting story and will use whatever techniques he needs to obtain it. You cannot win an argument with the reporter in whose power the published story lies. Since you have initially allowed yourself to be interviewed, you should use the interview as an opportunity to answer questions in a way that will present your story fairly and adequately.

Never ask questions of the reporter out of your own anger and frustration. If you become aggressive or hostile, the published interview will reflect the reporter's own hostility.

6. If a question contains offensive language or words that you don't like, don't repeat them, even to deny them

Reporters often like putting words into the interviewee's mouth. Politicians also like doing this. The technique works like this: the reporter includes colourful and provocative language in his question.

For example: "Mr Peters, wouldn't you describe your company's profits this year as excessive?" If Mr Peters does not spot the pitfall he will answer: "No, our profits are not excessive."

It would have been better to answer the question this way: "Our profits are not sufficient. To increase investment in plant and equipment, we shall have to earn much more money." The reporter knows that his questions will not be quoted in the article, only the respondent's answers. The important thing therefore is not how the question is asked, but how it is answered. As long as you do not repeat anything you do not want said, even to deny it, it will not appear in the published report.

7. Answer a direct question with a direct answer

Interviewees sometimes complain that although they answered all the questions, they did not make all the points they wanted to make – perhaps because, in their view, the reporter did not ask the right questions.

Management training teaches executives to be to the point when answering questions, and not to amplify unduly. Such behaviour, although appropriate in an office situation, should not be followed when talking to a reporter. Here amplification is often in order.

This rule does not suggest that you answer with either evasion or wordiness. But you should not stop with a one-word response. Instead amplify the point until you have said what you want to say.

8. If you do not know the answer to a question, simply say: "I don't know, but I'll find out for you"

This response does not make you look ignorant. Nor is your lack of knowledge newsworthy. Even in an interview filmed for television, such an answer would find itself "on the cutting room floor."

However, if you simply reply: "I don't know," it might appear to the reporter or the viewer that you are being evasive. So you are advised never to answer with this alone, but always to qualify the answer with a phrase like: "I'll put you in touch with someone else who can answer that for you," or similar words. Of course, you then assume the responsibility of following through to ensure that the requested information is provided promptly.

Occasionally, a reporter will ask a question which you do not wish to answer. There may be a legal reason, or the requested informa-tion may be a company secret. In such circumstances, the recommended course is to respond directly, without evasion or excuses: "I'm sorry, but I can't give you that information." Don't play dumb, deny knowledge, or give anything other than a forthright refusal.

9. Tell the truth, even if it hurts

Understandably, nobody likes to admit that business is bad, that employees must be laid off, that a new product introduction has been unsuccessful, etc. Yet telling the truth remains the best answer.

How much truth should a company tell? Experience answers: "As much as the reporter wants to know." When an executive change is announced, probably 99 out of 100 reporters will be satisfied with that bare fact, and ask nothing more. But once in a while a keen reporter may respond: "Mr Jones, I've heard that you held Mr Smith responsible for the severe drop in earnings your company had last year. Is that true?"

First of all, if the allegation is true, don't deny it. Denial will only lead to a loss of credibility later when the reporter confirms it from another source. However, don't invite a libel suit either, from Mr Smith, by blaming him for the company's problems. The question might thus be answered, factually but tactfully: "When economic conditions are difficult, companies frequently make management changes and that's what we have done."

While the press and the public do not like to hear bad news and will judge the company or its management adversely because of it, fair-minded people will understand that the difficulties of management make a certain number of errors in judgement unavoidable.

What the public will not understand or tolerate, however, is dishonesty. Concealment and lying will be neither forgotten nor forgiven by the press and public alike.

10. In conclusion

Telling the business story to an apathetic or hostile nation is not easy, but it is worth doing, and it can be done successfully. As one senior executive recently said: "I've been interviewed frequently over the past 10 years, and every time afterwards, I felt sorry for myself. But now, I realise that I just didn't know the rules of the reporter's game. Since I started playing the game too, I've had a much better press. In one case, I even got a sympathetic newspaper editorial on an issue where we always used to get clobbered. It's convinced me to look on a press interview as an opportunity, rather than as a cause for fear."

We despise no source that can pay us a pleasing attention
– Mark Twain

In a period of intense, accelerated change, all management assumptions about the outside world have to be rechecked for accuracy with the morning newscast
– Alvin Toffler

BODY LANGUAGE: THE IMPORTANCE OF NON-VERBAL COMMUNICATION

Strategic positioning in relation to other people is an effective way to obtain co-operation from them. Aspects of people's attitude towards you can be revealed in the position they take in relation to you.

Mark Knapp, in his book *Non-Verbal Communication in Human Interaction*, noted that, although there is a general formula for interpreting seating positions, the environment may have an effect on the position chosen. For example intimate couples prefer to sit side-by-side whenever possible, but in a crowded restaurant where the tables are close together, this is not possible so the couples may be forced to sit opposite each other in what is normally a defensive position.

The office desk

The following example relates primarily to seating arrangements in an office environment with a standard rectangular desk.

Person B can take four basic seating positions in relation to person A:

- B1: The corner position
- B2: The co-operative position
- B3: The competitive/defensive position, or
- B4: The independent position.

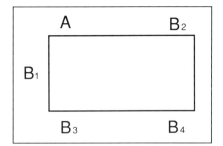

Figure 1   Basic seating positions

The corner position (B1)

This position is normally used by people who are engaged in friendly, casual conversation. The position allows for unlimited eye contact and the opportunity to use numerous gestures and to observe the gestures of the other person. The corner of the desk provides a partial barrier should one person begin to feel threatened, and this position avoids a territorial division on the top of the table. The most successful strategic position from which a salesperson can deliver a presentation to a new customer is position B1, assuming A is the buyer. By simply moving the chair to position B1 you can relieve the atmosphere and increase the changes of a favourable negotiation.

The co-operative position (B2)

When two people are mutually oriented, that is, both thinking alike or working on a task together, this position usually occurs. It is one of the most strategic positions for presenting a case and having it accepted. The trick is, however, for B to be able to take this position without A feeling as though his territory has been invaded. This is also a highly successful position to take when a third party is introduced into the negotiation by B, the salesperson. Say, for example, that a salesperson was having a second interview with a client and the salesperson introduced a technical expert. The following strategy would be the most suitable.

The technical expert is seated at position B3 opposite customer A. The salesperson can sit either at position B2 (co-operative) or B1 (corner). This allows the salesperson to be "on the client's side" and to question the technician on behalf of the client. This position is often known as "siding with the opposition".

The competitive/defensive position (B3)

Sitting across the table from a person can create a defensive, competitive atmosphere and can lead to each party taking a firm stand on his point of view because the table becomes a solid barrier between both parties. This position is taken by people who are either competing with each other or if one is reprimanding the other. It can also establish that a superior/subordinate role exists when it is used in A's office.

An experiment conducted in a doctor's office showed that the presence or absence of a desk had a significant effect on whether a patient was at ease or not. Only 10 percent of the patients were perceived to be at ease when the doctor's desk was present and the doctor sat behind it. This figure increased to 55 percent when the desk was absent.

If B is seeking to persuade A, the competitive/defensive position reduces the chance of a successful negotiation unless B is deliberately sitting opposite as part of a pre-planned strategy. For example, it may be that A is a manager who must severely reprimand employee B, and the competitive position can strengthen the reprimand. On the other hand, it may be necessary for B to make A feel superior and so B deliberately sits directly opposite A.

Whatever line of business you are in, if it involves dealing with people, you are in the influencing business and your objective should always be to see the other person's point of view, to put him or her at ease and make him or her feel right about dealing with you; the competitive position does not lead towards this end. More co-operation will be gained from the corner and co-operative positions than will ever be achieved from the competitive position. Conversations are shorter and more specific in this position than from any other.

Whenever people sit directly opposite each other across a table, they unconsciously divide it into two equal territories. Each claims half as his own territory and will reject the other's encroaching upon it. Two people seated competitively at a restaurant table for example, will mark their territorial boundaries with the salt, pepper, sugar bowl and napkins.

There will be occasions on which it may be difficult or inappropriate to take the corner position to present your case. Let us assume that you have a visual presentation; a book, quotation or sample to present to another person who is sitting behind a rectangular desk. First, place the article on the table (Figure 2). The other person will lean forward and look at it, take it into his territory or push it back into your territory.

Figure 2: A paper placed on territorial line

Figure 3: Taking paper into his territory signals non-verbal acceptance

If he leans forward to look at it, you must deliver your presentation from where you sit as this action tells you non-verbally that he does not want you on his side of the desk. If he takes it into his

Figure 4: Non-verbal agreement to enter buyer's territory

territory, this gives you the opportunity to ask permission to enter his territory and take either the corner or co-operative positions (B_1 and B_2). If, however, he pushes it back, you're in trouble! The golden rule is never to encroach on the other person's territory unless you have been given verbal or non-verbal permission to do so, or you will put them off.

The independent position (B_4)

This is the position taken by people when they do not wish to interact with each other; it occurs in such places as a library, park bench or restaurant. It signifies lack of interest and can even be interpreted as hostile by the other person if the territorial boundaries are invaded. This position should be avoided where open discussion between A and B is required.

Square, round, and rectangular tables

Square table (formal)

Square tables can create a competitive or defensive relationship between people of equal status. Square tables are ideal for having short, to-the-point conversations or for creating a superior/subordinate relationship. The most co-operation usually comes from the person seated beside you and the one on the right tends to be more co-operative than the one on the

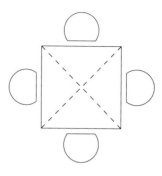

Figure 5: Square table (formal)

left. The most resistance usually comes from the person seated directly opposite.

Round table (informal)

King Arthur used the round table as an attempt to give each of his knights an equal amount of authority and status. A round table creates an atmosphere of relaxed informality and is ideal for promoting discussion among people who are of equal status as each person can claim the same amount of table territory. Removing the table and sitting in a circle also promotes the same result. Unfortunately, King Arthur was unaware that if the status of one person is higher than the others in the group it alters the power and authority of each other individual. The king held the most power at the Round Table and this meant the knights seated on either side of him were non-verbally granted the next highest amount of power, the one on his right having a little more power

Figure 6: Round table (informal)

than the one on the left, and the amount of power diminished relative to the distance that each knight was seated away from the king.

Consequently, the knight seated directly across the table from King Arthur was, in effect, in the competitive/defensive position and was likely to be the one who gave the most trouble. Many of today's business executives use both square and round tables. The square desk, which is usually the work desk, is used for business activity, brief conversations, reprimands and the like. The round table, often a coffee table with wrap-around seating, is used to create an informal relaxed atmosphere or to persuade.

Rectangular tables

On a rectangular table, position A has always commanded the most influence. In a meeting of people of equal status the person sitting at position A will have the most influence, assuming that he does not have his back to the door. If A's back were facing the door, the person seated at B would be the most influential and would be strong competition for A. Assuming that A was in the best power position, person B has the next most authority, then C, then D. This information makes it possible to structure power plays at meetings by placing name badges on the seats where you want each person to sit so that you may have the maximum influence over them.

Figure 7: Positioning at a rectangular table

The dining table at home

The choice of the shape of a family dining room table can give a clue to the power distribution in that family, assuming that the dining room could have accommodated a table of any shape and that the table shape was selected after considerable thought. "Open" families go for round tables, "closed" families select square tables and "authoritative" types select rectangular tables.

Getting a decision over dinner

Bearing in mind what has already been said about human territories and the use of square, rectangular and round tables, let us now look at the dynamics of taking a person to dinner where the objective is to obtain a favourable response to a proposition.

Firstly, whether you are dining at your home or at a restaurant, have your prospect seated with his back to a solid wall or screen. Research shows that respiration, heart rate, brain wave frequencies and blood pressure rapidly increase when a person sits with his back to an open space, particularly when others are moving about. Tension is further increased if the person's back is toward an open door or a window at ground level. Next, the light should be dimmed and muffled background music played. It would be best to use a round table and have your prospect's view of other people obscured by a screen or large green plant if you are to have a captive audience.

It is far easier to obtain a favourable decision under these circumstances than it will ever be in restaurants that have bright lighting, tables and chairs placed in open areas and the banging of plates, knives and forks.

Power plays

Power plays with chairs

Have you ever been for a job

interview and felt overwhelmed or helpless when you sat in the visitor's chair? Where the interviewer seemed so big and overwhelming and you felt small and insignificant? Certain strategies using chairs and seating arrangements can create this atmosphere in an office.

The factors involved in raising status and power by using chairs are: the size of the chair and its accessories, the height of the chair from the floor and the location of the chair relative to the other person.

Chair size and accessories

The height of the back of the chair raises or lowers a person's status and the high-backed chair is a well-known example. The higher the back of the chair, the greater the power and status of the person sitting in it. Kings, queens, popes and other high-status people may have the back of their throne or official chair as high as 8 feet to show their status relative to their subjects; the senior executive has a high-backed leather chair and his visitor's chair has a low back.

Swivel chairs have more power and status than fixed chairs, allowing the user freedom of movement when he is placed under pressure. Fixed chairs allow little or no movement and this lack of movement is compensated for by body gestures that reveal the person's attitude and feelings. Chairs with arm rests, those that lean back and those that have wheels are better than chairs that have not.

Chair height

Status is also gained if your chair is adjusted higher off the floor than the other person's. Some advertising executives are known for sitting on high-backed chairs that are adjusted for maximum height while their visitors sit opposite, in the competitive position, on a sofa or chair that is so low that their eyes are level with the executive's desk.

Chair location

As previously mentioned, the most power is exerted on the visitor when his chair is placed in the competitive position. A common power play is to place the visitor's chair as far away as possible from the executive's desk into the social or public territory zone, which further reduces the visitor's status.

Strategic office layout

You should now be able to arrange your office furniture in such a way as to have as much power, status or control over others as you wish. Here is a case study showing how we rearranged a person's office to help solve some of his supervisor/employee relationship problems.

John, who was an employee in an insurance company, had been promoted to a manager's position and was given an office. After a few months in the role, John found that the other employees disliked dealing with him and his relationship with them was occasionally hostile, particularly when they were in his office. He found it difficult to get them to follow his instructions and guidance and he heard that they were talking about him behind his back. Our observations of John's plight revealed that the communication breakdowns were at their worst when the employees were in his office.

For the purpose of this exercise, we will ignore management skills and concentrate on the non-verbal aspects of the problem. Here is a summary of our observations and conclusions about John's office layout:

1. The visitor's chair was placed in the competitive position in relation to John.

2. The walls of the office were wood panels except for an outside window and a clear glass partition that looked into the general office area. This glass partition reduced John's status and could increase the power of a subordinate who was sitting in the visitor's chair because the other employees were directly behind him and could see what was happening.

3. John's desk had a solid front that hid the lower part of his body and prevented the subordinates observing many of John's gestures.

4. The visitor's chair was placed so that the visitor's back was to the open door.

5. John often sat in the both-hands-behind-head position whenever a subordinate was in his office.

6. John had a swivel chair with a high back, arm rests and wheels. The visitor's chair was a plain low-backed chair with fixed legs and no arm rests.

Considering that between sixty and eighty percent of human communication is done non-verbally, it is obvious that these aspects of John's non-verbal communication spelled disaster. To rectify the problem the following rearrangements were made:

1. John's desk was placed in front of the glass partition, making his office appear bigger and allowing him to be visible to those who entered his office.

2. The "hot seat" was placed in the corner position, making communication more open and allowing the corner to act as a partial barrier when necessary.

3. The glass partition was sprayed with mirror finish, allowing

John to see out, but not permitting others to see in. This raised John's status and created a more intimate atmosphere within his office.

4. A round coffee table with three identical swivel chairs were placed at the other end of the office to allow informal meetings to take place on an equal level.

5. In the original layout (Figure 8) John's desk gave half the table territory to the visitor and the revised layout (Figure 9) gave John complete claim to the desk top.

6. John practised relaxed open arms and legs gestures when speaking with subordinates in his office.

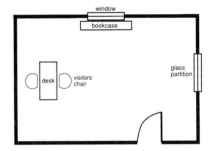

Figure 8 Original office layout

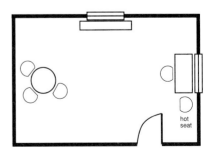

Figure 9 New office layout

The result was that supervisor/employee relationships improved and the employees began describing John as an easygoing and relaxed supervisor.

Status raisers

If you feel it is necessary, certain objects strategically placed around the office can be subtly used to increase your status and power. Clearly, it is not always appropriate or productive to go too far with such ploys. Some examples include:

1. Low sofas for visitors to sit on.

2. An expensive ashtray placed out of reach of the visitor, causing him inconvenience when tapping the ash from his cigarette.

3. A cigarette container from overseas.

4. Some red folders left on the desk marked "Strictly Confidential".

5. A wall covered with photos, awards or qualifications that the occupant has received.

6. A slim briefcase. Large, bulky briefcases are carried by those who do all the work.

All that is needed to raise your status, increase your power and effectiveness with others is a little thought given to non-verbal gymnastics in your office or home. Unfortunately, most executive offices are arranged like the one in Figure 8. Rarely is consideration given to the negative non-verbal signals that are unwittingly communicated to others.

We suggest that you study your own office layout and use the preceding information to make the positive changes needed.

Vision is the art of seeing things invisible
- Jonathan Swift

Our costliest expenditure is time
- Theophrastus

Man is still the most extraordinary computer of all
- John F. Kennedy

No advice on dressing for work could be given to women which is not only complex but also dates very quickly. For men, however, things are generally easier, but equally important to get right with regard to that most manipulative form of non-verbal communication, your appearance.

You control how you look each day. What you wear, how you wear it, and of course how you look is your own personal advertisement. It is a very important source of self-confidence as well, without which no person can hope to function successfully. To be successful in the corporate environment, you must look successful. Here are a few basic guidelines for managers. We are sure that if you follow them, you will definitely enhance your image.

Suits

Wear a suit. Although jackets and blazers are sometimes acceptable, more often than not your best bet is a suit. Get to know the different types of material, the ones which are crease-resistant, and can keep you cool in summer, warm in winter. Pure wool, wool/polyester blends and natural fibre blends are all good choices.

Suits are positive authority symbols. For business, select a relatively simple pattern. The pinstripe conveys the most authoritative image. Never wear the jacket of one suit with trousers of another. Make sure the arm length of your suit jacket reaches to your wrist bone. The collar and lapels should lie flat without curling or buckling and the under collar should be of felt and sewn on evenly. The bottom edge of a normal jacket should fit into the curl of your hand when your arms are extended. The choice of vent, single, side, or barrel back, depends on the wearer's build and prevailing fashions. Broad-hipped people should wear side vents as they allow for a better fall of the jacket and greater ease of movement.

When buying a suit, check the buttons and button holes. Buttons should be sewn on with a 'neck' to allow for easy fastening. Check the lining is stitched in cleanly and does not bag or sag. Check that you can move your arms comfortably.

The fit of trousers will depend on current fashions, but the leg should cover the top half of your shoe.

Shirts

Even in hot weather, long-sleeved shirts are the dress code. Plain collar, pin through or button-down collar shirts are acceptable. White shirts are often worn and in some corporate environments it is the only acceptable colour. Solid, light blue, grey and pinstripes are also popular. Generally speaking, your shirt should be lighter than your suit, and your tie darker, or of a contrasting colour.

The cuff of your shirt sleeve should cover the wrist bone. It should extend about 0,5 cm beyond the length of the sleeve jacket. Make sure that the neck is not too tight. The most popular fabrics for shirts are polyester and cotton blends. Pure silk, linen and cotton feel good, and are comfortable to wear, but tend to crease and need extra care in washing and ironing.

Ties

Ties are required for a good corporate image. When buying a tie make sure you select one that is long enough. Once knotted, the end of the tie should meet the top of your belt. Wear a neatly patterned tie, darker than your suit. Avoid bow ties except for formal wear.

Shoes

When buying shoes, remember two words: chic and comfort. Steer clear of shoes which are too conspicuous. They should blend in with the rest of your clothes. If you want to maintain the elegant look, do not wear shoes in a contrasting colour.

Wear closed shoes. Open toes and sandals are too casual and informal for business. Be sure that your belt matches the colour of your shoes.

Socks

Never wear white socks. Your socks must match the colour of your suit.

Jackets

A solid navy, black or camel blazer is the most formal style of jacketing and can sometimes be worn for business with a matching or complementary pair of trousers.

Traditionally, jackets are a smart form of casual wear and can be worn either with a tie for a more dressed-up appearance, or with a sport shirt or sweater for a more casual look.

Colour

When it comes to colour, the image experts all share a preference for grey, blue and navy. The top rating goes to pinstripe blue or grey suits worn with a white or cream shirt. Weak managers are often advised to build a more powerful image by wearing darker colours. Avoid wearing black – it is only suitable for funerals and formal dinner/dress occasions. Short men should avoid wearing checks which are too prominent.

Coats

A good camelhair or mohair coat is an investment. This type of coat is a classic – it will never date, it always looks good, and what's more it will keep you warm! When buying a coat, try it on over a suit, to ensure a correct and comfortable fit. A longer coat looks smarter than one that stops at the knees.

Accessories

Don't forget to complement your overall image with the right accessories. Good quality belts, gloves, wallets, briefcases, and pens project a look of success. Cheap accessories will ruin the image of success you want to create.

Jewellery and cologne

Be conservative when wearing jewellery or cologne. Most corporate executives wear only

---

When buying clothes for business

1. Plan your purchase well in advance. Evaluate your existing wardrobe. Decide what you need, how much you are willing to spend and what colour range you will be looking at.
2. Buy quality. Buying the best quality is essential. Clothes should be regarded as an investment.
3. Consider fit. Know your size and which makes fit you well. Clothes look best when they fit as perfectly as possible. Avoid making any major alterations to the garment to get a good fit, as it usually spoils the cut.

---

plain cufflinks, a plain watch and if applicable, a thin wedding ring.

Avoid overdoing cologne or after-shave lotion so as not to offend your clients or co-workers.

Formal occasions

The correct dress for formal occasions is the black dinner suit. Formal dress shirts must be worn, cufflinks or studs, and the traditional black bow tie.

Clothing and shoe size conversion tables

Clothing and shoe sizing can be confusing. These tables should be of some help in alleviating this confusion.

Men's sizes:

Collar		Chest		Waist	
cm.	in.	cm.	in.	cm.	in.
36	14	81	32	71	28
38	15	84	33	76	30
39/40	15½	86	34	81	32
41	16	91	36	86	34
42	16½	97	38	91	36
43	17	102	40	97	38
44	17½	107	42	102	40
45	18	112	44	107	42
		117	46	112	44
		122	48	117	46
		127	50	122	48
				127	50

Women's sizes:

	Bust/Hip		Waist	
	cm.	in.	cm.	in.
8	76/81	30/32	58	23
10	81/86	32/34	61	24
12	86/91	34/36	66	26
14	91/97	36/38	71	28
16	97/102	38/40	76	30
18	102/107	40/42	81	32
20	107/112	42/44	86	34
22	112/117	44/46	91	36
24	117/122	46/48	97	38
			102	40
			107	42

Shoe sizes (men and women)

British	American	Continental	British	American	Continental
3½	5	36	8½	10	42/43
4	5½	37	9	10½	43
4½	6	37/38	9½	11	44
5	6½	38	10	11½	44/45
5½	7	39	10½	12	45
6	7½	39/40	11	12½	46
6½	8	40	11½	13	46/47
7	8½	40/41	12	13½	47
7½	9	41	12½	14	47/48
8	9½	42	13	14½	48

The art of communicating

The good news for English-speaking managers is that the whole world speaks English. That's not entirely true, of course, but English has become an internationally accepted language of business.

The bad news is that they don't speak the melange of slang, business and technical jargon, colloquialisms, sport expressions, military metaphors, and local humour that constitutes the daily vernacular of commerce in the English-speaking world. What's more, even within the English-speaking world, some of the words you use can have entirely different meanings from those of other cultures, further complicating the communication for managers operating in other countries.

As a professional manager, you ought to be aware of the factor that can disturb or inhibit the process of getting your message across and distort its intended meaning. When the same words mean different things, and business customs and beliefs differ from your own, it presents quite a challenge to bridge the gaps in understanding. In such circumstances, the importance of not taking anything for granted, and making every effort to confirm that both you and the other party have understood each other correctly, cannot be overestimated. This is often critical to the success of ventures in other countries.

Here are some guidelines for communicating more effectively with people in other cultures.

Remember that people are people

In dealing with people from another culture the first step is to eliminate the terms "foreigner" and "alien" from your vocabulary. Think of your clients or business associates as individuals coming from a different country. Remember that to them *you* are the foreigner. Unfortunately, stereotypes, particularly those of the news media, can affect both your view of the other party and their view of you. Keep this potential for bias firmly in mind. Though the practices and procedures of the other party may be different from yours, they are no less important. Avoid judging others by your standards.

Check that what you say is appropriate

If you are in a country where you do not speak the language well, but nevertheless wish, as a courtesy, to address some remarks to a person or group in their own language always have your prepared text checked to make sure that it's in the proper vernacular of your regional audience. Get someone who is absolutely fluent both in English and the language of the target audience to check your words. The same applies to any written communications you make in a language you do not know.

Adapt your pace to your audience

When speaking to a group whose first language is not English, always speak plainly, clearly and slowly. Try to limit or totally avoid the use of colloquialisms and slang expressions in your conversation. Most people abroad have learned limited textbook English, and they simply won't understand if you depart too radically from what they have learned.

Be wise with an interpreter

Should you use an interpreter? That will depend on the English fluency of your counterpart and the complexity of your business transaction. In most cases, you'll probably need an interpreter only when your counterpart's English is extremely poor or non-existent. If you make use of an interpreter, be sure that he is familiar with both languages and cultures, and experienced in both the business you will be discussing and its technical terminology. Brief the interpreter ahead of time. When arranging for an interpreter to serve at a business negotiation, make sure to obtain a referral from your business counterpart on the other side of the negotiation. His translations may be subtly biased in ways you are not able to detect, even if you have studied the language.

Follow up meetings with a written confirmation

It is not only polite, but also good strategy to follow up every meeting with a written summary, including what was discussed and what was agreed on. If possible, you should also fax your messages immediately following telephone conversations. Don't count on the spoken word, but back up verbal agreements with written statements. At the same time, however, you should be aware that in some cultures this could be seen as a sign of distrust. In essence such written follow-ups should be aimed at ensuring understanding rather than checking up on the other party.

Be selective on topics

Exercise caution in discussing delicate topics such as politics or religion before you learn what are acceptable topics of conversation in that culture. For example, a question such as: "What do you do?" may be considered an ice-breaker in some cultures, but may constitute an invasion of privacy, similar to asking your age or how much money you make, in other cultures.

Body language

Remember too that words are just

one of the ways you communicate. You also send messages by gestures, body language, clothing and behaviour. These can differ from country to country. For example, the American "A-OK" gesture with the thumb and forefinger touching in a circle means money to the Japanese, zero to the French, and an obscenity to Brazilians. Similarly, formalities such as shaking hands, maintaining personal space and distance, and observing time standards, all differ in various cultures.

Don't be embarrassed by silence

Keep in mind that silence is acceptable in many countries, unlike others where you often feel that you have to "fill in" the gaps with chitchat. In some cultures, for example, you may be asked how you can think and talk at the same time.

Don't interrupt

Never interrupt a foreigner who is speaking. It may take him longer to formulate a thought in English, and breaking in could be interpreted as a reflection on his skill at the language.

Get to know the local customs

In every culture there are customs that regulate what can be discussed at which occasions. For example, do you or don't you discuss business at informal functions or sports venues? Also make sure what the customs are regarding the giving and receiving of business gifts. When dealing with groups of people in other cultures it is particularly important to be aware of the protocol regarding the seniority of the different group members.

Summary

The bottom line is to do your homework. Before dealing with a person or a group from another culture, learn all you can about that culture, including as much of the language as you can. They may (or may not) speak English, but if you expect the rest of the world to speak your language, you may find that competitors are going the extra mile and learning the language their customers and contacts are most comfortable with – their native tongue.

I can live for two months on a good compliment
- Mark Twain

I enjoy taking myself by surprise
- Peter Ustinov

The age of the customer is upon us. Advertisements, whether they are for service or products, keep talking about the customer and customer satisfaction. And most of us find ourselves rating organisations by our overall experience with them, not only by what we pay for their products or services.

For most progressive companies, customer care is not a new concept. You would be hard-pressed to find a company that gives it no attention at all. But using customer care to get a competitive edge over your competition is an idea that is fairly new. A crowded market, global competition, little difference in prices, and no differences (as perceived by the customer) in product attributes and quality, have made companies look for ways to differentiate their products or services from the rest of the market. In this context, customer care is emerging as a way for companies to stand out in the crowd, to give the customer added value for his money. In the past few years, customer care training programmes, with the emphasis on creating customer focus for the entire organisation, have sprung up in many companies.

The problem with mere satisfaction is that the customer expects to be satisfied. He finds nothing exceptional in mere satisfaction. In fact, it is the service the customer receives, rather than the price or the quality of a tangible product, that forms the determining factor in a customer's decision on what to buy and where to purchase it. The clear benefit is that good customer service increases customer loyalty. The point is that the customers value good service and are willing to pay for it again and again.

Guidelines for service excellence

1. Get total management commitment

Like the proverbial chain, good customer care in an organisation is only as strong as its weakest link. Therefore, management – from CEO downward – must be behind the effort, and must ensure that every part of the organisation is involved. Making a dedication to customer care, part of the organisation's policy, is management's responsibility. This also means that middle managers should know the goals of the customer care improvement effort. They should realise that they are responsible for setting the example. It is one thing to train employees to answer the phone courteously; what is really needed, however, is to show them that excellent customer service is an integral part of the departmental – and organisational – goal.

2. Think of yourself as the customer

One of the crucial elements in maintaining excellent customer care, is to define what customer care is. A certain way of knowing what customer care should entail in your company, is to put yourself in the customer's shoes. Executives should not only be committed to staying close to their customers; they should be able to identify with them. Successful business marketers put themselves in the customer's place and develop products or services that fill unmet or unrecognised needs, thus gaining a competitive edge. The same principle applies to customer care.

3. Make every employee aware of your vision

Senior management should not only have a consistent vision of what good customer service entails in their organisation, but should also constantly communicate this to frontline employees. Employees must know what products and services the organisation sells and what their particular relationship is with each product and service. Each employee should have a clear idea of who his customers are: with what customers, external and internal, does he have a direct or indirect relationship? How can these relationships be improved? Such data should be listed and can be incorporated into job descriptions, performance appraisals, etc.

4. Listen to your customers

As business becomes more and more competitive, organisations have to sharpen all their tools. Knowing what's on the customer's mind, is one of the most important things a company can do. Clearly, the best way to find out what the customers think is to ask them. This means that you have to go right to the source. Regular use of telephone surveys, questionnaires, point-of-service evaluation cards and other similar techniques can provide a wealth of information on what the customer thinks and wants. The amount of detailed information needed will vary, depending on the complexity of your business and the scope of your effort. In most instances, however, there will be a need to get your customers' views on three basic issues: the kind of service they expect, the kind of service they received from your organisation, and the improvement you can make. Customer satisfaction is a necessary goal for every organisation. If customers are not satisfied with a product or service, there is no reason for them to purchase it; and without customers and their money, the organisation has no profits.

5. Monitor internal customer relations

Most companies with a good service reputation monitor service at every level, including internally. They argue that workers who treat one another well, will treat customers better. Some companies make the mistake of merely telling employees what to do to get close to customers. However, good external service requires good internal service. In some instances, it is a good idea for regional offices regularly to rate the corporate staff on the quality of the service they get from the headquarters, and *vice versa*. Employees should be encouraged to feel good about themselves and to figure out how they would want to be treated as customers, and then treat internal and external customers the same way. When you want to increase customer satisfaction, technical training is easy. The quantum leap comes from improving employees' attitudes.

6. Pay attention to the entire distribution chain

Successful companies listen to everyone in the distribution chain – employees, dealers, distributors, retailers – as well as to the fellow who carries the package home. A good relationship with your customers requires you to pay attention not only to them and to employees, but also to every link in the distribution chain. This point is often lost on manufacturers, who have to use middlemen. The various sectors in your distribution chain often know what works well and what doesn't. As customer service becomes the focus for the total organisation, you'll find that these sections will come up with many suggestions for improvement – at the front desk, on the computer terminals, in the billing department. Not every suggestion will be good (or cost-effective), but distribution chain involvement generates excitement, which flows to the customer, internal and external.

7. Eliminate bureaucracy

Many companies have generated much goodwill by eliminating the bureaucracy that often makes it difficult or impossible for customers to register complaints or render suggestions. By maintaining an open line of communication, you will make sure that your company pinpoints and corrects trouble spots before customers choose to go to your competition. You need to have an objective and non-threatening approach for customers to be open and frank about their needs and concerns. Ultimately the judgement of the quality of your service occurs in the market place, and when the dust settles, the customer's definition of quality is really the only one that counts. This makes it imperative not to limit or inhibit customers from airing their views by creating bureaucratic obstacles.

Five dimensions of service quality

What should management look at? More important, what do customers look at? The Forum Corporation, using research from a report by the Marketing Science Institute (ServQual, 1986: Cambridge, MA), found five dimensions of service quality:

- *Reliability:* Is what was promised provided dependably and accurately?

- *Assurance:* Are the employees knowledgeable and courteous, and can they create trust and confidence?

- *Empathy:* Is caring and individual attention provided?

- *Responsiveness:* Is there a willingness to help customers and provide prompt service?

- *Tangibles:* Are the physical facilities and equipment customer friendly?

Summary

To look at the entire picture of customer care, you must find out who your customers are and what they want. A customer is anyone who is served, so that means you must define not only your external customers, but also the service relationships within your organisation. All your policies and procedures must be aligned; your internal systems must work to the benefit of your immediate and your ultimate customers. And you must continually try to enhance the value of your service in the customers' eyes.

The companies that have made a conscious effort to improve customer care, have a few things in common:

- top management is behind the effort and wants to make excellent service to the customer, the company policy;

- middle management has the power to make changes where it sees fit – obviously within bounds of other company policies;

- employees are given increased responsibility for satisfying the customer;

- the training departments are given the flexibility to try new things, use the ideas that work, and get rid of the ideas that don't.

CORRECT FORMS OF ADDRESS

How to address people correctly is always a problem, especially in business correspondence. To ensure that your company heeds the protocol with letter-writing and addresses VIP's correctly, consult the table below and follow these rules.

- Address letters to men as follows:
  Mr Smith, Mr T. Smith or
  Mr Thomas Smith.
- Esquire (Esq), the courtesy title has virtually gone out of use. It can be used on handwritten invitations as well as personal letters. In that case the surname must be preceded by the first name or initials, e.g.
  Thomas Smith Esq.
- The plural form Messrs is only used with the names of business firms which contain a personal name e.g. Messrs Smith & Sons.

- Socially, married women can be identified by their husband's first name or initial, e.g. Mrs T(homas) Tom Smith.
- In business, however, married women are known by their own first name, e.g.
  Mrs P(atricia) Smith.
- If a woman's marital status is unknown, or if the woman has signed herself Ms or expressed a preference for Ms, use Ms.
- Young girls are addressed as Miss Julia Parker, not just as Miss Parker.
- Young boys are addressed as Master James Brink. At eighteen they take the adult title Mister.
- Professional titles are used instead of Mr, etc. as in Dr Howard Simmonds, The Rev. Jack Murphy or combined as in Prof. Dr Henry Winston.
- Orders, decorations, degrees, qualifications and letters denoting professions appear in that order: degrees start with the lowest, but orders start with the highest, e.g. Joseph Halliday Esq., O.B.E., D.S.O.
- Orders and decorations are usually included in addresses, but qualifications, etc. are only used where appropriate, as when writing to a person in his official capacity.
- The forms given in the table below for beginning and ending letters are in general not of the highest degree of formality, but nor are they social. Social letters would include the name of the individual in the opening and would close
  Yours sincerely.
- Whitaker's Almanac and Who's Who are useful books when corresponding with people in important positions.

Title	Envelope address	Opening	Closing	Speaking about
The Queen	To Her Majesty The Queen	Madam	I have the honour to remain, Madam, Your Majesty's most humble and obedient subject	Her Majesty, the Queen
The Prime Minister	The Rt Hon. Mr John Smith MP The Prime Minister	Dear Prime Minister	Yours faithfully	The Prime Minister **or** Mr John Smith
Lord Chancellor	The Rt Hon. the Lord Chancellor	Dear Lord Chancellor	Yours faithfully	The Lord Chancellor
Lord Chief Justice	The Rt Hon. the Lord Chief Justice of England	Dear Lord Chief Justice	Yours faithfully	The Lord Chief Justice
Ambassadors	His Excellency Mr John Smith	Sir	I have the honour to be, Sir, Your Excellency's obedient servant	His Excellency
Consuls	To John Smith, Esq., H.M. Consul	Dear Sir	Yours faithfully	Mr John Smith

Title	Envelope address	Opening	Closing	Speaking about
Government Ministers	The Rt Hon. Mr John Smith MP Secretary of State for Employment	Dear Secretary of State	Yours faithfully	The Secretary of State for Employment or Mr John Smith
Mayor	The Rt Worshipful the Mayor of	Dear Mr Mayor	Yours faithfully	Mr Mayor **or** Mayor Smith
County Court Judge	His Honour Judge John Smith	Dear Sir	Yours faithfully	His Honour Judge Smith
Bishop Prostestant	The Right Reverend the Lord Bishop of Oxford	My Lord	Yours faithfully	His Lordship **or** The Bishop of Oxford
Clergyman Protestant	The Reverend John Smith	Dear Sir	Yours faithfully	Reverend Smith
Rabbi	Rabbi (name) Address of synagogue	Dear Sir	Yours faithfully	Rabbi (name)
Cardinal	His Eminence Cardinal Smith	Your Eminence	I remain, Your Eminence, Yours faithfully	His Eminence
Priest	The Reverend John Smith	Dear Reverend Father	Yours faithfully	Father Smith
University Prof.	Professor John Smith	Dear Professor Smith	Yours sincerely	Professor John Smith
Physician	John Smith, M.D. Office address	Dear Dr Smith	Yours sincerely	Dr Smith

An earl by right, by courtesy a man
– Alfred Austin

ORGANISING YOUR HUMAN RESOURCES

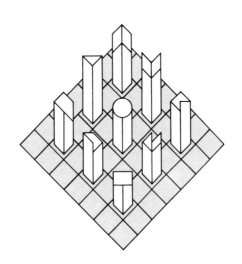

Supervisors, managers and anyone else in a hiring capacity should have a conscious awareness of sound, effective interview goals and techniques. Here are the basic areas of concern.

Interview objectives

Basically, the interview is an information-gathering process. The information that is obtained naturally becomes a part of and helps in the final decision of whether or not to hire. It can also be used in deciding whether or not to place an employee in a specific work assignment. This decision can be made when you are employing someone from outside the firm, or transferring or promoting an employee from within the company to a more challenging work situation. You can even use the interview information to help reshape an assignment to suit more accurately the talents of the capable individual.

Prior to any interview, the interviewer must have a clear picture of what he is looking for in the candidate being interviewed in relation to the requirements of the job. Many top interviewers find it helpful to set up a list of the "musts" and a list of the "wants" which will be explored during the interview. "Must" factors are those essential for a sound candidate-job match. "Want" factors strengthen the match but are not mandatory.

For example, for a senior sales manager, "musts" may be: actual sales experience, commitment to travel, language ability, ability to motivate subordinates, ability to run sales meetings, etc. "Wants" may include: familiarity with your product or service, territory knowledge, plus other specifics you feel would be desirable, but whose absence would not specifically rule out a candidate.

The interviewer has an important fact-finding checklist to cover:

- Gather information
- Form an impression of personality
- Pinpoint unique characteristics
- Establish whether or not the person has adequate communication skills

Learn something of the person's desires, needs and motivation. Assess whether or not the candidate is compatible with the proposed work group and expand on personal and professional information gained from other sources.

Leadership
Has the candidate held a leadership position? Is it similar to the one for which you are interviewing? Has the candidate been responsible for hiring, training, motivating other employees? Can the candidate lead without alienating others? Has the candidate been responsible for terminating the employment of others? Is this function important to the assignment that you have open?

Attitude
What does the candidate think of previous employers? Did he identify with the company's corporate values and policies?

Dependency
Does the candidate have a normal need for approval from superiors? Or is there a tendency to be overly dependent on the opinions of others?

Adaptability
Does past performance indicate a flexibility and ability to change as an employment situation changes?

Stability
Is the candidate resistant to stress, or would a high stress situation affect his ability to perform? What are the candi-

date's comments about stress and work pressure in previous jobs?

Motivation
Is work a source of personal satisfaction? Does the candidate have a wide range of interests other than work? Is there a reasonable grasp of current affairs? Does the candidate appear to be a social butterfly, or are there signs of being socially restricted?

Danger signs to look for

Interviewers, like the interviewee, are human. As a result, their objectivity can be swayed by the personal interplay within the interview situation. To help you maintain a balanced overall view of the candidate in relation to the employment position, here are a few "red flags" to look for; they indicate a need for caution:

- Are there indications of immaturity that could detract from work performance?
- Look for a tendency to blame others, criticise unnecessarily
- An inability to make unpopular decisions
- Unrealistic or over-blown claims of accomplishment
- Hypersensitivity
- Aspirations beyond ability
- Irresponsibility and demanding behaviour.

Interviewing techniques

If you are conducting the interview yourself, it is your responsibility to establish the best picture of the applicant *vis-a-vis* the position. If you draw out a complete picture from the candidate, you can reduce the risk that a promising candidate will be passed over.

Here are some proven guidelines for interviewing:

- Be as pleasant as possible to establish an early rapport, first impressions are important. Be sure to introduce yourself by name. Don't take an over-friendly or hearty approach, and avoid "chit-chat".

- If you are going to make notes, tell the interviewee the reason. Reassure the applicant that all information will be treated in professional confidence.

- Ask your questions clearly and concisely, while keeping your tone conversational.

- Interview ... don't sell.

- Don't ask questions that can be answered "yes" or "no". Probe for in-depth answers, but avoid leading or loaded questions.

- If you find contradictions in the answers, probe to find the reasons.

- The most important rule of all – Keep your own personal opinion, bias and/or prejudices out of the interview.

Suggested areas for in-depth probing

Intelligence
In addition to scholastic levels achieved, what can you discover about the applicant's effective range of applied intelligence?

Energy level
Does the candidate have the ability to sustain a high level of work activity? How has this been demonstrated?

Forcefulness
Is the candidate vigorous in the presentation and defence of opinions? Or is the candidate merely defensive?

Perception
How sensitive is the applicant to the feelings and motivations of others? Does the candidate reveal

an awareness of his impact on fellow workers?

Objectivity
How realistic is the candidate in assessing personal assets and liabilities, strengths and weaknesses?

Communication
Does the applicant communicate effectively with others? With you? How clearly does the candidate express himself? Does the candidate organise information to pass it on? Does he understand your views?

Organisation
What in the candidate's history indicates a well-organised person? Does it seem the candidate can plan effectively and carry out those plans?

Decision
Is the candidate systematic in his decision-making approach? Is there a tendency to play hunches and follow intuition or first opinions?

- Are there signs of personal or emotional instability?

- Has there been a recent marriage or divorce? How has your candidate responded?

- Has the candidate changed jobs frequently? If so, for what reason?

- Is the candidate personally attractive, yet not suited for the particular assignment?

- Does the age of the candidate correspond with the number and kinds of positions claimed? Be sure to verify dates of employment and number of positions with previous employers.

- Have there been frequent changes of residence? If so, what are the reasons for these changes?

- Does the applicant refuse to

answer some questions without giving an adequate reason for this refusal?

In interviewing, as with any worthwhile skill, practice makes perfect. Conducting a good interview is demanding, yet the results are rewarding, as you watch former applicants transformed into productive, achieving employees. Therefore, follow these rules and guidelines so that you are constantly improving your interviewing techniques.

EMPLOYMENT APPLICATION FORM

CONFIDENTIAL

Application for the position of _____

(1) PERSONAL INFORMATION

Full Name _____

Address _____

_____ Tel _____

Sex _____ Date of Birth _____

Age _____ Nationality _____

attach a recent photograph of yourself here

Marital Status _____ Valid Driving Licence ☐ No   ☐ Yes

(2) HEALTH
Please give details of any major operations or illnesses you have had in the last five years _____

_____

Are you willing to have a medical examination? _____

(3) EDUCATION

Secondary School	Qualifications/Subjects attained	Date
College/University		

Other Training

Type of Course	Institution	Qualifications	Date

Organising your human resources

(4) LANGUAGES

	Indicate Slight/Fair/Fluent		
	Speak	Read	Write

(5) LEISURE INTERESTS _____

_____

_____

(6) EMPLOYMENT HISTORY
Start with your present (or last) employer.

Name of Company _____ Tel _____

Type of Business _____

Position Held _____ From _____ To _____

Starting Salary _____ Last Salary _____ Bonus _____
  (including Commission)

Car Allowance _____ Car Provided ☐ Yes ☐ No

Housing Allowance _____ Housing Provided ☐ Yes ☐ No

Other Fringe Benefits _____

_____ Annual Leave _____

Reasons for Leaving _____

_____

Name of Company _____ Tel _____

Type of Business _____

Position Held _____ _____ From _____ To _____

Last Remuneration (including commission & bonus) _____

Reasons for Leaving _____

_____

Name of Company _____ Tel _____

Type of Business _____

Position Held _____ From _____ To _____

Last Remuneration (including commission & bonus) _____

Reasons for Leaving _____

_____

EMPLOYMENT HISTORY

Name of Company _____ Tel _____
Type of Business _____
Position Held _____ From _____ To _____
Last Remuneration (including commission & bonus) _____
Reasons for Leaving _____
_____

(7) REFERENCES
List two references below. Relatives should not be included.

Name	Address/Telephone	Period Known	Occupation

Do you have any convictions for criminal offences (other than spent convictions)?

☐ No   ☐ Yes (State nature) _____

_____

Remuneration expected _____ Earliest available date _____

I declare that the information provided above is true and complete in all aspects. I understand that any misrepresentation or omission of information may be considered sufficient for withdrawal of an offer, or subsequent dismissal from employment.

Signature _____   Date _____

INTERVIEWER'S ASSESSMENT FORM

Applicant's Name _____ Interview Date _____

Position Applied: _____

1. Academic Rating ☐ Poor ☐ Fair ☐ Good ☐ Very Good	7. Sincerity ☐ Doubtful ☐ Average ☐ Straight-forward ☐ Very frank and open
2. Relevant Experience ☐ None ☐ Some experience ☐ Good experience ☐ Considerable experience	8. Enthusiasm ☐ Pessimistic ☐ Indifferent ☐ Shows ready interest ☐ Contagious
3. Personality ☐ Antagonistic ☐ Too shy or too bold ☐ Likeable ☐ Very pleasant	9. Determination ☐ Lifeless ☐ Easily discouraged ☐ Average determination ☐ Persevering
4. Conversational Ability ☐ Unable to express self ☐ Can make self understood ☐ Clear and concise ☐ Effective use of language	10. Health ☐ Sickly ☐ Frail ☐ Normal ☐ Robust
5. Mental Alertness ☐ Slow ☐ Rather slow at times ☐ Quick thinking ☐ Very sharp	11. Appearance ☐ Untidy ☐ Needs improvement ☐ Neat ☐ Above average
6. Reasoning/Judgement ☐ Dull ☐ Jumps to conclusion ☐ Thinks clearly ☐ Very logical and capable	12. Potential ☐ Below Average ☐ Average ☐ Above Average ☐ Outstanding

Physical handicaps (where relevant) _____

Additional Remarks _____

_____

_____

Recommendation   ☐ Recommended for employment _____

                     ☐ Need not be considered _____

Interviewed by _____

TIPS ON INDUCTION OF NEW STAFF

A well-planned and maintained induction programme can result in reduced absenteeism and staff turnover, as well as greater productivity.

Many programmes focus on company policies, procedures and benefits. But they fail to spell out to new employees exactly what duties they are expected to perform; nor do they generate a feeling of welcome.

Here are some pointers for designing a successful induction programme:

Create a congenial atmosphere by ensuring that the new employee meets colleagues, feels welcome and is reassured that his job is important to the company. Assure him that the company will assist with any training needed to enable him to do a good job.

Explain the training plans. Tell the new employee you realise that during the first few days he will feel a little "lost" and "uneasy". But give the assurance that a specific programme has been planned to help him through the "learning" stages.

'Big Picture' *Organise*

Tell the new employee how the entire operation works and where his function fits in.

Take him on a guided tour of the premises, showing the facilities available. *Virtual Reality*

Make proper introductions. Introduce the new employee to colleagues and tell him what they do.

Explain the company's philosophy and tell the employee what it's objectives are.

Explain company history, rules, regulations and policies, as well as benefits.

Tell the new employee about the company's clients and it's competitors.

New employees are usually very keen to do a good job, to learn, and to improve their skills. For this reason it is important to establish an atmosphere that promotes good future performance. It is important to let the employee know what is expected, setting reasonable but high standards. To prevent complacency, ensure there is sufficient challenge for the new recruit by establishing goals and encouraging a competitive spirit.

Follow up periodically. Make sure the employee is making satisfactory progress. You should check closely during the employee's first few days on the job. After that, you can check less frequently if progress is satisfactory.

New employees in the office may benefit from a simple glossary of terms, combined with a directory of procedures. This is a way of communicating the "style" of the organisation. A glossary should contain any job titles, systems or machine names which are not self-explanatory.

Many organisations have a probationary period for new employees, but often don't take full advantage of this time during which superiors can help employees to adjust to the job and can evaluate their performance. It is important to explain the terms of the probationary period, and to show continued interest in the new employee's progress.

Use the employee's appointment to the permanent staff as an opportunity for positive feedback to the employee. Such acknowledgement will give the employee a sense of security in his new job and will also help to motivate him further.

It is worthwhile to remember that the company too, is on probation during these first weeks. The ability of management to project positive, competent leadership will greatly influence the employee's view of the company.

A thorough and well-planned induction programme competently carried out, will help build a productive and responsible work team.

This is only the beginning — not the end.

assign a Mentors G7 G5

Organising your human resources

CHECKLIST FOR NEW PERSONNEL

Here are a few simple, yet important items to bear in mind to present to new staff together with their letter of appointment:

- A guide to standards of business conduct
- Any special conditions of employment
- Copyright and "know-how" undertakings
- Forms for pension, health and insurance schemes.

The checklist below covers most items a newcomer needs to know. Some of the items may not be appropriate to your particular office and should be excluded. Again, in the smaller office some of the items are too obvious but they have been left in as it is easier to delete from a full list. You may, however, find the checklist helpful.

Checklist

Information (organisation)
    Name
    History
    Organisation chart
    Products/Services
    Customers
    Location

Information (departmental)
    What it makes or what services it gives

    Where it fits into the organisation

    Jobs done – trainee's job – where it fits

    Departmental rules (time-keeping, meal breaks, safety, smoking, etc.)

    Supervision – names

    Other employees – names

    Personal relationships

Employment conditions
    Remuneration

    Method of payment (how, where, when)

    Hours of work – overtime, week-ends, shifts

    Holidays

    Sickness payment scheme

    Pension scheme

    Bonus or profit sharing

    Notice period

    Time-recording and time-keeping

    Absence – notification – certificates pay

Health, safety, welfare
    Medical examination

    Medical/First-aid facilities

    Toilet and cloakroom facilities

    Hygiene (Personal/process)

    Safety (regulations/appliances)

    Protective clothing

    Fire-precaution procedures

    Smoking

    Canteen facilities

    Sports and/or social club

    Saving schemes

    Staff discount

    Parking facilities

    Travelling arrangements

    Telephone calls

    Time off

    Loans

    Personal problems

General
    Joint consultations (works/ staff advisory committee)

    Grievance/Disciplinary procedures

    Trade-union membership

    Education and training

    Promotion and transfers

    Suggestion schemes

    Security arrangements

Note: All this information cannot be given to new employees at once: give them the essential information about *their job* and *their department* first.

GUIDELINES FOR WRITING A JOB DESCRIPTION

How can you make sure that the people in your department understand their responsibilities? How can you hold your subordinates accountable? How can you narrow the gap between desired and actual results? Do your employees know their specific duties and the performance standards for each of their activities? Do your employees know the decisions they can make and when to defer to others?

All of these questions are related to the same issue: making employees accountable for results. The answer is also the same: every manager should maintain an accurate job description for each of the positions under his direction.

Most job descriptions are not much more than a statement of reporting relationships and a list of activities or duties that the person in the position is supposed to perform. These descriptions fall far short of a good job description, and a good one can be an excellent tool for enhancing communication and productivity.

A good position description should contain the following information:

Title

The title should describe the individual's position in the organisational hierarchy, as well as his function. If needed, a subtitle may be used to describe the product or division – for example, assistant manager sales, consumer products division.

Reporting relationships

This part of the description names the individual and his title who handles the personnel-related needs of the employee, including salary reviews, approval of overtime, performance reviews, and discipline. Usually this person is the employee's supervisor.

Responsibility

Here is stated the results for which the employee is responsible. This section answers the question: Why does this position exist? Without an answer to this question, an employee will not realise the total significance of his position and his contribution will not be what it could be.

Accountability

This section should answer two questions: How will the employee be held accountable? What will the criteria for accountability be? This is a critical issue. The answers to these questions provide a means of measuring the employee's performance. It also helps an employee to have specific and measurable criteria to aim for.

List of duties or activities

In this section is listed the actual activities and the standard of performance for each activity. The standard relates to the frequency, accuracy, timeliness, or the like of the activity. This section should answer a question of importance to both employee and supervisor: How will we know that the task has been satisfactorily completed?

Requirements

This includes the technical and interpersonal skills required to carry out the duties satisfactorily. Any required education or previous work experience should be mentioned in this section.

Authority

This specifies the decisions that the individual can make independently or in consultation with his supervisor. Also, the decisions that shouldn't be made by the individual should be specified. Thus the employee becomes aware of the constraints on his authority. For best results, the authority given should be consistent with the responsibility and accountability criteria.

Work relationships

The people who contribute to the accomplishment of the employee's tasks and responsibilities are listed in this section. It is important for an employee to know that even though he might *work* for one person, the successful completion of his work may require *working with* many people in different areas of the organisation.

The employee should be involved in the writing and maintenance of an accurate job description. After all, who knows the job better than the person who is doing it. The manager's job is to review the description at least at the time of the performance review (more frequently if possible) and make sure that there is agreement with the employee on its various sections.

While preparation of a job description like the one described here for each of your employees might seem too time-consuming, consider the employee productivity lost from being without objective criteria to measure employee performance and justify increased output.

Performance appraisal is the systematic evaluation of the individual with respect to his performance on the job and his potential for development.

A formal evaluation procedure minimises the likelihood of capable people being overlooked for training opportunities, pay rises, promotions and new assignments.

Purpose of performance appraisal

Employee appraisal is an essential part of effective personnel management. Its purpose and uses are as follows:

Employee performance

Appraisals are an aid to creating and maintaining a satisfactory level of performance by employees on their present jobs. When the actual evaluation process is followed up with an appraisal interview with each employee, it may contribute towards more effective or improved performance on the part of many individuals.

Employee development

The appraisal may highlight needs and opportunities for growth and development of the person. Growth may be accomplished by self-tuition, formal training courses or job-related activities, such as special broadening assignments and job rotation. It should be clear that training and development of employees and managers strengthen the organisation as well as aid the individuals.

Supervisory understanding

A formal and periodic appraisal encourages supervisors to observe the behaviour of their subordinates. Encouraged by the proper top-management attitude, they can be motivated to take an interest in and help each person. If carried out properly, the entire appraisal process can facilitate

The scenario for the traditional appraisal interview goes something like this

The boss or supervisor is cast in the role of judge and does most of the talking.

The interview usually focuses on the employee's major shortcomings.

Criticisms are usually "sandwiched" between compliments or praise.

Evaluation centres on aspects of the employee's personality, ability to work with others, initiative, dependability, etc.

Discussion centres on the past – specifically, performance over the past year.

What are the results of the interview?

The employee assumes a defensive attitude.

Criticisms have a negative effect on performance.

Praise has little effect one way or the other.

Performance remains unchanged.

mutual understanding between the supervisor and his subordinates.

Guide to job changes

An appraisal aids decision-making for promotions, transfers and discharges (for inadequate performance). Systematic assessments of an individual over a period of time and recorded in writing, help to make this process reasonable and sound. Appraisal should give due consideration to the needs of both the organisation and the individual.

Pay adjustments and other awards

Perhaps the most commonly expressed purpose for having performance appraisals is to provide equitable pay rises to all employees based on their contributions to the company. Employee appraisals that reward above-average performances will also have a significant impact on employee turnover and job productivity.

The appraisal interview

Most of us would agree that an employee needs to know where he stands – whether his job performance is measuring up or falling short. Surveys show that most people think the idea of regular performance reviews is good. Yet few operating managers ever conduct appraisal interviews on their own initiative. Most do so only after being told they must.

Supervisors and managers tend to resist appraisal interviews because of the experience they have had with them, both with their subordinates and with their superiors when they themselves were appraised.

What can the manager do to ensure that an appraisal of performance has a positive and desired effect on the employees concerned?

To achieve the best results, the performance appraisal should be used as a communication tool between the supervisor and his subordinates. Further, to use the appraisal as a motivational tool, several precepts must be kept in mind. Think about them:

- Discussing the appraisal with the employee is a medium for recognising the employee's positive contributions.

- The appraisal evaluates the employee's performance against the requirements of the job.

- It provides an opportunity to review developmental needs and outline career goals.

Preparation for appraising a subordinate should begin long before a performance discussion is actually held. Regardless of the type of appraisal document or rating system used, here are several suggested steps for successful appraisals, anytime, anywhere:

- Begin with a clear understanding of job duties, standards of expected performance, or objectives. This sets an objective basis for measurement during the evaluation period.

- To the fullest extent possible, quantify key aspects of the job. Elements of most jobs can be defined by some sort of quality or quantity measurements, such as timeliness of actions, quantity of output, project completion dates, accuracy or error rates, or other similar criteria.

- Avoid waiting to year's end to point out numerous errors which should have been communicated at the time of commission. Provide frequent informal feedback. For example, compliment the employee on a job well done and, of equal importance, point out and have the employee correct errors. Provide coaching and guidance as needed.

- Prepare for the appraisal discussion by reviewing performance and results in comparison with goals set at the start of the evaluation period.

- Document results on your company's evaluation or rating form. Be specific, use examples to highlight positive attributes as well as areas where improvement is needed.

- Direct your comments to the

way the employee does the job and not at him personally.

- Comment on improvements. Let the employee know that you are aware of his efforts to improve. Recognition of this progress will encourage the employee to do better in the future.

- Once you have discussed your rating of the employee's past performance, your next task is to establish new goals for the future. This should be a co-operative effort. Be specific and let the employee know how you will help. The employee can't do it alone – he must have your support and understanding.

- Take your time when doing an appraisal interview. Don't rush through it. If the interview is rushed, it will be non-productive.

Self-appraisals: the next stage in performance evaluations

Self-appraisals are becoming more and more common. This system of performance appraisal holds the following advantages:

To prepare for the appraisal meeting employees need to think critically about their performance; through such an analysis, they learn more about themselves. While most of us claim to know ourselves well, how often do we take an hour to analyse how we perform our jobs, to consider what "tools" we need to be successful, and what we should do to acquire these skills.

Secondly, preparing for the meeting through self-appraisal increases the chance that the meeting will be a real discussion, rather than a monologue by the supervisor. Both supervisors and employees can learn

something from this two-way communication.

The employees may present information of which the supervisor was unaware, leading to more accurate appraisals. And the employees will be more receptive to what the supervisors have to say because they may have arrived at many of the same conclusions through their own analyses.

The involvement of employees in the appraisal discussion also increases the likelihood of developing workable solutions to problems. The proposed solutions stem from a fuller analysis of the problems by both employee and supervisor and consequently are more likely to work. They are also more likely to be accepted by the employee because of his participation in their development.

For the self-appraisal system to work, employees need to be given guidelines on how to proceed. The supervisor must:

- See that the employee is knowledgeable about how performance will be measured. Supervisors and employees need to have the same yardstick for measuring performance. This should be established at the beginning of the performance period to guide employees' actions and enable continual self-monitoring.

- Provide employees with a structured format for preparing for the appraisal meeting. Just as supervisors need a standard form to help them think about their employees' performance, employees also need an aid to guide their thinking.

- A structured format will increase the chances that employees will be able to discuss specific examples of past performance and offer realistic suggestions for improvement.

- Ask the individual for "descriptive" rather than comparative information. The self-appraisal sessions should be structured around descriptions of what happened and how the job was accomplished. An individual should not be asked to compare himself with other employees. Other employees' work is irrelevant when one is considering what a person did (or did not) accomplish and the means used.

- Give the employee an incentive to provide an accurate self-assessment. If an employee believes the appraisal prepared by the supervisor to be fair and accurate, he will not feel the need to "inflate" or deflate the self-assessment. And one of the best ways to guarantee a fair appraisal is by having several sources of information contributing to the appraisal. Ideally, there should be some objective measures, for example, sales volume or units produced.

- The principal purposes of the assessment will also affect the honesty with which an employee approaches it. If the appraisal is only a means to decide on compensation, promotion or termination, it is obviously in the self-interest of the employee to push for the highest rating he can attain, regardless of its merits. However, if the main purpose of the assessment is individual development, career planning, or performance improvement, the employee will benefit from an honest, forthright look at his performance, strengths and weaknesses.

- Train both the employee and the supervisor. Active involvement by an employee in his own appraisal is something that may require some adjustment by both the employee and the supervisor. The employee needs to learn how to assess performance, analyse strengths and weaknesses, and think about career development. The supervisor must learn to listen objectively to what the employee says and to encourage the employee to participate in the discussion.

Start with good people, lay out the rules, communicate with your employees, motivate them and reward them. If you do all those things effectively, you can't miss

– Lee Iacocca

WHAT TO DO ABOUT HIGH STAFF TURNOVER

High staff turnover can be very costly to an organisation, yet it is often a misunderstood cost. Just because it's hidden – in other words doesn't show up on the balance sheet – doesn't mean it's not costly.

Employee turnover always has been, and probably always will be, one of the most important problems faced by a manager in his day-to-day activities.

We all know the joys of a well-trained, dedicated and motivated staff. Such a staff makes our job easy, and attaining such a staff is well worth the effort involved. It certainly doesn't happen overnight – and yet overnight it can be wrecked by a spate of unexpected resignations. Suddenly there are new people to train, new people to learn about, and new people to motivate.

Turnover costs money in decreased production, material spoilage and sometimes overtime. Then there's the cost of recruiting hiring and record-keeping.

Finally, there's the cost of low morale. People hate to see a great work team broken up. Sometimes one resignation inspires a rash of them. To combat the problem, you've got to know why people resign.

Improper selection techniques

You didn't get the right person in the first place ... and so a resignation was inevitable. Maybe you hired someone on somebody else's recommendation. Maybe you had no choice in the matter (or thought you didn't). Maybe your decision to employ the person concerned was based on unimportant issues.

Solution
Analyse the vacant job, what it demands in the way of physical and mental requirements, previous experience, qualifications, etc. *Then seek that person. Don't settle for less.*

Instead of buying, you sold

You liked a particular candidate for the job so much that you jumped the gun. Instead of buying his talents, you sold, or oversold, the job to the person. When the rosy picture you painted proved not to exist, he resigned.

Solution
Describe the job fairly, both its good and its bad points.

Poor training or poor acceptance

If a new employee is poorly trained, and so makes many initial mistakes, or doesn't feel accepted by his fellow workers, there's trouble ahead. His failure to understand the "big picture" at the company is another reason for resignation.

Solution
Train and orientate all new employees thoroughly. See to it that the right introductions are made. Call attention to similarities of interest between the new and the existing employees. Smooth the way for early acceptance.

Poor supervision

Sometimes the supervisor or manager who is excellent at meeting production targets, at scheduling or even trouble-shooting mechanical problems, is poor at handling people.

Solution
If you suspect there's a problem, ask your other supervisors to be frank with you – and ask them for their help in solving the problem.

Incorrect usage of skills

People overqualified for the job get frustrated very quickly working for you ... and those involved in work over their heads do so too. They tend to seek jobs more suited to their skills elsewhere.

Solution
Match a job candidate's skills as closely to those needed as you can, or be certain you've got a sound training programme that'll produce quick and superior results. Unless you have sound reasons for doing so, don't employ someone who's obviously overqualified for the job you have in mind.

Low morale

Politics ... cramped quarters ... low pay. All these are reasons for a drop in morale, and they all result in high staff turnover.

Solution
Do what you can to improve morale in your group. Often a manager can create an island of happiness for his people while others all around are adrift in a sea of discontent.

Other turnover problems are caused by wages, personnel policies, ineffective grievance procedures, and such outside causes as inadequate day-care facilities, poor transportation or parking problems.

To get to the bottom of any turnover problem, just keep accurate records on every new employee and every resignation that occurs in your department. Then study them, looking for the possible causes, some of which we've cited here. Next, implement the solutions we've suggested.

The use of temporary employees offers great potential for improving productivity. Business management has acquired a better appreciation of the role which temporary staff can play as a flexible supplement to permanent staffing as well as an efficient alternative to traditional personnel dilemmas.

The ways in which business employs temporary help are limited only by the creativity of management. The applications are virtually endless. The opportunities for expediting work-flow, for reducing overhead costs, for improving permanent staff morale, for controlling overtime expenditures and for the more efficient use of office space, are virtually unlimited. In addition, temporary employees enable an organisation to delay an employment commitment, obtain unique expertise needed only for a short space of time, or experiment with various types of skills and talents in determining what works well in a particular situation.

Organisational needs

When planning the possible use of temporary staff there are some "basic" steps you can take to predetermine needs, e.g.:

- Take a close look at every employee's role in your office system. Is there duplication? Is everyone fully employed? Each permanent employee should be working at close to maximum capacity ... not just sometimes, but throughout the year. Otherwise, you're paying a full-time salary for a part-time job.

- Establish your company's regular work-flow, charting where possible the cyclical peaks and troughs. Are you staffed to cope with the peaks? Many companies find temporary staff can handle work-load peaks at considerably less cost than full-time employees ... and do an equally good job.

- Observe what happens when sickness or holidays leave you short of people. If you're managing comfortably with people away, it could be a sign that you're overstaffed. The thing to do then is let natural staff turnover take its course, and before replacing anyone, consider whether or not flexible staffing with temporary personnel could do the same work more economically.

- Establish short and mid-term projections of your staff requirements for upcoming special projects such as systems conversion, inventory, special research, etc. Many of these are ideal for temporary staff. Because some projects call for specialised experience and talents, don't assume they are beyond the capabilities of temporary staff. The increased need for job specialisation in today's environment is causing temporary help companies to expand their recruiting and training efforts to meet the demand. Many companies offer a wide spectrum of employment classifications ranging from switchboard operators and filing clerks to accountants and systems analysts.

- Are you planning a completely new project? Consider the use of temporary staff during the yearly uncertain period.

- Check your present overtime requirements. Regular overtime every month or quarter, by permanent employees, is a warning sign. Those overtime hours are costing your company dearly in extra pay, poor morale and increased absenteeism.

- Make sure you understand the rate structures charged by temporary service organisations. Basically, you get what you pay for. A lower rate from one firm doesn't necessarily mean a saving – it could mean they're paying their employees less – so you're probably getting a poorer calibre of worker. In addition, these firms pay insurance costs, fringe benefits, deduct taxes, etc. You pay only for the hours a temporary employee works.

- Before selecting any company to fill your temporary staff needs, find out if their rates include all the complementary services of a top temporary service company. The company should provide recruiting interviews, reference checks, and pre-job testing services. In addition follow-up calls should be made to see if work is satisfactory. It's services like these that are largely responsible for making your flexible staff programme a success. Any temporary staffing service that doesn't provide them is giving your company less than full support.

Effective working relationships

Before you call

To get the best results at the most economical cost, give your agency as much detailed information as you can about the work to be done.

When arranging for temporary help, decide on the specific requirements and skills necessary to accomplish the job. Requesting a switchboard operator and neglecting to mention a typing requirement could produce a non-typist – plus a delay. To help evaluate your requirements, get a list of job classifications from your agency.

Remember, don't ask for someone with more qualifications than the assignment calls for; the extra cost is unnecessary. If you need a typist, don't order a secretary. On the other hand, don't try to save expense by requesting less qualified help than you actually require; the employee you receive may not be able to carry out all the duties that you expect.

Placing an order

When you're ready to call your agency, think carefully about your needs before you pick up the phone. To do a really first-rate job, they will need to know:

- Whether the temporary will be filling in for your permanent staff, or tackling extra work.

- Approximately how long you'll require his services.

- Exactly what the job involves.

- What type of office equipment will be used.

- The name and model of the word processors and the software package used, if word processing is required.

- The working hours.

- Who the temporary employee reports to on the first day, and where.

In addition, give your agency any other information that they should know about, like special parking or luncheon facilities.

Preparing for the temporary employee

To ensure that the assignment is a success for both you and the temporary employee, follow these simple steps before the job begins:

- *Notify your permanent employees*

Tell your staff about the temporary employee and explain why you need help. Enlist their co-operation to make the temporary employee feel more comfortable.

- *Prepare the working environment*

Thoroughly check the work station before the temporary employee arrives. Make sure that the requisite equipment arrives and is in good working order and that the necessary office supplies are readily available. Have someone organise the tasks to be completed so that the employee can get to work right away.

- *Organise the work schedule*

Plan the work schedule realistically. Although you'll want the job completed within the agreed time period, it's better to extend the assignment than to demand too much. Remember, the stress and pressure of an impossible workload can cause costly mistakes.

- *Appoint a supervisor*

Assign a "guardian angel" to supervise the temporary employee, answer questions and make occasional progress checks. Ensure that this supervisor understands his responsibility and what has to be done.

During the assignment

How do you get your temporary employee started and what can you realistically expect?

Here are a few pointers to ensure you get off to a good start:

- Brief the employee about your company. To ensure co-operation at all times, outline policies or procedures affecting the employee in advance, i.e. lunch periods, smoking, telephone manners, etc.

- Introduce the supervisor and co-workers. Make sure expectations are clear to both the temporary employee and the supervisor. A fellow worker should also be available to answer questions and solve problems.

- Outline job responsibilities in depth. When you point out the details and significance of each task, a good employee will see the total picture and anticipate problems.

- Inspect performance. Check work regularly to make sure that it is being performed to your satisfaction. If a problem arises, call your agency immediately. If the employee proves to be unsatisfactory, notify your agency within the first few hours, so that the employee can be replaced.

- Complete any performance review or quality control card sent to you by the agency. These results are important and become part of the agency's employee records.

When the assignment is complete

- Check the hours. Review the hours listed on the time slip carefully to be sure you are properly invoiced.

- Sign the timesheet. This is the employee's record. Without it, he cannot be paid. Be sure to check and sign the timesheet at the end of each week or assignment. If you won't be available, delegate this responsibility.

- Initial any corrections made to hours filled in by the temporary employee.

- Check on lunch hours taken. Ensure that the lunch hour column is filled in properly on the invoice.

- Be sure to retain your copy of the timesheet for validation when you receive your invoice/statement.

- Signing the timesheet is deemed acceptance of its terms and conditions, which should be listed with it. Direct any queries back to the agency, so that they can straighten out any problems that might arise.

DEALING
WITH
PERSONNEL ISSUES

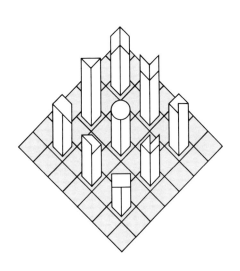

Putting together hundreds of strings to make challenging projects succeed, is easier, for many managers, than handling employee complaints.

Handling complaints is not easy because, as managers, we often feel we're personally attacked – even when it concerns a company policy over which we have no control.

Whatever the complaint, however, it must be dealt with – the sooner the better. The surest way of increasing employee unhappiness is to delay or leave the problem unanswered.

While many approaches are used, nine basic guidelines have been developed to help ease these uncomfortable management situations.

1. Listen to your employee

It sounds easy, but often while an employee is complaining, we're thinking of what our next response should be, not giving our full attention. Think of yourself as a sponge and absorb all the facts.

2. Get a handle on the complaint's emotional content

Employees frequently express unhappiness with a specific situation when something much larger is really the issue at hand.

For example, Grace, a bookkeeper, was feeling resentful towards a co-worker because she thought work on a new project had not been fairly divided. She felt that the other person had manoeuvered to receive more responsibility.

After a half hour of discussing Grace's unhappiness with the project, her job, and finally, with the company's standard operating procedures, she realised that she was not angry with her co-worker. Grace was extremely upset with the way the company selected project co-ordinators. In fact, she agreed with few of the company's management practices. Once the source of her anger was revealed, work could begin towards finding a solution.

3. Compliment your employees on the courage it took for them to speak up

After all, you are the superior. It isn't easy for employees to enter the boss's office unsure of whether voiced dissatisfaction will affect their jobs. Your recognition of their courage will boost employee confidence, and they will be able to give you the full story.

4. Don't get defensive

A hostile response will just exacerbate your employee's complaint. Show your wisdom by displaying open-mindedness. Only critical people repel critical comments. You will gain enormous respect by listening thoughtfully with sensitivity.

Incidentally, an employee will often be relieved simply because you acknowledged his personal feelings.

5. Ask questions before responding

Get a complete description. Enquiries such as: "Is this really the problem, Bob? I feel there may be other things you didn't bring up." Or: "Tell me more about your unfair workload. This is the first I've heard about it. I'd like to hear all of the facts."

Your concerned attitude will help employees explain their feelings.

6. Respond calmly and clearly

Without sounding defensive, tell your story. Although difficult, you must explain your motivations for laying off a best friend, or for demanding a report on Tuesday. One way of introducing your viewpoint is to ask: "Would you like to know why I arranged the schedule this way?". Or: "I understand why you're unhappy and I'm glad you brought it to my attention. Before we discuss solutions, here is the background on why I endorsed the change."

7. Ask how the employee would solve the problem

You might say: "Okay, Charles, I understand why you are frustrated. Now, if you could, tell me how would you resolve this conflict?"

An employee wants a voice towards a solution. More importantly, the employee, usually closer to the situation, might have the perfect solution. Remember, because an employee finds the answer, your reputation as a flexible, creative manager increases.

8. Design a specific action plan

If you can't immediately find the answer together, at least detail the first step towards a solution. Will you both gather more information? Can you speak to others about the matter? Will you, the manager, attempt to observe personally the troublesome situation?

9. Finally, report back to the complaining employee

Follow up the initial meeting with a phone call or memo. Tell Linda you have observed that Jeff is slowing production, and that you will speak to him about it. Arrange a meeting with Linda to review the situation after you have taken action. By setting and keeping appointments with your employees, you demonstrate that you are seriously seeking a solution that will satisfy all concerned.

If you follow these suggestions and take action, you need not feel apprehensive when an employee has a gripe. Not only will you be able to solve the problem, but your own cool will diminish office stress as well as increase your reputation as a fair, effective and sensitive executive.

POOR WORK DESERVES FAIR CRITICISM

None of us enjoy having holes poked in our work after we have invested time, effort and emotion in it. Nevertheless, pointing out errors and necessary corrections is an essential part of a manager's job.

However we phrase it, criticism hurts, and no amount of tact and diplomacy can eliminate the hurt. Such is the nature of all criticism. It has one virtue: only through criticism can we improve. It follows that criticism must focus on only those things the person is able to change. There is no point in criticising a person for having brown eyes or two arms. If a person is not able to alter the behaviour or the standard of his work then do not criticise it.

People often react to criticism. This must be expected. Your concern is not the immediate reaction, but the calm, reflective attitude that will emerge tomorrow. The criticism must be offered in such a way that upon reflection the person criticised comes to think: "They were right."

When you have to give criticism remember this rule: *Praise the worker, criticise the work.*

Effective criticism is offered with integrity. It is based on the wish to see the person perform better. Never begin your criticism by pointing out what is wrong. That puts people on the defensive, and defensive people don't listen. Instead, start out by praising the good points of the work and saying how you appreciate the person's effort and ability. Then shift the focus to what needs to be done to make things right or to keep them from going wrong in the future. Finally, end the discussion by again praising the person for his efforts, offering your support and expressing your confidence in him.

If someone is messing about and not doing the work expected, be more direct. Tell him how disappointed his work makes you feel because you know he is capable of doing a much better job. Then get to the specifics of what you expect from him in no uncertain terms and give him a deadline for doing it. End the discussion by offering your support and telling him: "You're much better than this."

Often people know when their performance is not up to standard. It is then enough merely to ask: "Do you think this is good enough?". They will look sheepish, hang their head and say: "No". Then it is a matter of discussing what they intend to do to correct the work or to prevent errors happening in the future.

A constructive critique leaves others with an understanding of the errors, the means to correct them, a feeling of appreciation and an eagerness to improve. Before delivering your criticism, be sure that it can provide these four things.

People cannot be supervised into getting it right. They have to bring the spirit of getting it right with them to the job

– John Naisbitt

DEALING WITH DIFFICULT PEOPLE

One of the most difficult and distasteful tasks that managers face is the need to make judgements about or confront difficult employees, especially when personality issues are involved. Even when an organisation has a formal procedure for dealing with such cases, it may often be that managers withhold their counsel when faced with sensitive issues because they feel uneasy about "sitting in judgement".

It is even more disquieting to many when an employee, either in confidence or openly and abrasively, initiates a discussion that opens up sensitive personal issues with a possible impact on the work situation. How should you as a manager react to these situations?

The traditional response has been to send the person along to the Personnel Department or to a higher organisational level in the hope that the problem can be solved elsewhere. Whilst this transfers the problem, it also cuts across the special relationship the manager has with employees and there is a danger that this may be seen as an abdication of authority where censure is involved, or as an act of rejection when someone has trusted you enough to reveal a delicate matter. Lack of skill in handling these encounters rather than lack of concern is usually behind a manager's reticence.

Whilst many organisations provide counselling services to deal with delicate and confidential personal problems, more serious problems are presented by the aggressive or abrasive employee who initiates actions that inevitably lead to negative confrontation and conflict. An essential first step is to familiarise yourself with the nature and dynamics of the abrasive personality.

The abrasive employee

One of the most common and troublesome employee behaviour problems is abrasiveness or lack of sensitivity to other people. Being perceived and experienced as abrasive or lacking in interpersonal skills often prevents otherwise hardworking or even talented employees from meeting their own career goals and fulfilling their potential. More serious, however, is that these persons can cause destructive tension and conflict affecting an entire division or the organisation as a whole.

People get labelled as abrasive for a variety of reasons. Some of the common abrasive types include the following:

The autocrat

The classic autocratic employee wants to do everything in his own way with total disregard for the input or opinion of either peers or superiors.

The rebel

The rebel cannot, or will not, abide by company rules. This individual possesses an anti-authoritarian streak and enjoys pressing against the organisation's rules and boundaries. Often tolerated begrudgingly by his peers because of their wish to avoid confrontation, the rebel eventually gets into trouble by offending or alienating people on higher levels.

The aggressor

The aggressor turns everything into a win-lose battle. This employee invariably plays the game of one-upmanship. They are often found not to be team players and to be overly protective of their own turf.

The bull in a china shop

This well-intentioned but ultimately destructive employee engages with other people and gives them feedback with a total lack of sensitivity to their feelings. This person is usually surprisingly heavily dependent on interaction with others, yet tends to communicate in a devastating way and seemingly never realising the impact. This employee isn't sensitive to underlying feelings and emotions in interactions, and usually underestimates the importance of the skills needed to interact properly with others.

The hard-to-predict

This inconsistent employee interacts well in one direction, but not in others. For example, some employees handle upward relationships well, but not peer or subordinate relations. In contrast, others have excellent relationships with their subordinates, but alienate peers and superiors by developing an us-versus-them orientation with their subordinates.

Assumptions about conflict

All of the above-mentioned types of employees are instrumental in increasing the potential for conflict in the organisation., To minimise the problems associated with conflict and to maximise the value associated with conflict, you should be aware of the following assumptions – they can guide you in effectively dealing with the difficult employee and the conflict associated with his behaviour:

Conflict is inevitable

This assumption is extremely important to keep in mind. People simply cannot exist together without experiencing conflict situations. It is natural for conflict to occur.

Conflict is not a dirty word

When conflict occurs, it is not a sign that those involved are bad people or that they are less worthwhile members of the organisation. Conflict can be extremely important and beneficial to relationships.

Conflict arises for many reasons and can take many forms

Although many approaches to conflict can be followed, you should be aware that there are many reasons for people getting involved in conflict and many ways that conflict can manifest itself. The key is your ability to recognise different kinds of conflict and to adjust your handling to the specific situation.

Conflict management approaches

There are many possible outcomes of conflict and they all require individual adaptation for effective management. There is, however, a number of general guidelines that can be applied in most situations:

Keep the conflict simple

Don't let the conflict evolve and accumulate all kinds of secondary baggage which may make it seem much more formidable than it did to start with. Try your best to prevent misunderstandings and do not attack the other person's pride or ego. Try to state the misunderstanding or difference of opinion as clearly as possible. Do not use emotional language or accuse the other person. Keep the conflict simple by using non-threatening language and stating the problem as clearly as possible.

Wait a while

If tensions are beginning to build up and you can put off making a decision, let the issue drop for a while. While waiting, analyse your reasons for the point of view you have selected. It may be that a solution that neither of you thought of, will materialise.

Face the problem together

Do not compete with the other person but try to work together on the problem. Mutually agree that the outcome of the situation will affect both of you. Nothing stifles problem-solving more than a dictatorial approach from one or both sides of a conflict. Work together to solve the problem.

Do not explain the conflict, describe it

When you are able to talk to the other person both of you should make an attempt to describe the conflict as best you can. Try not to explain what happened from any point of view, simply describe what happened. Do not allow competition or justification to enter into your description of the conflict.

Establish the sources of the conflict

After you have agreed about what caused the conflict in the particular situation by describing it, you can begin to determine what the general sources of the conflict were. If you can get to this point, you will probably be able not only to identify the underlying sources of the conflict, but also to agree on measures to avoid a recurrence of the same situation in future.

He that will not reason is a bigot. He that cannot reason is a fool. He that does not reason is a slave
- Anonymous

CONFLICT MANAGEMENT: HOW TO DEFUSE EXPLOSIVE SITUATIONS

Some people relish confrontations. Others avoid them like the plague. But the most successful people in this world have learned how to make the most of sticky situations.

What can you do to defuse and resolve potentially explosive situations? Here are some of the strategies that psychologists and business experts recommend:

1. Refuse to take things personally and don't get personal in return

Remember that the objective of the confrontation is to come up with a solution which meets the needs of both parties and defuses the bad feelings.

So don't name call, or play lay psychologist. A leading American human resources consultant Dr Kurt Einstein points out that subjective comments like "You are lazy, hostile, difficult or irresponsible" merely describe your perception of a person's character, and that these labels are really symptoms of a deeper underlying problem.

If you are having a problem with somebody, Einstein advises you to open the discussion by describing only the person's observable behaviours, which cannot be denied.

Example: "Kurt, at the last three sales meetings, you raised your voice and became argumentative every time anybody questioned your ideas."

Or: "Sue, there have been at least six errors in the last three letters you typed for me. Why do you think this is happening?"

2. Make an honest effort to understand the other person's point of view and his position

3. Sharpen your listening skills

Listen to everything the other party is saying and not just what you want to hear. All too frequently, we are so busy fuming over the issue which provoked the confrontation, or so pre-occupied with coming up with clever rejoinders in order to win the argument at all costs, that we fail to give the other person a fair hearing. He may well have legitimate grievances which need to be resolved. And for all you know, something which you are doing could well be exacerbating the problem.

4. Keep your cool

Even if you resolve not to become personal, the other party may well use this tactic. Some people purposely goad others and attack their weaknesses. Fine. Let them. Keep calm and tell your adversary that you would rather discuss the observable facts and not his or your personal opinions. This approach will serve you well and your opponent will remember your composure long after the argument has been resolved.

5. Seek agreement whenever possible, and downplay areas of disagreement

After hearing out the other party, demonstrate your understanding by saying something like: "Martha, the way I see it, you're making three major points. They are (then list them). Is that right? (Wait for a reply.) Good. Well, I heartily agree with you on points one and three, so let's concentrate on point number two."

Avoid saying things like: "You're talking nonsense." When you restate the other person's position

(as you did above), you gain a better understanding of it.

6. Determine if the argument can be settled here and now in an amicable fashion

There are many reasons why a confrontation may sometimes need to be continued at a later date, and yet you don't always realise this at the outset of the discussion. It may only become apparent as you begin to understand the other party's position more fully. You may need to consult last month's sales report, a report from a year ago, a receptionist who overheard a conversation, you name it.

So don't be reluctant to call a halt to things, and set a time and date for their resumption, if need be. This doesn't indicate that you've lost or backed down. It really means that you're taking the problem very seriously and want to resolve it in the fairest way possible.

7. If you can settle the argument here and now, by all means do so

If you're in the wrong, admit it. People will respect you for far more if you have the courage to admit your shortcomings than if you remain defensive and disagreeable. A sincere apology will also go a long way towards mending bad feelings and contrary to popular opinion, the other person will see this gesture as a sign of strength, and not of weakness, on your part. Only cowards don't have the guts to admit that they are sometimes wrong and that perhaps they too should change some of their behaviours.

The main point, however, is not to establish who is right or wrong.

In all likelihood, there is probably a little give and take on both sides. A successful outcome to a confrontation will rather consist of a tangible plan to remedy the causes of the initial problem. You and the other party need to come up with practical solutions to which you are both committed.

To achieve a win-win situation, you should therefore ask the other party questions like: "How do you think we can resolve this situation?" after you have both agreed on the facts.

8. Last, but not least, set up a follow-up meeting.

People don't change their behaviours overnight and it is often easier to slip back into old ways than to change. This is why it is critical that you ask the other party when he feels you should meet again to see whether the solution is working. (By asking him for a follow-up meeting, rather than imposing one yourself, you are likely again, to gain more commitment from him.)

Remember however, that as you resolve one problem, a new one will probably arise. This is why it is important to see confrontation as a healthy ongoing communications strategy, and not as something to turn to as a last resort.

Service without reward is punishment
– George Herbert

The reasonable man adapts himself to the world: the unreasonable one persists in trying to adapt the world to himself. Therefore all progress depends on the unreasonable man
– George Bernard Shaw

THE RIGHT APPROACH WHEN DISMISSING AN EMPLOYEE

Termination of employment is a traumatic experience, not only for the individual dismissed, but for the person handling the action. Moreover, for the organisation, it is potentially hazardous. Because people are proud and sensitive, employees who have been dismissed feel rejected, shocked, and bitter – regardless of how much they anticipated the dismissal. Also, for the company representative, releasing a worker is usually a painful and extremely uncomfortable experience.

If the situation is poorly handled, the company also incurs a risk. If this happens, the company's public image and legal stability may be adversely affected. In addition, there can be a great deal of erosion of the sense of security held by the other employees.

A dismissal, therefore, should not be handled in a haphazard way. Managers responsible must be prepared, and adhere to some fundamental points, including:

- avoid emotionalism
- plan the time and location of the interview
- have a written benefit package ready for the dismissed employee to take with him
- advise the individual of any available outplacement counselling services
- follow up on the progress of the individual until he finds a new job.

As with any other effective business activity, dismissals must be planned. A manager should be prepared to face a task with potentially significant consequences. Allowing emotionalism, rather than professionalism, to dictate will do both the company and the individual a major disservice.

All too often, personnel departments are informed of a termination much too late to be of valuable assistance. Somewhere in an unwritten code, managers seem to feel they must bear this burden alone. They feel that asking for help is a sign of weakness.

Yet, often, asking for help is a sign of strength, because displacing a person from a staff, or effecting a reduction in work force, is not something a manager does very often during a career. Therefore, all the help a manager can find in what to say, when to say it, where to say it, and so forth, is important

Avoiding emotionalism

It is to be expected that the person dismissed will exhibit an emotional reaction. One can imagine, therefore, the explosive potential in a situation where the manager is also in an emotional state.

A manager should be trained by personnel or an outside consultant on how to prepare for the exit interview. In coaching sessions over 80 percent of managers admitted they did not know what to say. Additionally, managers explained that they neither disliked the individual, nor were particularly upset with the employee's performance. In fact, they were hard pressed to explain where the person had gone wrong.

Managers must be clear as to why an individual is being fired, with two or three solid reasons for dismissal. Days are gone when a manager can simply get rid of someone because of a vague feeling that he is not performing well enough.

Planning when and where

Often decisions as to when and where the dismissal should take place are not even discussed, let alone planned. Yet, these factors are not unimportant. For example, the question of when a dismissal takes place should be carefully reviewed.

The best time for having a negative talk with someone is early in the week, preferably Monday or Tuesday morning. Unfortunately, most terminations still occur on Friday afternoon, around 4.30 p.m. From there, unfortunately, the individual goes home or to the local pub, and proceeds to drown his sorrows or take his frustrations out on loved ones.

If notice is given earlier in the week, a Monday morning at 10 a.m. for example, the individual has time to discuss personal feelings and even come back the next day to review benefits and career plans.

Terminations should always occur in the boss's office. Some consultants prefer the employee's office, because the manager can break the news and leave. This "hit-and-run" philosophy, however, is very destructive to the psyche of the dismissed individual.

The boss's office is usually more private. The employee, knowing that it is a final decision, can exit the office with the option of going back to the office or leaving the premises. Some people want to go home; others stay. However, they must feel the company still trusts them.

What not to say

When handling a dismissal, managers will get into trouble if they talk too much, don't listen, or ask questions. Most people assigned this task are terribly nervous as the bearer of bad tidings. The first error, therefore, is usually in not telling the individual the truth about his performance. Often the manager feels it is kinder not to bring up past errors, leaving the individual free to continue making the same mistakes.

Secondly, the manager might feel obligated to make promises of help, although they cannot be kept. The manager might say "I'll get you a job with another company," or "I will help you get a job through a personnel agency". If the manager does not come through, the employee feels he has been dismissed twice.

Managers are sometimes guilty of using certain offensive platitudes, such as: "I know how you feel," "this is not the worst day of your life," or "You're super – you'll find something else very soon". Since the employee is very sensitive at that moment, those statements may evoke a very negative reaction.

Finally, managers should be taught not to make untrue statements. Some examples: "Harry, you are getting along in years and should get out of this job because there is too much pressure," or "Mary, you have been with us several years, wouldn't you be happier at home with the children?" These types of statements are immoral. Dismissing someone because they are getting on in years, or to use their sex as a factor, is unjustifiable.

Human reactions

Years of experience have shown that there are basically four reactions to hearing the bad news: smooth, violent, shocked, and normal.

Smooth reaction
When informed they are no longer with an organisation, many people are so stunned, and their ego so damaged, that they appear to have everything under control. They imply that they have anticipated the news for a long time and are almost "happy" about the decision. The executive handling the termination is deceived into thinking the firing went quite well.

Individuals reacting this way are often those who do the most damage to the organisation and/or themselves. They do not ventilate their feelings, and instead lie to themselves as long as they can. Eventually, however, reality penetrates. Their reaction can come two weeks or a month later. All of a sudden something explodes inside, and they become extremely distraught. Remember this point, when someone reacts abnormally "well" to the news, be on the alert.

It is more normal to be hurt and express the hurt constructively than to keep it bottled up. These same people do not really think they have been fired and often hang around the organisation for quite a while after being dismissed.

When dealing with this type of response, the person handling the dismissal must ask enough questions to make sure that the individual is really hearing the news. There is a tendency – and a desire – on the part of management to think that the person is all right and to let him leave the office and head out on his own.

Violent reaction
In reality, a person who over-reacts is not the most dangerous or the most difficult to deal with. With this type of person, the manager himself cannot get out of control, regardless of whether the employee says something against the manager or the company.

Realise this is an acceptable reaction. Or course, if the individual gets truly violent and threatens harm, he must be restrained and warned about this behaviour.

Keep in mind that the person is letting out hurt, and very soon will calm down and start asking questions about the future, benefits due, and other specifics. Once these questions start, you have turned the corner and can deal with the rest rationally.

Shocked reaction
People who react in a very shocked manner may exhibit traits similar to reacting smoothly, or they may exhibit no expression at all. This type is often considered an easy termination. However, such people have the greatest tendency toward suicide and other forms of self-harm. With no apparent reaction, they are saying that this is one more bad experience in their lives and that they really cannot handle it.

Here the manager must take time to discuss the person's feelings and not rush. The manager should be prepared to ask questions about the person's home life, career, feelings, emotions, plans and desires. The objective is to get the employee to talk. Again, the warning: a person who just sits and stares, or shows little reaction, is not necessarily handling it well. Severe trauma should receive immediate professional counselling. A person who will not speak, or who cries uncontrollably, must get professional help right away.

Normal reaction
This is characterised by certain predictable responses, anger, hurt, and disappointment. But very quickly, individuals move to practical questions about what the company will do for them, or if support services will be available. These people may truly have anticipated the action and are sufficiently together to ask for protection, help, or assistance. They may express disappointment in the company, but are primarily concerned about self-survival. This is the typical, more normal reaction of persons who have been dismissed.

What to say and do

Do the dismissal in the first five minutes. Take the rest of the recommended half-hour to put the person back together by listening to the other side of the issue.

Do not change your stance during the exit interview. If you

are going to change your opinion, let the exit interview go by and get back to the individual later.

Do not go beyond 10 to 30 minutes in the exit interview. Psychologists agree that it is not helpful to spend long hours discussing what is wrong with an individual.

Don't use platitudes or make promises you can't keep.

Get the personnel department or the personnel agency involved before the dismissal.

Don't ever get defensive and try to justify the decision. This type of action encourages the person to agree with you, because they think they have a chance to change your mind. Dictate the facts, then listen, listen, listen.

Plan thoroughly, and know what you are going to say, where you will say it, and when you are going to say it. Also, have a structure established for the individual, once he is dismissed. He will feel disoriented, out of control, unsure as to what he should do next. You must help him restructure his life as much as possible.

As painful as the experience of dismissal might be on both sides of the desk, your remembering to approach it in a businesslike manner will help ease this tense situation all around.

People don't dislike work ... help them to understand mutual objectives and they'll drive themselves to unbelievable excellence
– Bim Black

When angry, count ten before you speak; if very angry, a hundred
– Thomas Jefferson

HOW TO CONTROL ABSENTEEISM AND IMPROVE ATTENDANCE

Absenteesim is not just a problem for the company, but a phenomenon that could waste billions of pounds in the national economy. When it comes to dealing with the problem, however, it still remains the responsibility of each individual company.

There are two main reasons why employees stay away from work: either because they have no choice, due to illness and other authentic and legitimate reasons, or simply because they choose not to go to work. Although the latter reason obviously presents the major problem to employers, leave due to sickness can also become a serious concern if not guided by a sensible policy.

If asked for their opinion, most employees would probably feel that there are often legitimate reasons for not being able to attend work, including their own or their children's illness, or other personal problems. In many companies, there would, at the same time, be a perception among employees that general company policy seems to be intolerant of anything less that perfect attendance.

In the end, the question whether absenteeism is a problem will tend to vary substantially, depending on how the policy and the culture of the organisation define attendance abuse.

Facts on absenteeism

Research reveals predictable patterns of absenteeism across a wide spectrum of business and industry. The following are some observations that shed light on the phenomenon:

- Emotional factors are involved in 25 percent of all absences.

- Skilled employees are absent less that unskilled or semi-skilled workers.

- Most absenteeism is concentrated in a small segment of the total work force.

- Long-service, older employees are absent less than the under-25-year-old group.

- Approximately 50 percent of all one- and two-day absences precede or follow otherwise legitimate time off for holidays or weekends.

- There is a high correlation between employee "illness" and major sports events.

- About 30 percent of employees are seldom absent.

- Absenteeism increases with prolonged overtime and extended working weeks.

- Surprisingly, warnings to workers who are frequently absent are seldom effective.

- In many instances management's approach to attendance is punitive and policing rather than facilitating.

- Absenteeism policies often penalise legitimate needs while abuse still continues.

- There is often little recognition of good or even perfect attendance.

Hints for dealing with absenteeism

Although major differences may exist between the specific content of attendance policies in different companies, there are guidelines that can be applied in most situations.

Formulate a simple policy
Establish a written policy for absenteeism and indicate the disciplinary action to be taken if absenteeism becomes excessive. Most important, however, is that the policy should be easily understood and administered. The conditions, procedures, benefits and penalties of the system should not be mystified through impressive but unintelligible terminology. The fact is that the better it is understood, the more likely employees will be able to adhere to it.

Communicate the policy

As with any other important company policies, the effectiveness of the policy on attendance and absenteeism is totally dependent on whether those who have the major interest in the issue, the employees, have received, understood and accepted the policy, and whether they would be prepared to apply it in their daily work contexts. The point is that, for all of this to become possible, at least the existence, but preferable the content, of the policy has to be communicated effectively to all employees.

Apply the policy consistently

In many companies, the belief is widespread that the attendance policy is administered differently by different supervisors. This leads to employees finding justification for misusing the system. Therefore it is absolutely imperative that the policy be consistently applied throughout the organisation.

Form an evaluating task force

No policy is or should ever be unalterable. This is especially true for something as sensitive as the policy on absenteeism. It is a good idea to form an evaluating task force, with representatives from middle management, supervisory and other grades to review the effectiveness and appropriateness of the policy regularly.

Identify concerns about existing policy

The first assignment of the task force should be to find out from all the represented groups what problems they experience with and what perceptions they have of the existing policy. However prejudiced or invalid these may be, it will still provide a useful benchmark for both improving the policy and correcting misconceptions among the employees.

Reduce the types of absenteeism

Some policies are characterised by a complicated array of types of absenteeism. Although, comprehensiveness may contribute to more effective control, it may also lead· to a measure of confusion with both employees and supervisors. In some settings there is no differentiation among the types of absences. A given amount of paid time off replaces all vacation, holidays, sick days, and so on. This system provides a brake on abuse because when sick time is taken fraudulently, the employee has less vacation time. In addition, such systems appear to avoid much of the upset that occurs when supervisors counsel and reprimand employees for absenteeism.

Record patterns of absenteeism

A basic approach to controlling absenteeism is to keep good records of absences, study them to ascertain the reasons for absences, and discuss them with each employee. Often employees are surprised when they see how their six-month record of absences compares with those of others. Find out the reasons for absenteeism and take decisive action immediately after each absence occurs.

Publicise absence rates

It can prove very useful to publicise regularly absence and attendance rates of the company as a whole and of the different divisions. One important provision, however, is that this should serve the purpose of encouraging rather than degrading employees. The absence rates should ideally be accompanied by a reminder that absenteeism lowers productivity, increases costs and thus negatively affects the income of individual employees.

Integrate attendance with promotions and appointments

Perfect attendance can be made a major part of the annual performance appraisal process on which pay rises and promotions are based. Screen new employees closely and do not hire those known to have questionable attendance records at other companies. Ensure these measures are seen as a sincere attempt to improve attendance to the benefit of all employees.

Allow employees leave to appeal

Consider implementing a safety valve in which normally outstanding employees who experienced unforeseen circumstances leading to excessive absenteeism, and who would be penalised under the policy, could have their situations reviewed.

How to award good attendance

There is ample research evidence to confirm that positive reward systems may be more effective than punishment. A number of applications in industrial settings substantiate this point. For example, a large manufacturing firm with more than 7 000 hourly employees showed an increase in attendance by offering non-monetary privileges for good attendance combined with progressive discipline for excessive absences.

A few employees will probably have perfect attendance regardless of the situation; conversely, a few employees will always have poor attendance. Reward systems tend to affect employers in the middle. Improved attendance comes from average attenders. Here are a few ways in which good attendance can be rewarded:

- Institute a monthly perfect attendance draw. Each employee with perfect attendance and no tardiness should be eligible for the draw. Include a limited number of big prizes, such as a TV, VCR or substantial gift certificates, and a number of smaller monetary prizes or appliances.

- Have quarterly or semi-annual perfect attendance luncheons hosted by the CEO

- Present qualifying employees with letters of recommendation and have their pictures posted on the bulletin board or published in the personnel journal.

- Finally, it should be kept in mind that excessive absences and tardiness are often a reflection of company morale, and an award system can go a long way in boosting employee confidence and company climate.

SOME ASPECTS OF EMPLOYMENT LAW IN THE UK

Ideally neither employer nor employee should feel the need to seek assistance from the law. Your organisation must ensure, however, that its labour policies are always within the law so that if there is ever a dispute with an individual or a union, the company will not be vulnerable.

We outline here a few important points of employment law. Further information on all aspects of employer-employee relationships can be obtained from the Advisory Conciliation and Arbitration Service (ACAS) whose address is given at the end of this article. This body was established by the Employment Protection Act, 1975, to:

(a) improve employer-employee relationships

(b) help solve disputes when requested

(c) investigate voluntarily any industrial relations problem and publish the findings

(d) investigate terms and conditions of employment and the recognition of trade unions

(e) prepare codes of practice for the conduct of employer-employee relations.

If your company ever finds itself in an actual dispute with an individual or a union it should immediately consult its solicitors.

Contracts of employment

Any employee working more than 16 hours a week must receive, within 13 weeks of commencing employment, written particulars of the contract of employment. These must state: the names of employer and employee, the date when employment began, whether employment counts towards the period of employment for notice purposes, scale or rate of pay, when payment is made, hours to be worked, holiday entitlement, side pay arrangements, details of pension scheme, length of notice, job title, disciplinary procedures, grievance procedures, trade union rights. The laws affecting contracts of employment are:

> Contracts of Employment Act, 1972
> Employment Protection Act, 1974
> Employment Protection (Consolidation) Act, 1978

Reasons for dismissal

In the UK industrial tribunals decide on cases of possible unfair dismissal. To claim unfair dismissal, an employee must normally have been continuously employed for two years up to the date of termination. It is important to note while a dismissal may not break the contract of employment (i.e. the required notice may have been given), it can still be considered an unfair dismissal by an industrial tribunal.

Reasons for dismissal which are acceptable to the industrial tribunals are:

(a) lack of ability or qualifications

(b) bad conduct

(c) redundancy

(d) that the employee's continued work would break another law

(e) some other substantial reason.

Bad conduct, such as stealing from an employer, fighting on the premises, refusal to obey reasonable instructions and neglect of duties, can justify dismissal without notice. Otherwise the statutory notice (or contractually agreed notice if that is longer) must be given.

Although these are all acceptable reasons for dismissal, the tribunal must also be satisfied that the employer was reasonable in dismissing for the particular reason alleged. For instance, theft of a blank piece of paper, no matter how well proven, would not be reasonable grounds for dismissal.

Dismissal for taking part in a strike is allowed as long as there is no selective re-engagement of those dismissed within a three-month period.

Examples of unacceptable reasons for dismissal are:

(a) Trade union activity

(b) Pregnancy

(c) Spent convictions

(d) Transfer of business to a new owner (unless there are 'economic, technical or organisational' reasons requiring changes to the workforce).

Note that if an employee leaves employment because of unreasonable behaviour on the part of the employer (for example, sexual harrassment), it can be construed by an industrial tribunal as a 'constructive dismissal'. And if it is a dismissal, it can also be an unfair dismissal calling for some form of compensation from the employer.

Laws relating to discrimination in selection, promotion and pay

Equal Pay Act, 1970 & Employment Act, 1982
Men and women must be paid the same rates for equivalent jobs.

Sex Discrimination Act, 1975
Female employees may not be discriminated against in recruit-

ment, selection, promotion and training or unfairly selected for dismissal. The Equal Opportunities Commission investigates possible breaches of the law.

Race Relations Act, 1976

Similar to above as regards race. The Commission for Racial Equality investigates possible breaches of the law.

Disabled Persons (Employment) Acts, 1944 and 1958

Employers with more than 20 people employed are required to employ a quota of registered disabled people.

Industrial disputes

Above employee level, companies have to deal with unions. In some trades and industries working conditions and rates of pay are agreed by unions and individual companies or employers' associations/federations. This process can be completed either by joint consultation or by collective bargaining (a negotiation that ends in a more formal agreement than joint consultation).

If your organisation has terms and conditions less favourable than the agreed terms for your industry, the matter can be referred to ACAS to be settled by conciliation or, in the last resort, to the Central Arbitration Committee (CAC), which can make an award against a company.

If you find yourself in a dispute, you will certainly need the advice of legal experts. To avoid such situations is best, and to further that end, you must make sure you or the relevant people in your company are properly informed. A useful starting point is the Department of Employment's 'Directory of Employers' Associations, Trade Unions and Joint Organisations', available from:

Department of Employment
Statistics Division B2
Hampton Court
Manor Park
Runcorn
Cheshire
WA7 1TT

The following addresses and telephone numbers may also prove useful, particularly that of ACAS, if you are formalising procedures in employer-employee relations:

Central Arbitration Committee
S. Gouldstone
39 Grosvenor Place
London
SW1X 7BD
Tel. 071-210 3737/
 3738/3741

Industrial Court Northern Ireland
Industrial Court
2nd Floor
Bedford House
16-22 Bedford Street
Belfast
BT2 7NR
Tel. 0232-327666

Central Office of Industrial Tribunals
England and Wales:
93 Ebury Bridge Road
London SW1W 8RE
Tel. 071-730 9161

Northern Ireland:
2nd Floor
Bedford House
Bedford Street
Belfast
BT2 7NR
Tel. 0232-327666

Scotland
St. Andrew House
141 West Nile Street
Glasgow
G1 2RU
Tel. 041-331 1601

Advisory Conciliation and Arbitration Service
D.B. Smith, C.B.
27 Wilton Street
London
SW1X 7AZ
Tel. 071-210 3625

Labour Relations Agency
Windsor House
9-15 Bedford Street
Belfast
BT2 7NU
Tel. 0232-321442

Certification Office for Trade Unions and Employers' Associations
27 Wilton Street
London
SW1X 7AZ
Tel. 071-210 3733/4

RUNNING
YOUR
OFFICE

DESIGNER OFFICE—THE EASY WAY

If you are moving to new offices, or it has been decided that the old ones are to be refurbished, you could well be expected to become involved in the plans, so it might be a good idea to familiarise yourself with the options.

An architect, interior designer or planning consultant may be called in to organise the entire project. Or you may be called on to co-ordinate the job.

Should an outside consultant be called in, you should have a clear idea as to what your office requirements are. In this way you can ensure that time is not wasted re-doing work that is not suitable. The same holds true if you are to organise the job yourself.

In either case the following information will be useful.

A little forethought and planning should be your starting point for a pleasant working place. You should ascertain which style will be acceptable to help promote the image your company would like to project. A slick high-tech environment may be perfect for an advertising group while a solicitor may prefer the solid, dependable atmosphere associated with polished wood and walls of books behind leaded glass doors. These criteria should be well established before you start shopping for an interior designer, architect or planning consultant. Many of these professionals do have distinctive styles and will be happy to show you examples of their work. This way you will be able to make an informed choice as to which "look" would suit your company best.

Planning

The consultant chosen should be given a detailed brief and have access to all key personnel to ascertain work flow and communication habits which could possibly be improved upon. Future development and expansion of information systems such as computers, word processors and fax machines should be a major consideration.

Ergonomics, the science of designing furniture to adapt to the human physique, should be of optimum importance as it can only improve the efficiency of the workforce. The height of work surfaces is an excellent example: desk tops should be 750 mm high and those for keyboards 700 mm. Adjustable chairs will eliminate a lot of costly back aches. Items in daily use should be within easy reach of the user, while dead files can be stored on high shelves. Remember vertical space for storage is free while every square centimetre of floor space wasted is expensive.

Lighting

Lighting should be carefully planned and the user should have individual control over task lighting to avoid eye fatigue which is often the result of inadequate lighting. Artificial lighting should be well shaded to eliminate glare on work surfaces and display terminals. Natural light, if available, should fall over the left shoulder of a right-handed worker and the opposite for a left-handed employee.

Noise

Acoustic control is an often neglected area in office design. Soft sound-absorbing surfaces will help to control the inevitable clatter of keyboards and printers. Carpets, wallpaper and curtains will all help to soften the sound effects.

Floor coverings are varied but carpeting will be softer underfoot.

Walls

Wall coverings are available in a wide range of textures and designs and really help to create a polished look. Heavy-duty wall coverings should be chosen and designs be kept soft and small. Paint is an excellent alternative but should be easy to maintain. High gloss enamel paint should be used in utility areas for easy maintenance.

Window coverings can vary from venetian and vertical blinds which are generally easy to operate to heavy draperies which may need elaborate cording systems to move smoothly. Loosely woven fabrics both lined and unlined are popular choices for offices. If you have the advantage of a beautiful view, frame it with simple side-curtains. Never forget the usefulness of curtaining where natural light conditions need to be controlled in different ways as the sun follows its path across the sky.

Maintenance

Regular cleaning and maintenance will protect your company's investment. Use only reputable firms as inexperienced cleaning techniques can mean many pounds worth of damage. Spot testing should be routinely done before cleaning commences.

Colour

After all these practical considerations have been taken into account you can now start with the choosing of colours. The first thing to remember is, it is impossible to please everyone in the group. Start by selecting a neutral colour like grey or beige for the carpets and walls. Accents can be in any strong colour but remember not to overdo it. Often the company colours can be used or a lighter shade if the original combination is too bold to spend all day with. Peach and apricot shades will help to warm cold, dark rooms usually on the north side of the building, while blues and greens will create a coolness in rooms which will appear hot if warm colours are used. Colour choices need not be dull and boring but do follow basic guidelines for colour co-ordination. Dark and murky shades must be avoided unless you need to camouflage dust and dirt.

Colours should flow to expand visually the space available. Contrasting bands of colour are often used to indicate traffic flow or demarcate different work areas.

No company is ever static and changes in requirements will affect the lay-out of the office. This could mean that traffic paths will be obsolete before the carpet needs replacing. Quality should be an important consideration. Wool, being naturally flame resistant and inherently antistatic, should be top of your list. Many synthetic fibres now have these features included. The carpet should be rated for heavy or medium commercial use.

Accessories

Accessories should be chosen with care. No painting, lamp or even ashtray is too insignificant. Remember, even the cutlery and crockery are part of your company image.

HOW TO MAKE BETTER USE OF AVAILABLE OFFICE SPACE

- **Revamping offices**, if handled in a systematic manner, can be relatively easy. And, one of the first steps involves analysing the entire space as it exists at present.

  There may be unused offices, or areas that employees simply spread into because they had not been occupied before. Perhaps one employee now occupies an area that was originally designed for two or three.

  There's no point, however, in attempting to place many people into too small a space. When employees are positioned too closely together you start to lose quality in the work product. Ultimately, the efficiency you hoped to achieve through space planning is defeated through lack of efficiency on the part of employees, who cannot work at their maximum in an ill-conceived work environment.

- Another area that can be of critical concern is a firm's use of **automated equipment**. For example, many firms have allotted one word processor for each employee station. Where applicable, a word processor can be mounted on a revolving table to service several clerical workers. Not only does this save square feet by removing the need for additional secretarial returns, but it also eliminates the need for a multiplicity of equipment. However, space-saving and money-saving ideas such as this revolving table, can only be considered if equipment is truly capable of being rotated and operated efficiently.

- For firms requiring extensive research facilities, we suggest making better use of the **hallways** instead of expanding library space. One law firm added a foot to the width of the office hallways to accommodate old oak shelving, which previously had been considered unsalvageable. Law books and reference material became part of the office decor, and the space that was designated for library expansion was used in a more cost-effective manner.

  Naturally, the number of files which must be maintained by a firm generally will increase as the size of the firm increases and it becomes more mature and established. However, there is no need for the size of the file room to increase.

  This could be the time to analyse your firm's filing system, and determine if it is growing out of control. Switching from the conventional method of filing to a computerised data-retrieval system will reduce the necessary filing space, and allow for easy retrieval of information.

- Almost all companies can cut their space in the **coffee room**. All that is really needed is a coffee machine alcove, or several strategically located alcoves.

  Another area that can be evaluated is the employee **lounge-lunch-room**. Today, studies show that almost all employees eat their lunch outside of the office. The space allotted to the lunch-room can be put to better and more profitable use.

- The vertical space around **desk areas and open-office systems** can save considerable space. For instance, the use of bookcases and small storage spaces above work areas is a simple way of using vertical space while also providing easier access to materials.

HOW TO MAKE OFFICE MOVES EASIER

There are three elements involved in moving company premises:
- pre-move planning
- communication, and
- the actual move.

Your main objective is to move with as little disruption of work as possible. This can only be achieved by working out each detail in advance.

It may be a good idea to elect one executive as moving coordinator, with total responsibility and authority to organise the move. A committee of departmental heads can be formed to carry out details and provide staff backing.

Careful planning and coordination with the removal company chosen for the job will ensure that normal productivity and efficiency are not hampered by the move.

Pre-move planning and communication, careful selection of a qualified mover, and staff assistance and support can help put the complexities of an office move in a more realistic and manageable perspective. Here are some practical tips:

The new office

Once you have finalised the layout of the new office, tell all the members of the staff the following:
- the general decor to be used
- where each staff member will be located in the new lay-out
- the part each staff member will play in the moving operation
- the approximate time of the move. Arrange this over a weekend or public holiday in order to upset normal business as little as possible.

Preparing for the move

- Book a reputable furniture removal company to do the move and have the actual date of the move reserved.

- If it is difficult for a stranger to find your current office premises and/or the destination, a simple plan or diagram will help a lot and save time. Make sure the removal company has your full address, with the name of the building and/or the street, as well as the office numbers.
- Advise the removal company of any known difficulties, e.g. stairs, passage or doorways which are very narrow.
- By arrangement, cases or cartons for your packing can be hired from the removal contractors prior to the removal date. They generally require a deposit on these containers, which is refunded on return by you, less hire, delivery and collection fee.
- Drawers, filing cabinets and cupboards must be emptied. The contents must be securely parcelled and clearly labelled.
- Breakable items must be carefully packed and marked "Fragile".
- All furniture and equipment should be labelled and coded to indicate its exact location as shown on the lay-out plan. Use different colours for different rooms.
- Each departmental manager or head should be responsible for the labelling and coding of furniture and equipment in his department.

Insurance

- Carefully consider the question of insurance. Do not under-insure. Under-insurance in the event of a claim results in only part settlement of the claim. Make sure therefore, that each and every item to be moved is insured for the full replacement value – less depreciation, where applicable.
- Should there be any reason to make an insurance claim for loss or damage in transit, you must make your claim as soon as possible. Most removal com-

panies have set a limit to the period in which you must submit a claim.
- At the time of delivery you must indicate to the removers any obvious damage and details of this must be specified on the delivery note.

Checklist

Have you:

Identified the new location of every piece of furniture and equipment?

Cleaned all furniture, carpets and curtains that are not to be replaced?

Purchased all new furniture, etc. required?

Arranged for electricians, carpenters, etc. to be at the new premises when you move in?

Bought new stationery?

Arranged for the redirection of mail?

Arranged for the transfer of the telephone, telex and fax service?

Transferred the bank account to a more convenient branch?

Followed up on the delivery of all new carpets, equipment, etc.?

Sold obsolete furniture, etc.?

Notified:
- customers and suppliers
- branches and agents
- shareholders and debenture holders
- government departments
- the tax office
- the Stock Exchange
- the insurance company or broker
- the auditors
- the advertising agents
- publishers of periodicals to which the company subscribes?

HOW SECURE IS YOUR OFFICE?

Introduction

The rising crime rate and increasing possibility of terrorist attacks in recent years has seen the introduction in many places of access control systems. A security guard at the door, a signing-in process and in some instances a checking-out process to ensure the visitor has left the building.

In many instances, however, this is only playing lip service to security. In all our major cities there are large multi-occupancy buildings with many staff and visitors and it is these buildings which have become the target of the criminals who prey on the office.

Perhaps in the first instance it is necessary for us to look at what we have to protect. In the office environment this can range from the office furnishings, the expensive office electronic equipment, the security of confidential files and data and of course employees' personal effects and the protection of people themselves.

The next question that arises is who have we got to protect against. There are several categories:

1. The office thief. The professional who makes a regular living from what he can obtain in an apparently casual visit.

2. The terrorist and bomb hoaxer – large corporate organisations experience this problem.

3. The violent criminal, not to be found very often in an office environment but certainly financial institutions and premises with large cash holdings, can experience this form of attacker. The wage office is an exellent example of a target area for the violent criminal.

4. The dishonest employee. Having one rotten apple in your midst can cast a complete blight over the whole working environment.

Good security in any environment must revolve around an attitude of mind. The secretary and receptionist who are aware of the need for security and being suspicious can do much to enhance the security of the office. The checklist which follows deals with most of the more common situations which you are likely to encounter with office crime, security and safety.

It is well to remember that the number one intruder, the opportunist thief, can be easily deterred by a few simple precautions. The removal of temptation and opportunity is a must for good office security

Portable desk-top machines, handbags, briefcases, should be put in drawers or cupboards which can be locked before offices are vacated. Closed passages and interconnecting doors would also deter the opportunist thief who tends to "hang around" to spy out the items he can easily conceal on his person.

If you see a person looking "lost" ask him who or what he is looking for and offer to help. If he is honest, the offer will be taken, if not, he will look for easier pickings elsewhere. Remember, the opportunist thief can come disguised, as a repairman, serviceman or other regular visitor.

The best deterrent must always be adequate access control, doors which are electrically controlled and can only be opened by the receptionist on the identification of the caller.

Security will always cause a certain amount of inconvenience, but without that inconvenience you will never have security. The practice of security today must become a daily activity and must always be in the forefront of a person's mind.

Checklist

Hold-up

- If there are other people in the room, convince them to stay calm.

- Do not make any sudden movements, the violent criminal is often nervous and could mistake sudden movement as a possible attack.

- Do not try to outwit the criminal. You do not know how serious the threats are.

- Try to reach the panic or attack button you have in your office. Make sure the attacker does not suspect your intention. You should only make the attempt if the panic button is situated where you are absolutely sure the thief will not be able to see any movement.

- Listen carefully and try to ensure that you will be able to recognise the thief in future. Look for any distinguishing features. Note the clothes he is wearing and try to determine the age, weight and height. Remember, after the attack the police will want help to compile an identikit. As soon as the attacker leaves the office, raise the alarm.

A fire

- On discovering a fire, raise the alarm by reporting immediately to the switchboard.

- Call for assistance and attack the fire with the fire-extinguishing equipment provided.

- On hearing the fire alarm, either leave the premises and report immediately to the assembly area or join the fire party if you are a member. **Do not stop to collect personal belongings unless it is obvious there is a clear escape to the outside**.

- On being notified of an outbreak

of fire, you should call the fire brigade immediately, and notify a senior member of the staff.
- Notify other departments and offices in the building.
- When instructed, sound the fire alarm or pass on the order to evacuate the premises. In the event of a fire involving the switchboard, alternative methods of raising the alarm will be necessary.

Action by management
- On being notified of an outbreak of fire, a senior member of the staff should ensure that the fire brigade has been called.
- Clear everyone except those actually engaged in the fire fighting from the immediate vicinity of the fire.
- Evacuate the building as soon as it becomes apparent that fire or smoke is spreading. Do not wait until the fire is out of control.
- Take a roll call of all staff when the premises have been evacuated.
- With a large organisation, this should normally be done by the head of each department.
- Instructions should be given to the personnel, setting out the action that should be taken in the event of a fire. These instructions should include bringing all lifts to the ground level and shutting down all services not essential to the escape of occupants.

Bomb threats

- Bomb threats can cause panic and disorder in any business establishment. Making a concerted effort to prepare for such a threat will help ease the tension which results in such an incident. For this purpose each company should develop bomb and bomb-threat procedures as well as an evacuation manual.

A bomb threat usually comes in the form of a telephone call. The call will usually be made during times when someone can react to the threat. The telephone provides a sense of security to the antagonist because it offers a cloak of secrecy and the chance to make other bomb threats.
- The first action to a bomb threat might be a feeling of panic or fear. A good training programme will help employees get the proper information from the caller in spite of their emotions. If the threat is received by telephone, it is usually a call to the switchboard operator, the security chief in the building, or a selected member of the staff. If you receive such a call:
  — Stay calm.
  — Try to determine where the bomb is and what it looks like, a description of the container, the internal construction of the bomb and when it is timed to go off. Keep the caller talking and note down the answers in writing. Write down the date and time the call came through and the exact wording used. Try to assess the accent if any, the sex, race and age of the caller. Listen carefully for background noises such as trains, machinery or conversations.
  — Inform the police without delay, inform the security chief in your building. Senior management personnel should have prepared an emergency plan that determines whether an evacuation of the building is required.
  — A bomb can be camouflaged in a number of different ways - it can be hidden in a briefcase, carton box, thermos flask, or even disguised as a book.

Should you see something sus-

picious, take the following action:
- Don't touch it or pick it up.
- Warn people in the immediate vicinity.
- Open all doors and windows and evacuate the area.
- Inform the police and your security personnel as soon as possible.

Mail bombs

The use of the mail bomb has gained popularity among terrorist groups. The following procedures should help personnel responsible for handling mail to recognise and react appropriately to suspicious mail.

Checklist
Watch for the following signs of suspicious parcels:
- Oil stains on the parcel.
- Evidence of the parcel having been opened and retaped.
- Peculiar odours.
- Wire or strings sticking out or attached to the parcel.
- Feeling of springiness in the sides or bottom.
- Heavier than usual package for its size.
- More rigid container than normal.
- Uneven thicknesses.
- Addressed to an executive but poorly typed, handwritten, or incorrect.
- An unsual postmark.

Confidential information

Information that may be regarded as vulnerable is information which, if disclosed, could:
- Be prejudicial to the national interest.
- Be damaging to the interest of shareholders, customers, clients or associates.
- Be administratively embarrassing to management, or cause a loss of public confidence.

All this information must be regarded as vulnerable and protection given accordingly until the release of the information is authorised.

Classification

This may be indicated as follows:

- According to the nature of the document or other item, and the possible consequences of disclosure: **top secret, confidential, secret, restricted**.
- The meaning of the first three is self-evident. Restricted material may be defined as material which, while not intended for general circulation, may be made known, wholly or partially, on a broader basis. **Strictly confidential** may be used where none of the above is considered appropriate. **Personal** or **Private** may be used when it is intended that correspondence be opened personally by the addressee. It is usual in reply to classified correspondence to use the corresponding classification.
- File covers, film, microfilm and computer tape containers in which classified material is kept should be clearly marked according to the maximum classification of their contents.
- In some companies where employees have access to classified material, clauses should be included in the employment contracts, binding them to refrain from disclosing to people outside the company any information that may come into their possession in the course of their employment. Breach of such a clause may enable the employer, or former employer, to take civil court action against them. However, this may have less force in law than value as a deterrent.

Protective measures

- Secretaries who may be handling classified material should

be trained to identify "nosey parkers", whether employees or or visitors, and to ensure that these people are unable to get sight of this kind of material. They should lock this material away during any period of absence from their place or work. This includes diaries and partly typed correspondence.
- Security "pairing" is a useful drill. In this, an executive and secretary or two colleagues, arrange to check each other's security.

Industrial espionage

- It is impossible to estimate the extent to which industrial espionage is now being practised, but it is known that it does occur, and the scope may be said to be unlimited. Obviously, the best way to prevent the loss of trade secrets, like anything else, is to look after them.
- Keep confidential papers out of sight when not actually working on them. Papers should be kept face downwards, or in a folder, or preferably inside a drawer. An untidy desk is an invitation to snoopers.
- Never leave papers on a desk when leaving an office, even for a few minutes. Lock them away and see that subordinates do the same. The office door may well have been locked on departure, but most doors have master keys so that window cleaners and others can have access. They, in turn, could leave the door open. Alternatively, someone may have acquired a duplicate key.
- It is sound practice never to leave any safe, filing cabinet or cupboard standing open, even when the office is occupied. Do not leave keys in safes while at work. Do not leave keys lying about on top of a desk.
- Ensure that desk drawers and cupboard locks are reliable and

that keys for them, including duplicates, are fully accounted for. If there is any doubt about this, change them. The use of a key chain is recommended.
- Arrangements should be made between executives and their secretaries for the safety of correspondence and other material received during the executive's absence from the office, or work left for the secretary's attention. The use of a locked receptacle, such as a desk drawer or cupboard, the keys to which are held by the executive and the secretary, should be considered.
- The whereabouts and planned movements of senior executives should be regarded as confidential information. While it is important that secretaries, and other people who may be concerned, should know the whereabouts of the executives at all times, this information must not be disclosed to others unless specific instructions have been given in this regard.
- Executives should be particularly careful to see that security requirements are met when a secretary is on leave or has the day off, resulting in the executive having to do without a secretary or making use of someone else.
- Interviews should never be conducted across a desk if this can be avoided. If possible, use furniture placed well away from the desk, or use another room. Never leave a briefcase in a car, no matter where the car is parked. Never leave office papers lying out at home, and avoid taking classified papers home if possible.
- When staying at an hotel, see that classified material is locked in a briefcase or suitcase, and that this is placed in a locked cupboard or wardrobe. Be careful to lock the room. Alternatively, consider depositing the

briefcase in the hotel safe. If staying with friends, treat classified material in the same way as if staying at home.

- Do not, on any account, allow strain, fatigue, anxiety or pressure of work to cause personal precautions to be relaxed.

- Ensure that all printed material is shredded before being given to the cleaning staff for disposal. Paper shredders are one of the most effective tools for improving security and they must be made readily available to everyone in the organisation. All executives and managers, together with their secretaries should have their waste bins replaced with a small personal shredder, while larger departmental shredders should be installed in the financial area, data processing, personnel department and any other department where sensitive information may be generated. Ensure that the correct shredder is purchased for each area, taking account of the degree of security necessary and the volume and type of material to be shredded.

  Material to be shredded includes discarded notebooks for shorthand, typewriter ribbons, carbon paper and dictaphone tapes. Remember to destroy telexes and faxes too. Remove or destroy all messages from the telex/fax machine overnight.

- Remember that many listening devices have been planted by people posing as technicians. Ask for positive proof of identification and check whether a service call has indeed been made. Never issue keys to the telecommunication room without ascertaining that it really is a technician. A vast majority of telephone bugging is done at that point. If you suspect bugging or have positive proof of spying and bugging, warn your boss in a public area where

there is no likelihood of bugging. Do not confide this information to anyone else. Do not report the matter from your boss's telephone. Rather telephone from outside the company.

Ensure floppy disks, tapes, etc. are confined to locked cabinets when not in use, treating them as if they were normal documents and ensure that some form of security is introduced on your PC or word processor. There are a number of different approaches that can be adopted for securing a PC, some addressing the actual hardware, others the software. The simplest method is to use the PC lock where it exists, locking the unit and removing the key whenever you are not present. If your PC or word processor does not have a lock, there are proprietary products available that cover the on/off switch to prevent access or alternatively there are software packages that enable you to encrypt your data or to lock out unauthorised users by requiring a password to be entered before allowing access. You should discuss your particular circumstances with your computer dealer and get his advice.

Finally, as stated earlier, good access control will lead to greatly enhanced security. A properly enforced system of access control within the business premises is vital to good security. Employee identity cards, and permit systems are a good idea. Visitors should be accompanied the entire period they are on the premises. Report the presence of individuals giving rise to suspicion.

Other vital aspects of access control should be high quality and functioning door locks, external and internal as well as those of desks, cupboards and cabinets, which must be completely reliable. Ensure there is effective key control over keys and duplicates.

Magnetic card key locks are recommended for entrance to high security areas, such as computer rooms and areas used for research and development projects.

Remember, good office security is thinking and acting securely and safely.

OFFICE SECURITY — 10 POINTS TO REMEMBER

1. **Never leave handbags on desks or wallets in coats in your absence**
Take them with you or lock them away.

2. **Always keep money in a safe place**
Even if it is only the tea money, never leave it in an unlocked drawer during the day. And at night put it in a safe or remove it from the building altogether.

3. **Be careful with keys**
Always put them in a safe place and don't put spare keys for safes, etc. in desk drawers. Deposit them at the bank.

4. **Fasten vulnerable windows in your absence**
It's easy to forget, particularly in the summer, and a thief can come and go in a couple of minutes.

5. **Never assume that a stranger wandering in the building is a member of staff**
Challenge him. Even :"Can I help you?" will often deter the dishonest.

6. **Don't accept that a stranger is authorised to be in the building just because he says so**
Check with someone in authority. If the stranger really is there to service the telephones or computers, someone in your firm will know. And never allow anyone to remove office equipment without checking first.

7. **Don't be overawed by callers**
Even if he does want to see the managing director make sure he is known and expected.

8. **Never leave callers alone in your office**
Use the telephone to enquire whether someone can see him.

9. **Don't disclose confidential information to a stranger**
No matter how important he may seem. Always report any such requests for information to your employer.

10. **Don't assume all staff are as honest as you**
Take care of your property and that of your employer.

Advice is seldom welcome: and those who want it the most always like it the least
  - Philip Dormer Stanhope, Earl of Chesterfield

The reward of a thing well done is to have done it
  - Ralph Waldo Emerson

Common sense is the most widely shared commodity in the world, for every man is convinced that he is well supplied with it
  - Rene Descartes

With the number of businesses and individuals using mini, micro and personal computers rapidly expanding, a serious security problem also is spreading. Many users of computerised systems simply cannot afford the security devices and the computer-audit techniques available to large computer companies. However, several effective measures are available, without the high cost, which will increase the security of small business and personal computers.

Sensible procedures

The majority of large corporations and major financial institutions take the necessary steps to achieve a high level of security, using techniques such as security software and back-up computer facilities. These procedures are for the most part not a cost-justified answer for the personal computer owner or user. However, with common sense and practical knowledge, minis and micros can be as safe as the huge mainframes of large companies.

There are three major types of security hazards for the small or personal computer:

- environmental disasters
- accidental errors and
- deliberate criminal schemes

It is vital to protect data from these hazards.

Environment

Environmental disasters include natural catastrophies such as fires and floods. First, the computer should be stored in a safe and secure location, away from outside windows or doors. It should not be located near any potential fire hazards. Second, it would be wise to check with an insurance agent about the cover needed for the computer.

The combination of a computer's electrical wiring and the presence of paper and other combustible items in the room increases the danger of fire. To reduce these risks, several measures can be taken. A fire extinguisher (specifically designed for electrical fires) should be located near the room housing the computer. A heat, smoke or ion detector is also necessary in this area. A main power-off switch, which turns off power to the computer and peripheral equipment, should be located in the vicinity of the computer area.

Accidental errors

Accidental errors include faulty programming as well as poor practice on the part of the user. The "guilty" party could be the programmer or the user. Thorough testing of the program before installation is the key to prevention.

Operating errors include the mishandling of computer equipment, mounting the wrong tape or disk and accidental deletion or change of data. Operational mistakes do happen, but they can and should be minimised.

Personnel controls need to be considered. Employees using the computer should be identified and held accountable. If possible, the programming and operating functions should be separated to help prevent accidents and, possibly, collusion. Changes in the program or software should be fully documented and tested by an independent source.

Criminal schemes

Deliberate criminal schemes include the theft of funds and information, and sabotage.

The theft of funds could include a change or deletion of the computer's records for personal monetary gain. This could be the wrongful manipulation of accounts-receivable information.

A thief could possibly change the payroll program to pay himself a larger sum each pay period. Many smaller companies have gone bankrupt because of dishonest employees.

The theft of information can be far more damaging than the theft of funds. For example, an individual could possibly steal confidential financial data, special mailing lists or entire programs. Some employees have used company minicomputers to run their own service bureaux during off-hours. External threats, such as the interception of data transmissions by telephone circuits, have happened.

The mere thought of sabotage is frightening. Actual sabotage, however, has occurred at several computer sites and will probably happen again. Computer-related sabotage can be physical (bomb explosions or vandalism), or the software-type (malicious destruction of files and programs). With the vulnerability of the computer in particular and the entire company in general, safeguards are necessary.

The hazards, whether environmental, accidental or criminal, can be lessened and the after-effects of loss or damage reduced by observing the points made in the following checklist.

A business computer security checklist

Physical protection and back-up

- Is your computer and peripheral equipment in a safe and secure location?

- Is your computer and peripheral equipment protected against fire, natural disaster, water damage, temperature and humidity changes, electrical power surges and electrical power losses?

- Do you have secure storage of on-site floppy disks and tapes?

- Do you have and use back-up procedures?

- Do you have secure off-site storage of back-up disks and tapes?

- Do you have an up-to-date inventory of programs and master files, on-site and off-site?

- Do you have the right insurance cover for your computer equipment and data?

Prevention of errors

- Do you have separation of duties with respect to the data-processing function?

- Are changes to the software reviewed by someone other than the programmer?

- Are programs fully tested before implementation?

- Does your computer system provide verification of input?

- Is the documentation sufficient to maintain and operate the computer system?

Prevention of theft and deliberate damage

- Where possible, do you lock personal computers and main-frame terminals when not in use and after work?

- Are passwords required before programs or data files can be entered?

- Is a daily log of computer use and job runs kept and checked by management?

For mainframe or network computer rooms

- Is access to the computer room restricted to authorised personnel only?

- Is the computer room locked after working hours?

A problem for all

Computer security is not only for the large computer centre. It is important to realise that today's minis and personal computers are as sophisticated and vulnerable as the large main frames of only a few years ago. These small computers also require protection against loss, or change of data and equipment.

Experience is a good school, but the fees are high
– Heine

If you would know the value of money, go and try to borrow some
– Benjamin Franklin

Today's office is the nerve centre of industry. This is as true in manufacturing as it is in service industries. Without the office, not a factory wheel would turn. Small wonder, then, that the efficiency of an entire organisation often parallels that of their offices.

The importance of record-keeping and filing systems cannot be too highly stressed. A well-planned system contributes significantly to efficiency of operation as well as to a company's image.

The true test of any filing system is its ability to give an affirmative answer to the question: "Can I find what I want when it is needed?"

Whether records are filed in a computer or in a steel cabinet, they have to be readily accessible. The cost of misplaced records can be staggering.

Make a study of your system. Conducting such a study is no more than taking an inventory of the records in your files.

Here are some of the questions you should ask:

- What are the records?
- Where should they be filed?
- Who uses the records?
- How often are they used?
- How are they used?
- How are the records referred to?
- What is the size of each record?
- How many of each record are filed?
- Who else has copies of the same record?

Also check if your filing system shows any of the following symptoms:

- You find the information you need is difficult to obtain due to your system or lack of one.
- You are always having to expand your filing system's capacity.
- You are maintaining duplicate files of the same information.

- You are filing material to protect the function and not because of information or legal requirements.
- You are using your filing system or equipment for storage of unnecessary information.
- Your file folders are too full for easy access.
- Your filing drawers or shelves are too full for easy access.
- You are not finding the information you require in the first place you look.

Your analysis is now complete – your records inventory reveals the strengths and weaknesses of your record-keeping system.

Once you have analysed your records inventory, you should determine:

- Best arrangement of the records.
- Type of media to be filed (paper, microfilm, magnetic, etc.).
- Proper equipment for adequate storage and retrieval.
- Proper systems to complement the equipment.
- The required record retention schedule and facility.

From the simplest manual filing system to the latest automated record filing and retrieval equipment, a systems consultant can assist you in setting up and maintaining an optimum filing and retrieval system.

What follows are the basic rules for filing systems and procedures on which your future operations should be based.

Some helpful filing tips

Changing a filing system or devising one from scratch needn't be complicated, especially if you observe the following guidelines. If you are computerising your files, the computer should follow the same rules. It's a matter of giving information space in which to grow and of devising the best

way to flag information.

Space
A file drawer or shelf should be filled to no more than 90% of its capacity. Tightly packed files slow filing and finding to a crawl. They also cause paper cuts and torn cuticles, to say nothing of low morale.

Index guides
All active files should have a guide every 10 to 15 folders. Anything less means the operator is wasting time pushing and pulling folders back and forth, looking for the required record.

Folder tabs
Folder tabs should be visible immediately upon opening the file. A well-run file must have folders of uniform size and tab styles. Be sure you order supplies for your files that match the ones originally chosen. Mixing folder heights and tab positions can reduce the efficiency of a filing system tremendously.

Folder tab identification
Identification on the tabs should be typewritten. Handwritten labels or labels with the names crossed out and re-typed should never be permitted.

Overloaded files
Standard folders are scored to hold 25 mm of material. Ideally, no more than 25 records should be placed in one folder or the tab will slump down and out of sight.

Basic filing procedure

- Inspecting: Each document is inspected to see that it has been released. If not, it should be returned to the interested party.
- Marking: The file operator must determine under what name or caption the paper is to be filed.
- Follow-up and cross-reference: If the letter is marked for

follow-up, then a record should be made and placed in the follow-up file. If there is more than one place in which to file the document, make a cross-reference.

- Sorting is the last step prior to actual filing.
- Documents should be arranged in sequence so they can be placed in the proper folders quickly, without moving back and forth.
- Sorting makes documents easy to find if needed while out of the file.
- Filing: What is filing? It is the actual placing of documents in folders in a pre-determined plan.
- Torn papers should be mended before they are filed.
- Folders should be raised slightly in the file drawer (or removed if on shelves) when placing papers in them so the papers will go entirely to the bottom of the folder.
- Check the caption of the document and folder as a precaution against misfiling.
- All documents should be placed with the tops to the left as you face the folder.
- Never overcrowd folders. Break them down by date, name or subject, using additional folders.

Filing systems utilise one of the following methods:
Alphabetic
Numeric
Geographic
Subject
Chronologic

All these methods have advantages and disadvantages. A systems consultant can help you select the system that's right for you, as well as the proper storage and handling equipment.

Alphabetic systems group documents together by letters of the name. These systems can be used for any volume of records; such a system should be determined by

your need. Its advantages include the fact that it gives direct reference, it also groups common and/or family names together.

By the same token, common names do not occur evenly throughout the alphabet. There are, for instance, more names beginning with S than with Q. As an alpha file grows – say to hundreds or thousands of names – identification and location become more cumbersome.

Numerical filing refers to all systems in which documents are prenumbered to distinguish them from each other or from alpha documents. Numerical systems can be as simple as numbering and filing from the lowest number to the highest, or as sophisticated as the many variations of terminal digit filing.

Terminal digit filing is a method of arranging numbers in a file so all numbers ending with the same last digits are grouped together. When filing by the last two or four digits, these numbers are read in groups starting with the last two digits at the extreme right.

The last two digits of the number are called the primary number. There are one hundred primary numbers, 00 through 99. The third and fourth digits from the right are called secondary numbers. These also run 00 through 99, for a total of one hundred secondary numbers for each primary group. The remaining figures to the left of the secondary number are filed in straight numeric sequence within each group and are called the final numbers.

All numbers ending in the same last digits thus fall into one group in the file. A six or seven digit number would be separated into three groups, either by the use of a hyphen or a space. If the number is less than six digits, a zero is usually added to the front of the number to make a six digit number:

01-20-00 11-20-00 110-20-00

10-20-00 12-20-00 264-20-00
These numbers would be filed in the 00 primary and the 20 secondary group.

Advantages of terminal digit:

- All sections of the system will expand evenly.
- Eliminates periodic back-shifting to take up empty space where records have been removed to make space for new records at the end of the system.
- There are less misfiles, even without colour coding, because it is easier to read the number separated into groups.

Advantages of numeric filing:
The greatest benefit of a numeric system is speed of filing and finding. It is twice as fast to file and find by number than by name. Even though a numeric file requires a cross index, it can increase production time by 40 to 50%.

Numeric systems provide both a positive identification of the record and a degree of confidentiality.

Several other systems are sometimes required by the nature of the business or by the nature of a department within a business. A brief discussion of these follows:

Geographic filing

Geographic filing systems operate generally by province or country, and then alphabetically or numerically by account name or number. Reasons for this type of filing can be several. Since countries have differing laws, a commercial enterprise may have to consider these constraints as of primary importance.

Subject filing

Obviously, this is the arranging of material by given subject. It is filing by descriptive feature instead of by name or number. Such filing involves choosing a word or phrase to stand for each subject or to point out some one phase of it. A subject folder may contain any combination of correspondence, bulletins, clippings, pictures, statistics, trade journals, and other printed information relating to the subject.

Subject filing is considered the most difficult of all methods of filing. It is a system which demands that the person installing such a system has a complete knowledge of the business. The greatest problem is knowing under which subject an item will be filed.

Because a subject file is expensive to maintain, subject filing should be used only where absolutely necessary.

The majority of subject files are not large, complicated libraries. They are in the 5, 10 and 20 drawer category.

Chronologic filing

Chronologic filing is filing by date. Usually you will find this used for bills of lading, copies of freight bills, cancelled cheques or as a reserve file. It is normally used only where there is little or no reference made to the record once the transaction is complete.

Use of colour coding

Colour coding is not new and has become extremely popular during the past few years. Colour coding is probably the greatest cost-saving feature that has ever been developed for the filing and retrieval of records. There are colour-coding systems that can be applied to every method of filing.

Colour coding converts numbers or letters to colours. Each digit 0 to 9 is assigned its own specific colour. Each letter is assigned two colours. The simple process of filing the folders in a desired sequence therefore creates colour blocks. If a folder is filed out of sequence the colour band does not match, which automatically flags a misfile.

Benefits of colour coding
• Eliminates hidden misfiles
• Speeds filing and finding
• Folders are easier to find while out of the system
• Eliminates the need for index guides.

Colour coding for computer disks and tapes
The same colour coding can be used to index computer disks and tapes as is used on the folders. With tapes, identical colour-coded number labels are provided for the tape box and the side of the reel. This allows you to spot a tape that is misfiled as well as providing fast retrieval by colour.

There are virtually no problems with colour coding. Folders should be ordered with colour coding applied at the factory to avoid extra work. The next folder in the box is the next number to be used. Or, alphabetic folders are stored in a handy location to enable you to take out the folder coded with the proper letter whenever it is needed.

Information storage in today's office

Information management today has become a complex science with the advent of computers. In addition to housing papers in letter, legal and card sizes, we must house information stored on magnetic tapes, cassettes, microforms, floppy disks and printouts. Such media come in a multitude of shapes and sizes.

Look for these features in the equipment you choose for media storage:

• Flexibility – the equipment must be flexible enough to meet your needs as a volume of records increases.
• Versatility – cabinets should be made to accommodate any me-

dium and allow you to mix different sizes in one unit.
• Easy access – since labour is the greatest cost in any media storage system, the equipment must provide easy access. Filing and retrieval time can be reduced to save many pounds in file-room costs.

Choose a cabinet that has been designed not only to fit your needs, but to fit in with your office decor.

Standard filing cabinets

You are familiar with vertical filing cabinets. These range from two to four drawer and are available with and without locks, and with or without insulation for fire protection.

Lateral filing cabinets, now in wide use, offer an improvement in ease and speed of filing when compared with a regular four-drawer vertical filing cabinet. Most come in four, five and six shelf heights.

Open-shelf filing

Open-shelf filing has an obvious advantage in ease of access; it also usually permits filing of odd-size items such as artwork, photographs and drawings.

Wire inserts

Wire inserts are available for shelves or drawers, keep files and documents completely vertical and in many instances displace the expensive suspended pocket-system.

Filing is a complex and vital activity giving quick and easy access to information – the life-blood on which business efficiency depends. The right system, the right media and the right housing combine to allow optimum handling of information for greater productivity. It is, however, a science calling for expert advice. Ask for it.

Generally printers can be classified into three broad categories:

- The big printers who cater for large volume printing.

- The medium to small size printers who are usually involved in book, magazine and stationery printing.

- The 'quick' printers who are geared to do simple and very quick printing. They are best suited to print office stationery. If necessary, printing can sometimes be completed within a day.

Choose the right type of printer

Bear in mind the following points if you need to shop for a quick printer.

- Are they reliable?

- Is their printing quality good?

- Are they conveniently located?

- Do they charge reasonable prices?

Choose the right paper

The choice of paper depends on what you want to print.

Use standard sizes. Do this to avoid wastage. The most common standard sizes for stationery printing are the 'A' series and the DL size of the 'C' series for envelopes. For details see the information section on 'International Paper Sizes'.

Another advantage of using international paper sizes is that artwork for stationery can be reduced and enlarged proportionately without having to redo it.

Check that the name cards you design fit into standard name-card holders.

Use of colours

Use as few colours as possible for your stationery. Each additional colour means additional cost and time in completing your printing. If you have to use colours try to select standard ink colours. Special colours require time to match. Also, you may have problems in maintaining colour consistency if subsequent repetition is required for logos/trademarks.

If you must have embossed printing, take note that this is more expensive than normal printing and it also takes a longer time to complete.

Combine your colour printing

If the opportunity arises, organise your colour printing such that you can print the same colours together. It is cheaper to print the blue of your letterhead and the blue of your invoice together than to print them on separate occasions. It costs money each time the printer changes the ink. In this connection it is wise to use the same colour for all your company stationery and for all departments.

Choose the right type size

Save paper by accommodating more copy into less space. Typeset in smaller point size or select the smaller pitches that are now available with most electronic typewriters and computer printers. Alternatively, you can always get the printer to reduce your text. Proportionate reduction can best be achieved if you work on international paper sizes. For example, an A4 text when reduced by 30% fits into an A5 paper.

Use your letterheads wisely

If you are printing a large number of documents where text is to appear in the same colour as your letterhead, then type your text onto your letterhead and print both the letterhead and the copy at the same time. Do not overprint your text on pre-printed letterheads. This is tantamount to printing twice and will eventually cost you twice as much.

Keep your frequently used artwork

Reproduce multiple copies of artwork that you need to use time and again like your company logo, trademarks, letterheads, name-card setting, etc. This is for safe-keeping in case your printer loses or damages the artwork. It is expensive to replace artwork.

A Series

The A series is based on A0 (841 × 1 189 mm), which is the equivalent of a square metre in area, and each smaller size, A1, A2 and so on, is equal to half the area of the preceding larger size.

A3 is suitable for 4-page leaflets which will be folded into A4.

A4 is ideal for letterheads, invoice forms, and many other office forms

A5 is often used for memo pads and booklets.

A6 is for postcards, invitation cards and index cards

A7 is used for compliment slips and labels.

A8 could be used for name-cards and labels.

A9 and A10 are often used for name-tags and price-tags.

Code	millimetres
A0	841 × 1 189
A1	594 × 841
A2	420 × 594
A3	297 × 420
A4	210 × 297
A5	148 × 210
A6	105 × 148
A7	74 × 105
A8	52 × 74
A9	37 × 52
A10	26 × 37

B Series

The B series is intended primarily for posters, wall charts and similar items where the difference in size of the larger sheets in the A series represents too large a jump.

Code	millimetres
B1	707 × 1 000
B2	500 × 707
B3	353 × 500
B4	250 × 353
B5	176 × 250

C Series

This is for envelopes or folders suitable for enclosing stationery in the A series.

Code	millimetres
C3	324 × 458
C4	229 × 324
C5	162 × 229
C6	114 × 162
DL*	110 × 220

*Dimensional lengthwise

The common size folder would be C4. A special envelope B4 is recommended for enclosing this folder.

Below are figures illustrating how the standard sizes A4 and A5 flat or folded can be fitted into the proposed standard size envelopes.

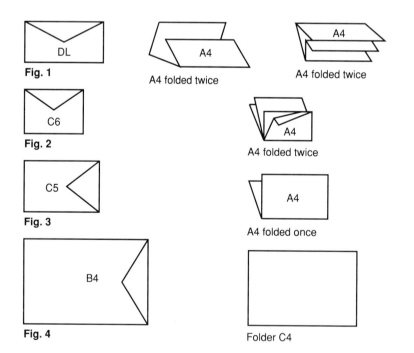

Fig. 1 — DL

Fig. 2 — C6

Fig. 3 — C5

Fig. 4 — B4

A4 folded twice

A4 folded twice

A4 folded twice

A4 folded once

Folder C4

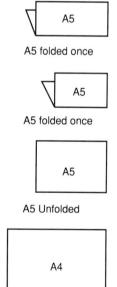

A5 folded once

A5 folded once

A5 Unfolded

A4

A CHECKLIST FOR FORM DESIGN AND EXAMPLES OF SOME USEFUL FORMS

Establish the purpose of the form

What   – identify the form
Why   – is the form necessary
When   – is the form used
Where   – is the form prepared
What   – is the form content
By whom   – is the form prepared and to whom is it circulated
How   – is the form completed: manually, typewriter, etc.

Establish the content of the form

• Be thoroughly conversant with the clerical procedures of which the form is a part.

• Consider associated forms, their generators, receivers, processors, filers, etc. Is the information contained elsewhere?

• Can existing forms be modified to suit the purpose of the proposed new form?

• Consider the information which is subsequently added to a form as well as the original content.

• Obtain samples of completed, not blank forms when redesigning existing ones.

• Reduce to a minimum the information which is to be included on the form.

• Decide what information is constant and therefore worth pre-printing.

• Determine the sequence of entries, make them as logical as possible.

• Determine the average number of entries, not minimum or maximum.

• Determine the number of copies of each form or set.

Design and layout

• The form must be functional.

• Consider the visual effect of the form.

• Consider paper sizes: standard paper sizes, sizes for reproduction, filing, etc.

• Ensure that the form is self-explanatory for compilation and that questions and headings are not ambiguous.

• Design to aid filing, indexing and information retrieval, e.g. if filing numerically, place number at top right-hand corner.

• Do not number forms unless really essential since it adds considerably to the printing cost.

• Try to group entries in a logical format.

• Keep ruling faint – for large number of lines every fifth line should be heavily ruled.

• Provide for 6 mm lines horizontally for desk-compiled forms and 8 mm lines for forms compiled away from desks.

• Give the form a title and/or reference.

• Keep examples of amendments/changes which arise between printing runs.

Colour of forms and printing

Order of legibility	Printing	Background
1	Black	Yellow
2	Green	White
3	Red	White
4	Blue	White
5	White	Blue
6	Black	White
7	Yellow	Black
8	White	Red
9	White	Green
10	White	Black
11	Red	Yellow
12	Green	Red
13	Red	Green

Useful forms

On the following pages are examples of some of the more common forms required in an office. They have been designed so that they may be photocopied.

A good photocopy can also serve as artwork for printing. Space has been provided at the top of each form for you to place your company name and logo before you print.

Forms	Recommended print size
Leave Application	A5
Leave Record	A4
Transmittal Slip	A4
Message Slip	A6
Despatch Request	A6
Supplies Requisition	A5
Payment Voucher	A5
Petty Cash Voucher	A5
Employment Application	A4
Interviewer's Assessment	A4

LEAVE APPLICATION

To: _____

From: _____

Department: _____

I wish to apply for leave as follows:

    ☐   Annual Leave

    ☐   Compassionate Leave

    ☐   Maternity Leave

    ☐   Others, please specify _____

_____

From _____ to _____

Leave Due _____ days

This Application _____ days

Balance _____ days

Approved by

_____   _____
Applicant's Signature/Date   Signature/Date

LEAVE RECORD

Name _____

Department _____

   Leave entitlement for 19 _____ days

   Balance b/f from 19 _____ days

   Total leave due _____ days

Leave Taken		Balance	Remarks
Dates	Duration		
5			
10			
15			
20			

TRANSMITTAL SLIP

To: _____

From: _____ Date: _____

_____

☐ Confidential   ☐ Please make ____ copies

☐ Urgent   ☐ Please reply

☐ For your action   ☐ Please return

☐ For comments/discussion   ☐ As requested

☐ For signature/approval   ☐ For your information

☐ Investigate & report   ☐ For filing

☐ Please advise   ☐ For your retention

☐ Please circulate   ☐ Returned with thanks

Message: _____

_____

_____

_____

_____

_____

MESSAGE

To: _____

While you were out

M _____

of _____

Tel _____ Extn _____

Time _____ Date _____

☐ Urgent   ☐ Will call again

☐ Telephoned   ☐ Returned your call

☐ Please return call   ☐ Came to see you

Message _____

_____

_____

_____

_____

Taken by _____

DESPATCH REQUEST

Person to see _____

Company _____

Address _____

_____

Tel _____

☐ To deliver _____

☐ To collect _____

☐ Recipient to sign _____

☐ Job deadline _____

Remarks _____

_____

_____

Requested by _____

Department _____

Time _____ Date _____

SUPPLIES REQUISITION

Department _____ Date _____

Please supply the items listed

Particulars of Items	Quantity Required	For Stock Control		
		Supplied	Unit Cost	Total Cost
		Total £		

Requested by _____ Date _____ Authorised by _____ Date _____

PAYMENT VOUCHER

Payee _____ Voucher No _____

_____ Date _____

Invoice No.	Description	Account	Amount	
		Total £		

Cheque No. _____

Prepared by _____

Approved by _____ Date _____

Authorised by _____ Date _____ Received by _____ Date _____

PETTY CASH VOUCHER

Payee _____ No _____

Department _____ Date _____

Description	Account	Amount	
	Total £		
£			

Prepared by _____

Approved by _____ Date _____ Received by _____ Date _____

KEEPING COSTS DOWN

With just about everything continuing to mushroom in price, the proper use, maintenance and control of materials, equipment and supplies is more important than ever. In some factories and offices, day-to-day problems and crises involved in getting the work out, tend to make managers overlook the seemingly less pressing task of keeping the lid on equipment and material costs and ensuring proper procedures. Yet, in well-managed companies, all employees learn pretty fast that expenses must be closely – and constantly – watched lest they rapidly get out of control.

How efficiently does your department function in this vital aspect of your operation? The following questionnaire will help you work out the answers:

	Yes	No
1. Do you have multiple supply sources for key items to avoid reliance on a single source?	☐	☐
2. Can nearby suppliers be used instead of distant ones to reduce transportation – and overall – costs?	☐	☐
3. Do you use standard equipment and supplies wherever possible instead of more expensive special or custom-made units?	☐	☐
4. Do you have a training programme set up to ensure that employees understand the proper use of equipment and materials?	☐	☐
5. Do you regularly monitor your staff to make sure the right tool or equipment is used the right way for the job?	☐	☐
6. Do you have a procedure established whereby you automatically notify the purchasing department about unsatisfactory products and unreliable suppliers?	☐	☐
7. Is the operating condition of equipment reviewed on a periodic basis?	☐	☐
8. Do you tend to ignore repair-work or forget to replace defective equipment?	☐	☐
9. Are tools, materials and supplies stocked in a convenient, centrally located place?	☐	☐
10. Is there a control established to ensure your company takes advantage of suppliers' warranty provisions rather than performing repairs at your own expense?	☐	☐
11. Do you analyse errors, mistakes, or rejects to determine if the possible cause is defective equipment or materials?	☐	☐
12. Do you have loose controls in keeping track of requisition supplies?	☐	☐
13. Do you conduct periodic unannounced inventory checks to control and minimise "shrinkage"?	☐	☐

How do you rate? A right answer is worth 1, a wrong answer 0. "Yes" answers to all but Questions 8 and 12 are correct. These two should be answered "No". A score of 12 or 13 is great, 11 is acceptable – but anything below that is a signal that you should take immediate steps to institute tighter controls.

USEFUL
REFERENCES

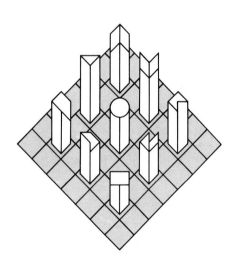

A COMPREHENSIVE TRAVEL CHECKLIST

Preparing for a business trip involves a lot of careful planning and attending to last-minute details that could easily be forgotten in the rush to get away.

Here are a number of aspects you should bear in mind before travelling:

Passport

Check whether it is still valid or due to expire and if there is enough space for stamping of visa or entry endorsements.

It is advisable to renew the passport if it is due to expire within the next three to four months. Some countries do not accept visitors if their passports are due to expire soon, i.e. in less than six months.

Health documents

Some countries require the visitor to have valid vaccination and health papers, e.g. for smallpox, yellow fever or cholera. Check with your travel agent to find out what the countries to be visited require.

According to the World Health Organisation the following countries are on the infected areas list:

CHOLERA:

in Africa:
Angola, Benin, Burkina Faso, Burundi, Cameroon, Equatorial Guinea, Ghana, Guinea (Rep.), Ivory Coast, Liberia, Mali, Mauritania, Nigeria, Rwanda, Sierra Leone, Tanzania, Zaire.

in Asia:
India, Indonesia, Iran, Malaysia, Thailand, Vietnam.

YELLOW FEVER:

in Africa:
Burkina Faso, Gambia, Ghana, Guinea (Rep.), Mali, Mauritania, Nigeria, Sudan, Zaire.

in S. America:
Bolivia, Brazil, Colombia, Peru. (Source: TIM Travel Information Manual.)

Visa requirements

Find out which countries to be visited require a visa. As delays can occur, apply well in advance for your visa, e.g. as much as six weeks for Australian and Canadian visas.

Business itinerary

When arranging appointments try to organise them by area. Remember to reconfirm appointments two days in advance.

Preparation of itinerary

When all has been arranged have the itinerary typed. It may be in the form of a booklet or a neat list which can be placed in your pocket. (Leave a copy with your secretary and spouse or partner and keep a copy for yourself.)

In the itinerary make sure to put all the information necessary and helpful for the trip, for example:

- List of appointments, including contacts and telephone numbers

- Method of reaching that particular town for the appointment (by train, taxi, tube and the approximate travelling time)

- List of topics and questions for discussion

- Hotel accommodation (name of hotels, rates, discounts, etc.)

- Flight details (arrival and departure times, telephone number of airline office in that country, a note to remind yourself to reconfirm onward bookings).

Booking flights — efficiently

Get exact travel information first
When asking your secretary to make a reservation, also give her the following information:

- Nationality of traveller

- Exact destination(s)

- Date of travel and preferred time

- Airline preference

- Class of airticket

- Sleeper/bed requirements for long-distance flight (1st class only)

- Preference for stop-over or direct (non-stop) flight

- Preference for seat (window or aisle), smoking or non-smoking section

- If travelling with children, is a bulk-head seat required

- Special request for food (e.g. Muslim, Kosher, vegetarian)

When making reservations

Call your travel agent and supply the necessary information. Check on visa requirements and, if necessary, take action.

After making the seat reservation you should request the following:

- Airline flight number and type of aircraft

- Departure and arrival times

- Connections/stop-overs, if any

- Computer access code (reference number of the reservation)

- Name of reservation officer

The last two items serve as evidence of your reservation in case of dispute when the passenger checks in.

Type of airtickets

First class
This is the most comfortable and the most expensive. Sleeper seats are provided.

Business class
This is a combination of first and economy class with more space and higher-graded cuisine. Seats are wider and there is more legroom.

Economy class
This offers an average price range. The ticket has no restrictions, and can be used on any airline.

Apex fare
Apex means Advance Purchase Excursion. It must be purchased at least 14 days before departure. The earlier you reserve and pay for your ticket the higher the discount allowed.

Dates for both forward and return journeys may not be changed. If you cancel the flight, a 25% cancellation fee is charged. There is also a minimum-maximum stay restriction.

Excursion fare
One of the cheaper types, it is restricted to minimum and maximum stays. One must travel within a certain time period, e.g. minimum 14 days, maximum 75 days, etc.

Airlines have also introduced other fare packages, e.g. family fare plans, group fares, senior citizen fares, sporting group fares, national servicemen's airfare, etc. Contact your local travel agent for further details.

Accommodation

The hotel reservations department will require the following information:

- The dates of arrival and departure.

- The type and number of rooms required, e.g. single or double rooms or a suite? Also state any preference regarding sea-facing, pool-facing, etc.

- Your name and initials and the address and telephone number of the company.

- Time of arrival. This is most important, particularly if you will be arriving late. Reservations are usually held until 18h00 without charging or the room being let to someone else, unless it has been clearly stated at the time of making the reservation that it will be a late arrival – guaranteed payment. This means that the room will be held all night, but the person or company will be debited with the cost of one night's accommodation irrespective of whether they arrive or not.

Remember that when you want to book into the hotel before 12h00, you may be required to pay for the previous night as well. Be sure to check this with the hotel in advance and to make special arrangements if this should happen. When making a reservation also consider the following:

- If the room is ready well before noon the hotel may allocate it to the client earlier as a good-will gesture.

- If the hotel must meet you at the airport, give the name of the airline, flight number and expected time of arrival.

- Who is responsible for paying the account – you or the company?

- Method of payment, i.e. cash, credit card or company account. In the case of the latter, most hotels require you to present on arrival (in addition to the voucher) a telex or fax, and official order or a letter from

the company to this effect. If you are a corporate card holder the card number must be quoted at the time of booking.

- Make any necessary restaurant reservations.

Ask the reservations clerk to send you a confirmation voucher confirming your reservation. This will enable you to check whether your instructions have been understood and carried out. When a hotel overbooks, the guest with the confirmation voucher also stands a better chance of being accommodated.

Finally, remember to cancel the accommodation booked, if you should for one reason or another, not require it any longer. The cancellation period is generally 24 hours before check-in time.

Business data

All documents and correspondence regarding the appointments together with relevant papers, should be attached together, filed and labelled.

Make a note of your company's telex and fax numbers.

Supplies

Do not forget to pack stationery, e.g. letterheads, memos, pens, paper clips, folders, etc. In addition, for sales trips include:

- Sales kit
- Catalogues
- Price list
- Order forms, etc.

Make sure name cards and a name and address list of clients as well as your own name cards are included.

Insurance

- Buy travel insurance (e.g. for loss of money or baggage, medical expenses, flight cancellation, personal accident or liability)

- Check if additional insurance is required for important luggage
- Medical costs overseas are expensive. Make sure you have sufficient cover.

Funds

There are a number of ways for an overseas traveller to have a supply of funds:

- Letter of credit
- Credit cards e.g. Diners, American Express, Visa, etc.
- Travellers' cheques: These can be purchased from most banks
- Currency of the country you are visiting: It is important and necessary to have some foreign currency in small denominations for taxi fares, tips, airport tax, etc. Check if there is a maximum amount of local currency that can be taken in and out of the country.

Baggage

On international flights, there are two different regulations for the free baggage allowance depending on your route.

On most international flights, you have an allowance of 20 kg in the economy class, 30 kg in business class and 40 kg in first class (except for direct flights to/ from USA, Canada and Brazil when the piece concept applies if no stopover is made).

There is a limit on number and size of items on routes to and from the USA, Canada, the South Atlantic and Rio de Janeiro, from Germany to Mexico, from Germany to the Caribbean via San Juan or Miami.

The allowance is two pieces of checked baggage and one piece of hand luggage which will be carried free of charge. In first class, neither pieces of checked baggage may be larger than 158 cm (62 inches) in length plus width plus height, nor may each weigh more than 23 kg. In economy class the measurements of both pieces may not exceed 298 cm.

Hand baggage

The following items will be carried free of charge over and above your applicable free baggage allowance provided they remain in your custody during the flight:

- One piece of hand baggage with outside dimensions not exceeding 45 x 35 x 20 cm
- An overcoat, wrap or blanket
- A small handbag or wrist bag
- A walking stick or umbrella
- A small camera and a pair of binoculars
- A reasonable amount of reading matter for the flight.

Excess baggage

As excess baggage regulations are subject to change at short notice it is better to contact the airline for details before you start your journey.

Larger amounts of excess baggage may be sent off beforehand as unaccompanied baggage or as air freight at more favourable rates. There are also special rates for ski, golf and other sport equipment.

Baggage contents

For security reasons, the following items may not be included in your baggage.

- compressed gases
- corrosive materials
- explosives, munitions, fireworks and flares

- flammable liquids and solids (such as a lighter or heating fuels, matches and articles which are easily ignited)
- irritating materials (bleaching powders, peroxides)
- radioactive and magnetised materials
- poisons.

The only exceptions are:

- up to 2 kg or 2 l of medicine or toilet articles which you may need during the journey
- up to 2,5 kg of dry ice for packing perishables (in hand baggage only)
- alcoholic beverages
- small oxygen cylinders worn by passengers for operation of mechanical limbs

Weapons

Any weapons you wish to take along for sporting or hunting will be carried under the following conditions:

- Weapons should be checked beforehand
- They must be packed in unbreakable and impact-proof containers
- Firearms must not be loaded

Identification

Every piece of your checked luggage must be marked with your name and home address. Suitable tags and stickers are usually provided by the airlines and these should be attached to your baggage before departure. Stickers and tags left from previous flights should be removed as they could cause confusion. It is a good idea to have your name and address stuck inside the lid of the case in the event of the label on the handle being lost.

Departure

Before leaving your baggage, check if it is locked. When accepted each item of baggage is given a tag with destination and flight number; the identification portion is then affixed to your ticket. Check the correct tag has been attached.

Make sure that your baggage has been checked to your final destination.

Always decline to do anyone a favour at the last moment by taking along some package with unidentified contents. Should you be asked to do so, please notify the police, or customs.

Customs and transfers

If you have booked a connecting flight, your baggage will normally be transferred to your final destination automatically. There are, however, exceptions: you have to pick up your baggage and clear it through customs yourself:

- If you have to change airports to catch your connecting flight
- If you have to transfer from an international to a domestic flight (except in Germany, Austria, Italy, Morocco, Portugal, Spain and Switzerland where you clear your baggage through customs at your final destination)
- If you have to transfer to an international flight in the following countries: Argentine, Bahamas, Bolivia, Canada, Chile, Columbia, Ecuador, Ghana, Hungary, Iran, Libya, Mauritius, Mexico, Paraguay, Saudi Arabia, Uruguay, USA and Zaire as well as at the airports of Ankara and Rio de Janeiro.

Should you fail to clear customs in these cases, your baggage will not be transferred to your connecting flights. If you have any doubts, it is better to inquire at your transfer point.

Claiming your baggage

Many suitcases look identical and mistakes are easy to make. Make sure, if necessary, that the baggage you claim is in fact your own by comparing the number on the tag of your suitcase with the one on the identification portion affixed to your ticket. If your baggage is missing or damaged on arrival, notify a member of the airline staff at once.

Private baggage insurance

The Warsaw Convention automatically insures all travellers while in the air, but it is safer to take out private baggage insurance to cover all your belongings including those which remain in your custody. The insurance is valid not only during the flight, but also for the complete length of your trip.

Car hire

For the executive on a business trip a hired car is often essential – and you must arrange everything to the last detail. But how do you do it? And what will the company have to pay?

What you pay for a hired car, depends on what you are looking for. A classy model, such as a Mercedes Benz, will obviously cost more than a smaller model which is economical and easy to run. Do you want it for a few hours or a few weeks? Do you need a driver or not?

Most car rental firms will hire out cars on a daily, weekly, monthly, yearly and even – in some overseas countries – hourly basis. To get the best deal, ask well in advance especially if you are travelling in peak seasons, for a few price quotations and decide on the most favourable terms. But remember, read the fine print of the contract and beware of liabilities that may be hidden in it.

Rates are usually calculated on a daily basis. The minimum charge is usually for 24 hours. This includes insurance, oil, maintenance, windscreen breakage, etc. Although petrol is not included, the cars are delivered with a full tank. The client only pays for a refill when returning the car. (In some cases hiring on an unlimited mileage basis is available.)

Reservations

Reservations are free of charge – and so are cancellations. Remember to book well in advance: international bookings, made locally, may sometimes take up to three days to confirm.

When making a reservation supply the following information:

- Your full name.
- The car group required. The car group refers to the size and type of car required, i.e. small, medium or luxury. The time and date – also flight number, if necessary, for collecting the car.
- The city or airport where the car should be delivered to, as well as the place to which it will be returned.
- A full street address and telephone number if the car must be delivered.
- How your company is paying for the service.

Paying

Cash
Bank-guaranteed or travellers' cheques will be accepted as cash. If you are paying in cash a minimum deposit is required. The car rental firm can brief you on what deposit is required.

Credit cards
Most credit cards are accepted. If you use a rental service often, it will pay to apply for the car

rental companies' own cards: you will receive a discount when using them.

Purchase orders

These are accepted once it is verified that you have been authorised by your company to rent a car. Rubber stamp orders are not acceptable. The purchase orders, valid for a month only, should be numbered.

Miscellaneous charge orders (MO) and Supplementary service vouchers (SSV)

Airlines and most travel agencies issue these. Once again, the value allocated for car rental must be clearly stated. Produce these forms at the time of the rental.

Insurance

Collision Damage Waiver (CDW)

CDW is optional. Most car rental companies offer it on a daily or weekly basis. Although it relieves the client of financial responsibility for the car if involved in an accident, he is liable for excess amounts (the car rental companies specify the excess limit).

Personal accident insurance

Buy peace of mind at a nominal cost. This insurance covers both the client and passengers. Other benefits are:

- Instant payment in the country where the car is rented.

- There is no need to prove guilt of any party: the insurance is paid out within seven working days.

- Cover is provided for injuries or death resulting from an accident.

One-way rentals

When a client rents a car at office A and returns it to office B it is referred to as a one-way rental.

There is usually no additional charge for this rental between offices in the same country, but check with the car rental company first. A "collection fee", for example, will be made if the client returns the car to a city where there is no representative office of the rental company.

Clients wishing to rent cars in Europe to use in various countries, may apply for one-way rental. A large number of countries participate in the European one-way-programme, but once again, first check with the car rental company.

Points to remember

- Parking and traffic fines are the responsibility of the renter.

- If there is any mechanical problem, the rented car can be exchanged immediately.

- Rental agreements can be terminated at any time, without costing the company anything.

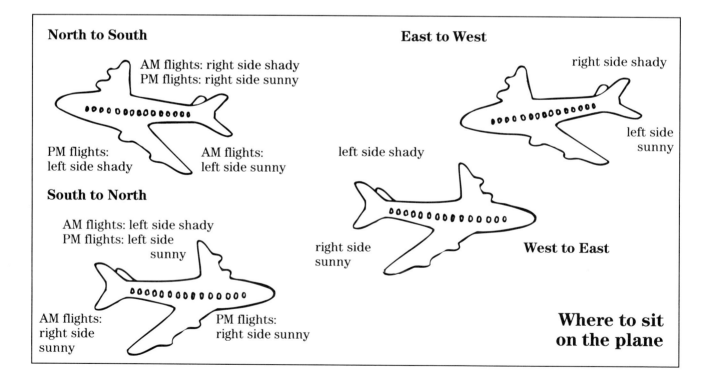

North to South

AM flights: right side shady
PM flights: right side sunny

PM flights: left side shady

AM flights: left side sunny

South to North

AM flights: left side shady
PM flights: left side sunny

AM flights: right side sunny

PM flights: right side sunny

East to West

right side shady

left side sunny

left side shady

right side sunny

West to East

Where to sit on the plane

KEEP FIT IN YOUR SEAT

Sitting is the activity - or rather non-activity - in which we engage most during our lives. We sit at the desk, in the car, in conferences, in trains, in planes, in restaurants, in front of the TV. Nearly every other activity is linked with movement, but not sitting.

In our modern life there's not much we can do to get around all this sitting: our world requires such a lifestyle. One way we can do so, however, is to plan fitness into our work style. Exercises have been created which can be fitted into the busiest of lifestyles, and often can be done without anyone else being aware of them. You can perform them while making a phone call, driving your car or sitting in a meeting. These exercises include:

- **Muscle tone exercises:** Tighten up a muscle or muscle group with about one-third of your maximum strength. Repeat six times, rhythmically. Use systematically for those parts of the body particularly affected by long sitting: thighs, buttocks, back, shoulders, stomach.

- **Stair-climbing:** Every staircase gives you a little fitness training, so ignore every elevator and escalator. Stair-climbing particularly exercises leg, stomach and buttock muscles. It contributes to flexibility of foot, knee and hip joints.

- **Hot seat:** Never sit on a chair too long. Stand up frequently, take a few steps to and fro; work standing up whenever you can. Get up out of your chair using only one leg (first lift other foot slightly off the floor). This keeps the leg muscles in shape.

- **Every joint once:** Make use of everyday opportunities to move every joint through its full scope at least once. Stretch as high as you can, bend over, do a deep knee bend, twist your torso and rotate your shoulders. After

every long period of sitting (office, conference, flight, drive, television), really stretch your limbs.

- **Stomach press:** Clasp your hands firmly together, placing the palms against the slightly pulled-in abdomen. Tense up your stomach muscles, using about two-thirds of your strength. Press your hands firmly against the tightened stomach muscles. Count to seven, then relax.

- **Shake hands:** Grasp the left hand with the right, as if you wanted to shake hands with yourself. Squeeze both hands, using two-thirds of your strength. Count to seven, then relax.

- **Moving walls:** Stand one pace away from a wall, place hands against wall at shoulder height. Press forcefully against wall, as if you could move it. Count to seven, then relax.

When sitting at your desk the following few guidelines will help you maintain a good posture and prevent stress on your back. Your posture should be maintained with the minimum of muscular effort, i.e. the body should be symmetrical and the centres of gravity of the various trunk segments should be situated as near as possible to a vertical line through the lumbo-sacral joint at the base of the spine.

Avoid chairs with low, adjustable backrests and no arms. These can strain your lower back and hamstrings. Instead, get a firm, straight-backed chair that allows your hips and knees to bend without effort while both feet touch the floor. A backrest should support your back 10 to 15 cm from the seat, at belt level.

If you sit most of the day, take a short walk at least once every hour. If you spend a lot of time reading at your desk, use a reading stand or prop your books so you look forward, not down. Don't

balance the telephone receiver with one shoulder. This can cause neck cramps and muscle strains. Switch sides frequently or use a telephone cradle.

Apart from health and comfort, posture is another reason to be aware of how you sit. Posture can reveal the way you feel about yourself. It's a form of body language; when your shoulders droop, your feet drag and your head hangs forward, you can't help appearing insecure and unhappy. With your shoulders back and your head held high, though, you look confident, poised and successful.

Finally, exercises you can do at your desk to relieve strain include:

- **Neck stretch:** Place your fingers at the back of your neck, just below the hairline. Pull your chin in tightly, straightening your neck against your fingers. Keeping your chin tight, look downward, moving your head only an inch or so. Now feel the stretch behind your neck and hold the tautness for six seconds. Repeat five times each day.

- **Neck circles:** Relax your neck and upper back by gently letting your head drop forward. Begin rotating it to the right, forward, to the left, back and then forward again. Repeat. Do this two more times in the opposite direction.

- **Shoulder shrugs:** Raise both shoulders forcefully up toward your ears. Hold this position for five seconds. Relax. Now round your shoulders forward, hold for five seconds and relax. Finally, press your shoulders back, trying to make the blades of your shoulders touch. Hold this position for five seconds. Repeat this entire sequence five times a day.

Useful hints

1. When carrying a heavy object use both arms and hold the object close to you.
2. When sitting, sit well back against a firm-backed chair and support your head too.
3. Do not slide forward and slump in an armchair.
4. Do not sit in one position for a long time.
5. If reading, typing, knitting, for any length of time, do the shoulder girdle exercise at regular intervals. When doing it, try to sit up straight and not stoop forward.
6. When driving:
   (a) make sure car seat is far enough forward
   (b) if neck is painful – support while driving with towel or soft collar
   (c) sit up straight.
7. When reading, books must be placed at 45° in front of you.
8. Working surfaces:
   High enough not to have to stoop or bend neck forwards, but not so high that neck moves beyond the neutral position which is halfway between the bent and stretched position.
9. Avoid draughts.
10. Keep neck warm – wear a scarf in cold weather.
11. Do exercises regularly.

DEALING WITH JET LAG

Although air travel may seem like a glamorous mode of transport, the novice air traveller might disagree with this statement, feeling bloated, tired and uncomfortable both during and after a long flight. A few simple precautions will ensure a pleasant flying experience and rapid acclimatisation to the demands of a new time zone.

After take-off the atmospheric pressure reduces to the equivalent of 2 400 m above sea level. The humidity drops to about three percent (the ideal is 45 percent) and a continuous noise and vibration level sets in. In modern aircraft this level is less than 70 decibels. Only when the noise level exceeds 85 decibels, does one's hearing begin to suffer.

Not only does the immediate environment change, but the international traveller is then lifted from one climate and time zone and displaced in another which may differ completely from the zone his body and mind have been adjusted to.

The reduction in air pressure prevents the normal absorption of oxygen by the body, which over an extended period, may cause mild hypoxia (lack of oxygen) and fatigue. This problem is exaggerated if the passenger is suffering from a heart-lung disease or smokes.

Alcohol consumption may further complicate the issue. Enjoy a cocktail or a glass of wine with your meal, but don't overdo it. One's tolerance to alcohol reduces with increased altitude and further adversely affects the quality of sleep.

Some travellers also experience flatulence or stomach discomfort from the reduction in air pressure. Avoid fatty foods and acidic fruits before flying and be careful not to overdose yourself with vitamin tablets (especially C and A).

Beware of flying with a cold or ear infection. The change in pressure is normally accommodated by the Eustachian tube. However, if this area is blocked by discharge, it could prevent the equalization of pressure between the middle and outer ear, causing pain because of the inward flexing of the eardrum. Ask your doctor to recommend appropriate treatment.

The low humidity could cause eye irritation and dehydration. Drink as much liquid as possible before and during the flight to prevent a backlog in dehydration. Also carry a small bottle of mild eyedrops in your handbag. (Do keep in mind that alcohol also dehydrates body tissue.)

Other effects of the cabin atmosphere could be irritation of the mucous membranes, inability to wear contact lenses and swelling of legs, feet and hands. Blood tends to accumulate in the extremities of the body when a person is immobile for more than two hours.

Most problems, of course, are generated by the notorious jet lag.

The shift in time zones produces a number of problems. Our bodies are cyclic, biological machines undergoing myriads of fluctuations in temperature, enzymes, hormones, gastric secretions, brain functions, work-rest cycles, etc.

As long as these are in harmony, we remain unaffected. But as soon as these cycles are disrupted, problems arise. Sleeplessness, chronic and acute fatigue, irritability, loss of concentration, depression, are just a few possible results.

There is a very real and effective solution to these disturbances in the body rhythm. If an air traveller observes a few simple rules, he can readily adjust. The solution is exercise!

Regular, free-flowing exercise remains the most effective antidote. The executive should follow regular exercise programmes designed to improve circulation, muscle tone and cardio-vascular function. Cycling, swimming, jogging and a brisk walk are all excellent forms of rhythmic aerobic exercise.

If you need an alert mind in order to prepare for a lecture or meeting overseas while still in flight, try to exercise for half an hour about three hours before the journey.

Similarly, while on board, walk the aisles every half hour and if possible, do some stretching exercises. You will find your mood improves, and in general your relaxed alertness and well-being will astound you.

If you wish to overcome that inevitable spongy, post-flight feeling, set aside 45 minutes for a good aerobic workout. Regardless of how you felt previously, you will spring back into life and feel elated and energetic well into the evening, by which time you should be ready to drift into a new sleep/work cycle compatible with the specific country's time zone (although you may still awake at 3 a.m. after travelling west and oversleep after an east-bound flight).

Similarly, find time each day to exercise, preferably each morning, but don't overdo matters. Once again, try to avoid consuming too much alcohol or taking sleeping tablets, pep pills or tranquillisers. These habits will only reduce the quality of your sleep and result in irritation, clouded thought and fatigue. If sleep is a problem, try meditation by concentrating on a single colour or word, or plug into the in-flight music.

The quality of your decisions and level of concentration are of vital importance and could have major implications for you and your company. Maximise your potential by following these simple rules. You will not only perform better, but feel better and thus enjoy the whole business trip that much more.

Being people oriented is not about being nice to people
– John Naisbitt

The world is full of willing people; some willing to work and the rest willing to let them
– Robert Frost

TEMPERATURES YOU CAN EXPECT
ELSEWHERE IN THE WORLD

For the convenience of travellers, below are the average daily temperatures of major international cities from January to December measured in degrees Celsius. It should be noted that the daily minimum and maximum temperature will vary from this average temperature.

	Jan	Feb	Mar	Apr	May	Jun	Jul	Aug	Sep	Oct	Nov	Dec
Adelaide	27	26	25	21	17	13	12	15	17	21	25	26
Amsterdam	3	3	5	9	14	15	17	18	16	11	7	4
Athens	9	10	12	15	20	25	27	27	24	20	15	11
Auckland	20	20	19	16	14	12	11	11	13	14	15	18
Bahrain	17	18	21	25	30	32	33	34	31	28	25	18
Bangkok	26	27	29	30	30	29	28	28	28	27	27	27
Bombay	24	24	26	28	30	29	27	27	26	28	27	26
Brisbane	29	28	24	21	19	17	15	17	20	22	25	27
Brussels	2	3	6	8	13	16	18	17	14	10	5	3
Buenos Aires	23	22	20	17	12	10	12	14	14	15	19	21
Cairo	13	15	18	21	25	28	28	28	26	22	20	15
Chicago	−4	−3	2	9	14	20	23	22	19	12	5	−1
Colombo	26	27	27	28	29	27	27	27	27	27	26	26
Copenhagen	0	0	2	7	12	15	18	17	13	9	4	1
Delhi	14	17	23	29	34	34	31	30	29	26	20	16
Djakarta	26	26	27	28	28	27	27	27	27	27	27	26
Frankfurt	1	3	6	10	14	18	16	18	15	9	5	2
Geneva	1	3	6	10	14	18	20	19	16	11	6	2
Hong Kong	15	15	18	22	25	27	29	29	27	25	21	18
Honolulu	22	22	23	24	25	26	27	27	27	26	25	23
Jeddah	23	22	25	27	28	29	30	31	30	29	27	24
Johannesburg	26	26	23	20	18	17	17	19	20	22	24	26
Karachi	19	21	24	28	30	31	30	28	28	28	22	20

	Jan	Feb	Mar	Apr	May	Jun	Jul	Aug	Sep	Oct	Nov	Dec
Kuala Lumpur	27	28	28	28	28	27	27	28	28	27	27	27
London	5	5	7	9	12	16	18	17	15	11	7	5
Los Angeles	13	14	15	16	18	20	22	22	22	20	17	14
Madrid	4	6	9	12	16	21	24	23	19	14	8	6
Manila	26	26	28	29	29	29	28	28	28	27	27	26
Melbourne	20	20	10	16	13	11	10	11	13	15	16	18
Mexico City	12	13	16	18	19	19	17	18	18	16	14	13
Milan	2	5	8	13	17	22	23	23	19	14	7	3
Montreal	−11	−9	−4	6	13	19	21	19	15	8	1	−7
Moscow	−9	−6	−4	4	13	17	19	17	11	4	−3	−8
München	−2	−1	3	5	12	16	17	17	13	8	3	−1
Nice	10	8	10	15	18	21	23	24	21	16	12	10
New York	−1	0	3	9	16	21	23	23	21	15	7	2
Osaka	3	4	7	13	17	21	25	26	23	17	11	6
Oslo	−4	−3	1	6	12	16	18	16	12	6	1	−2
Paris	3	4	7	11	13	17	19	18	16	11	6	4
Perth	23	23	21	19	16	14	13	13	14	16	19	21
Rio de Janeiro	26	26	26	24	22	21	21	21	21	22	23	25
Rome	8	9	11	14	18	22	25	25	22	18	13	9
San Francisco	10	12	13	13	15	15	15	15	16	16	14	8
Singapore	27	27	27	27	28	28	28	28	28	27	27	27
Stockholm	−3	−3	0	7	9	14	17	16	11	7	2	−1
Sydney	22	22	21	19	15	13	12	13	15	18	20	21
Taipeh	17	19	25	25	30	30	30	31	30	30	27	23
Tel Aviv	14	14	17	19	23	26	28	28	27	25	21	16
Tokyo	3	4	7	13	17	21	25	26	23	17	11	6
Toronto	5	5	1	5	12	17	20	19	15	9	3	3
Vancouver	3	4	6	9	13	16	18	18	14	10	6	4
Vienna	−1	1	4	9	14	18	19	19	15	10	4	1
Washington	1	3	7	12	18	23	25	24	20	14	8	3
Wellington	17	18	16	13	11	10	9	9	10	13	15	16
Zürich	0	2	6	9	14	17	19	19	16	10	5	1

Britain (UK)												
Nov—Feb	0600	0700	0800	0900	1000	1100	1200	1300	1400	1500	1600	1700
Mar—Oct	0700	0800	0900	1000	1100	1200	1300	1400	1500	1600	1700	1800
Australia												
Freemantle, Perth	1400	1500	1600	1700	1800	1900	2000	2100	2200	2300	0000	0100
Adelaide												
Feb—Sept	1530	1630	1730	1830	1930	2030	2130	2230	2330	0030	0130	0230
Oct—Jan	1630	1730	1830	1930	2030	2130	2230	2330	0030	0130	0230	0330
Darwin	1530	1630	1730	1830	1930	2030	2130	2230	2330	0030	0130	0230
Brisbane, Tasmania	1600	1700	1800	1900	2000	2100	2200	2300	0000	0100	0200	0300
Canberra, Melbourne, Sydney												
Apr—Sept	1600	1700	1800	1900	2000	2100	2200	2300	0000	0100	0200	0300
Oct—Mar	1700	1800	1900	2000	2100	2200	2300	0000	0100	0200	0300	0400
Austria												
Oct—Mar	0700	0800	0900	1000	1100	1200	1300	1400	1500	1600	1700	1800
Apr—Sept	0800	0900	1000	1100	1200	1300	1400	1500	1600	1700	1800	1900
Bahrain	1000	1100	1200	1300	1400	1500	1600	1700	1800	1900	2000	2100
Bangladesh	1200	1300	1400	1500	1600	1700	1800	1900	2000	2100	2200	2300
Belgium												
Oct—May	0700	0800	0900	1000	1100	1200	1300	1400	1500	1600	1700	1800
June—Sept	0800	0900	1000	1100	1200	1300	1400	1500	1600	1700	1800	1900
Brazil	0300	0400	0500	0600	0700	0800	0900	1000	1100	1200	1300	1400
Brunei	1400	1500	1600	1700	1800	1900	2000	2100	2200	2300	0000	0100
Burma	1230	1330	1430	1530	1630	1730	1830	1930	2030	2130	2230	2330
Canada												
Halifax												
Oct—Mar	0300	0400	0500	0600	0700	0800	0900	1000	1100	1200	1300	1400
Apr—Sept	0400	0500	0600	0700	0800	0900	1000	1100	1200	1300	1400	1500

This chart has been designed for instant determination of the time in 46 countries against British time listed in hourly breaks. For countries spreading over different time zones, the cities are grouped in their respective time zones.

Britain (UK) Nov—Feb	1800	1900	2000	2100	2200	2300	0000	0100	0200	0300	0400	0500
Mar—Oct	1900	2000	2100	2200	2300	0000	0100	0200	0300	0400	0500	0600
Australia Freemantle, Perth	0200	0300	0400	0500	0600	0700	0800	0900	1000	1100	1200	1300
Adelaide Feb—Sept	0330	0430	0530	0630	0730	0830	0930	1030	1130	1230	1330	1430
Oct—Jan	0430	0530	0630	0730	0830	0930	1030	1130	1230	1330	1430	1530
Darwin	0330	0430	0530	0630	0730	0830	0930	1030	1130	1230	1330	1430
Brisbane, Tasmania	0400	0500	0600	0700	0800	0900	1000	1100	1200	1300	1400	1500
Canberra, Melbourne, Sydney Apr—Sept	0400	0500	0600	0700	0800	0900	1000	1100	1200	1300	1400	1500
Oct—Mar	0500	0600	0700	0800	0900	1000	1100	1200	1300	1400	1500	1600
Austria Oct—Mar	1900	2000	2100	2200	2300	0000	0100	0200	0300	0400	0500	0600
Apr—Sept	2000	2100	2200	2300	0000	0100	0200	0300	0400	0500	0600	0700
Bahrain	2200	2300	0000	0100	0200	0300	0400	0500	0600	0700	0800	0900
Bangladesh	0000	0100	0200	0300	0400	0500	0600	0700	0800	0900	1000	1100
Belgium Oct—May	1900	2000	2100	2200	2300	0000	0100	0200	0300	0400	0500	0600
June—Sept	2000	2100	2200	2300	0000	0100	0200	0300	0400	0500	0600	0700
Brazil	1500	1600	1700	1800	1900	2000	2100	2200	2300	0000	0100	0200
Brunei	0200	0300	0400	0500	0600	0700	0800	0900	1000	1100	1200	1300
Burma	0030	0130	0230	0330	0430	0530	0630	0730	0830	0930	1030	1130
Canada Halifax Oct—Mar	1500	1600	1700	1800	1900	2000	2100	2200	2300	0000	0100	0200
Apr—Sept	1600	1700	1800	1900	2000	2100	2200	2300	0000	0100	0200	0300

For countries where the hours are sometimes changed, the months are indicated when the different times apply. The months indicated may be subject to alteration.

Britain (UK)												
Nov—Feb	0600	0700	0800	0900	1000	1100	1200	1300	1400	1500	1600	1700
Mar—Oct	0700	0800	0900	1000	1100	1200	1300	1400	1500	1600	1700	1800

Canada												
Montreal, Ottawa, Quebec, Toronto												
Oct—Mar	0200	0300	0400	0500	0600	0700	0800	0900	1000	1100	1200	1300
Apr—Sept	0300	0400	0500	0600	0700	0800	0900	1000	1100	1200	1300	1400
Winipeg												
Oct—Mar	0100	0200	0300	0400	0500	0600	0700	0800	0900	1000	1100	1200
Apr—Sept	0200	0300	0400	0500	0600	0700	0800	0900	1000	1100	1200	1300
Calgary, Edmonton												
Oct—Mar	0000	0100	0200	0300	0400	0500	0600	0700	0800	0900	1000	1100
Apr—Sept	0100	0200	0300	0400	0500	0600	0700	0800	0900	1000	1100	1200
Vancouver												
Oct—Mar	2300	0000	0100	0200	0300	0400	0500	0600	0700	0800	0900	1000
Apr—Sept	0000	0100	0200	0300	0400	0500	0600	0700	0800	0900	1000	1100
China	1400	1500	1600	1700	1800	1900	2000	2100	2200	2300	0000	0100
Denmark												
Oct—Apr	0700	0800	0900	1000	1100	1200	1300	1400	1500	1600	1700	1800
May—Sept	0800	0900	1000	1100	1200	1300	1400	1500	1600	1700	1800	1900
Egypt	0800	0900	1000	1100	1200	1300	1400	1500	1600	1700	1800	1900
France												
Oct—Apr	0700	0800	0900	1000	1100	1200	1300	1400	1500	1600	1700	1800
May—Sept	0800	0900	1000	1100	1200	1300	1400	1500	1600	1700	1800	1900
Germany, West												
Oct—Apr	0700	0800	0900	1000	1100	1200	1300	1400	1500	1600	1700	1800
May—Sept	0800	0900	1000	1100	1200	1300	1400	1500	1600	1700	1800	1900
Greece												
Oct—Mar	0800	0900	1000	1100	1200	1300	1400	1500	1600	1700	1800	1900
Apr—Sept	0900	1000	1100	1200	1300	1400	1500	1600	1700	1800	1900	2000
Hong Kong												
Nov—Mar	1400	1500	1600	1700	1800	1900	2000	2100	2200	2300	0000	0100
Apr—Oct	1500	1600	1700	1800	1900	2000	2100	2200	2300	0000	0100	0200
Hungary	0700	0800	0900	1000	1100	1200	1300	1400	1500	1600	1700	1800
India	1130	1230	1330	1430	1530	1630	1730	1830	1930	2030	2130	2230
Indonesia	1500	1600	1700	1800	1900	2000	2100	2200	2300	0000	0100	0200

This chart has been designed for instant determination of the time in 46 countries against British time listed in hourly breaks. For countries spreading over different time zones, the cities are grouped in their respective time zones.

Britain (UK)												
Nov—Feb	1800	1900	2000	2100	2200	2300	0000	0100	0200	0300	0400	0500
Mar—Oct	1900	2000	2100	2200	2300	0000	0100	0200	0300	0400	0500	0600
Canada												
Montreal, Ottawa, Quebec, Toronto												
Oct—Mar	1400	1500	1600	1700	1800	1900	2000	2100	2200	2300	0000	0100
Apr—Sept	1500	1600	1700	1800	1900	2000	2100	2200	2300	0000	0100	0200
Winipeg												
Oct—Mar	1300	1400	1500	1600	1700	1800	1900	2000	2100	2200	2300	0000
Apr—Sept	1400	1500	1600	1700	1800	1900	2000	2100	2200	2300	0000	0100
Calgary, Edmonton												
Oct—Mar	1200	1300	1400	1500	1600	1700	1800	1900	2000	2100	2200	2300
Apr—Sept	1300	1400	1500	1600	1700	1800	1900	2000	2100	2200	2300	0000
Vancouver												
Oct—Mar	1100	1200	1300	1400	1500	1600	1700	1800	1900	2000	2100	2200
Apr—Sept	1200	1300	1400	1500	1600	1700	1800	1900	2000	2100	2200	2300
China	0200	0300	0400	0500	0600	0700	0800	0900	1000	1100	1200	1300
Denmark												
Oct—Apr	1900	2000	2100	2200	2300	0000	0100	0200	0300	0400	0500	0600
May—Sept	2000	2100	2200	2300	0000	0100	0200	0300	0400	0500	0600	0700
Egypt	2000	2100	2200	2300	0000	0100	0200	0300	0400	0500	0600	0700
France												
Oct—Apr	1900	2000	2100	2200	2300	0000	0100	0200	0300	0400	0500	0600
May—Sept	2000	2100	2200	2300	0000	0100	0200	0300	0400	0500	0600	0700
Germany, West												
Oct—Apr	1900	2000	2100	2200	2300	0000	0100	0200	0300	0400	0500	0600
May—Sept	2000	2100	2200	2300	0000	0100	0200	0300	0400	0500	0600	0700
Greece												
Oct—Mar	2000	2100	2200	2300	0000	0100	0200	0300	0400	0500	0600	0700
Apr—Sept	2100	2200	2300	0000	0100	0200	0300	0400	0500	0600	0700	0800
Hong Kong												
Nov—Mar	0200	0300	0400	0500	0600	0700	0800	0900	1000	1100	1200	1300
Apr—Oct	0300	0400	0500	0600	0700	0800	0900	1000	1100	1200	1300	1400
Hungary	1900	2000	2100	2200	2300	0000	0100	0200	0300	0400	0500	0600
India	2330	0030	0130	0230	0330	0430	0530	0630	0730	0830	0930	1030
Indonesia	0300	0400	0500	0600	0700	0800	0900	1000	1100	1200	1300	1400

For countries where the hours are sometimes changed, the months are indicated when the different times apply. The months indicated may be subject to alteration.

Britain (UK)												
Nov—Feb	0600	0700	0800	0900	1000	1100	1200	1300	1400	1500	1600	1700
Mar—Oct	0700	0800	0900	1000	1100	1200	1300	1400	1500	1600	1700	1800
Indonesia	1300	1400	1500	1600	1700	1800	1900	2000	2100	2200	2300	0000
Ireland, Rep of												
Nov—Mar	0600	0700	0800	0900	1000	1100	1200	1300	1400	1500	1600	1700
Apr—Oct	0700	0800	0900	1000	1100	1200	1300	1400	1500	1600	1700	1800
Israel	0800	0900	1000	1100	1200	1300	1400	1500	1600	1700	1800	1900
Italy												
Oct—Apr	0700	0800	0900	1000	1100	1200	1300	1400	1500	1600	1700	1800
May—Sept	0800	0900	1000	1100	1200	1300	1400	1500	1600	1700	1800	1900
Japan	1500	1600	1700	1800	1900	2000	2100	2200	2300	0000	0100	0200
Korea, South	1500	1600	1700	1800	1900	2000	2100	2200	2300	0000	0100	0200
Kuwait	0930	1030	1130	1230	1330	1430	1530	1630	1730	1830	1930	2030
Malaysia	1400	1500	1600	1700	1800	1900	2000	2100	2200	2300	0000	0100
Mexico												
Nov—Mar	0100	0200	0300	0400	0500	0600	0700	0800	0900	1000	1100	1200
Mar—Oct	0200	0300	0400	0500	0600	0700	0800	0900	1000	1100	1200	1300
Netherlands												
Nov—Feb	0700	0800	0900	1000	1100	1200	1300	1400	1500	1600	1700	1800
Mar—Oct	0800	0900	1000	1100	1200	1300	1400	1500	1600	1700	1800	1900
New Zealand												
Apr—Sept	1800	1900	2000	2100	2200	2300	0000	0100	0200	0300	0400	0500
Oct—Mar	1900	2000	2100	2200	2300	0000	0100	0200	0300	0400	0500	0600
Norway												
Oct—Apr	0700	0800	0900	1000	1100	1200	1300	1400	1500	1600	1700	1800
May—Sept	0800	0900	1000	1100	1200	1300	1400	1500	1600	1700	1800	1900
Pakistan	1200	1300	1400	1500	1600	1700	1800	1900	2000	2100	2200	2300

This chart has been designed for instant determination of the time in 46 countries against British time listed in hourly breaks. For countries spreading over different time zones, the cities are grouped in their respective time zones.

Britain (UK)												
Nov—Feb	1800	1900	2000	2100	2200	2300	0000	0100	0200	0300	0400	0500
Mar—Oct	1900	2000	2100	2200	2300	0000	0100	0200	0300	0400	0500	0600
Indonesia	0100	0200	0300	0400	0500	0600	0700	0800	0900	1000	1100	1200
Ireland, Rep of												
Nov—Mar	1800	1900	2000	2100	2200	2300	0000	0100	0200	0300	0400	0500
Apr—Oct	1900	2000	2100	2200	2300	0000	0100	0200	0300	0400	0500	0600
Israel	2000	2100	2200	2300	0000	0100	0200	0300	0400	0500	0600	0700
Italy												
Oct—Apr	1900	2000	2100	2200	2300	0000	0100	0200	0300	0400	0500	0600
May—Sept	2000	2100	2200	2300	0000	0100	0200	0300	0400	0500	0600	0700
Japan	0300	0400	0500	0600	0700	0800	0900	1000	1100	1200	1300	1400
Korea, South	0300	0400	0500	0600	0700	0800	0900	1000	1100	1200	1300	1400
Kuwait	2130	2230	2330	0030	0130	0230	0330	0430	0530	0630	0730	0830
Malaysia	0200	0300	0400	0500	0600	0700	0800	0900	1000	1100	1200	1300
Mexico												
Nov—Mar	1300	1400	1500	1600	1700	1800	1900	2000	2100	2200	2300	0000
Apr—Oct	1400	1500	1600	1700	1800	1900	2000	2100	2200	2300	0000	0100
Netherlands												
Nov—Feb	1900	2000	2100	2200	2300	0000	0100	0200	0300	0400	0500	0600
Mar—Oct	2000	2100	2200	2300	0000	0100	0200	0300	0400	0500	0600	0700
New Zealand												
Apr—Sept	0600	0700	0800	0900	1000	1100	1200	1300	1400	1500	1600	1700
Oct—Mar	0700	0800	0900	1000	1100	1200	1300	1400	1500	1600	1700	1800
Norway												
Oct—Apr	1900	2000	2100	2200	2300	0000	0100	0200	0300	0400	0500	0600
May—Sept	2000	2100	2200	2300	0000	0100	0200	0300	0400	0500	0600	0700
Pakistan	0000	0100	0200	0300	0400	0500	0600	0700	0800	0900	1000	1100

For countries where the hours are sometimes changed, the months are indicated when the different times apply. The months indicated may be subject to alteration.

Britain (UK)												
Nov—Feb	0600	0700	0800	0900	1000	1100	1200	1300	1400	1500	1600	1700
Mar—Oct	0700	0800	0900	1000	1100	1200	1300	1400	1500	1600	1700	1800
Philippines	1400	1500	1600	1700	1800	1900	2000	2100	2200	2300	0000	0100
Portugal												
Oct—Mar	0600	0700	0800	0900	1000	1100	1200	1300	1400	1500	1600	1700
Apr—Sept	0700	0800	0900	1000	1100	1200	1300	1400	1500	1600	1700	1800
Saudi Arabia	0930	1030	1130	1230	1330	1430	1530	1630	1730	1830	1930	2030
Singapore	1400	1500	1600	1700	1800	1900	2000	2100	2200	2300	0000	0100
South Africa	2000	2100	2200	2300	0000	0100	0200	0300	0400	0500	0600	0700
Spain	0700	0800	0900	1000	1100	1200	1300	1400	1500	1600	1700	1800
Sri Lanka	1130	1230	1330	1430	1530	1630	1730	1830	1930	2030	2130	2230
Sweden	0700	0800	0900	1000	1100	1200	1300	1400	1500	1600	1700	1800
Switzerland												
Sept—May	0700	0800	0900	1000	1100	1200	1300	1400	1500	1600	1700	1800
Jun—Aug	0800	0900	1000	1100	1200	1300	1400	1500	1600	1700	1800	1900
Taiwan	1400	1500	1600	1700	1800	1900	2000	2100	2200	2300	0000	0100
Thailand	1300	1400	1500	1600	1700	1800	1900	2000	2100	2200	2300	0000
United Arab Emirates	1000	1100	1200	1300	1400	1500	1600	1700	1800	1900	2000	2100
USA												
Atlanta, Boston, Cleveland, Detroit, Indianapolis, New York, Washington DC												
Oct—Mar	0100	0200	0300	0400	0500	0600	0700	0800	0900	1000	1100	1200
Apr—Sept	0200	0300	0400	0500	0600	0700	0800	0900	1000	1100	1200	1300
Chicago, Dallas, Houston, New Orleans												
Oct—Mar	0000	0100	0200	0300	0400	0500	0600	0700	0800	0900	1000	1100
Apr—Sept	0100	0200	0300	0400	0500	0600	0700	0800	0900	1000	1100	1200
Denver, Salt Lake City												
Oct—Mar	2300	0000	0100	0200	0300	0400	0500	0600	0700	0800	0900	1000
Apr—Sept	0000	0100	0200	0300	0400	0500	0600	0700	0800	0900	1000	1100
Los Angeles, San Francisco, Seattle												
Oct—Mar	2200	2300	0000	0100	0200	0300	0400	0500	0600	0700	0800	0900
Apr—Sept	2300	0000	0100	0200	0300	0400	0500	0600	0700	0800	0900	1000
Honolulu	2000	2100	2200	2300	0000	0100	0200	0300	0400	0500	0600	0700
USSR												
Oct—Apr	0900	1000	1100	1200	1300	1400	1500	1600	1700	1800	1900	2000
May—Sept	1000	1100	1200	1300	1400	1500	1600	1700	1800	1900	2000	2100

This chart has been designed for instant determination of the time in 46 countries against British time listed in hourly breaks. For countries spreading over different time zones, the cities are grouped in their respective time zones.

Britain (UK)												
Nov—Feb	1800	1900	2000	2100	2200	2300	0000	0100	0200	0300	0400	0500
Mar—Oct	1900	2000	2100	2200	2300	0000	0100	0200	0300	0400	0500	0600
Philippines	0200	0300	0400	0500	0600	0700	0800	0900	1000	1100	1200	1300
Portugal												
Oct—Mar	1800	1900	2000	2100	2200	2300	0000	0100	0200	0300	0400	0500
Apr—Sept	1900	2000	2100	2200	2300	0000	0100	0200	0300	0400	0500	0600
Saudi Arabia	2130	2230	2330	0030	0130	0230	0330	0430	0530	0630	0730	0830
Singapore	0200	0300	0400	0500	0600	0700	0800	0900	1000	1100	1200	1300
South Africa	2000	2100	2200	2300	0000	0100	0200	0300	0400	0500	0600	0700
Spain	1900	2000	2100	2200	2300	0000	0100	0200	0300	0400	0500	0600
Sri Lanka	2330	0030	0130	0230	0330	0430	0530	0630	0730	0830	0930	1030
Sweden	1900	2000	2100	2200	2300	0000	0100	0200	0300	0400	0500	0600
Switzerland												
Sept—May	1900	2000	2100	2200	2300	0000	0100	0200	0300	0400	0500	0600
Jun—Aug	2000	2100	2200	2300	0000	0100	0200	0300	0400	0500	0600	0700
Taiwan	0200	0300	0400	0500	0600	0700	0800	0900	1000	1100	1200	1300
Thailand	0100	0200	0300	0400	0500	0600	0700	0800	0900	1000	1100	1200
United Arab Emirates	2200	2300	0000	0100	0200	0300	0400	0500	0600	0700	0800	0900
USA												
Atlanta, Boston, Cleveland, Detroit, Indianapolis, New York, Washington DC												
Oct—Mar	1300	1400	1500	1600	1700	1800	1900	2000	2100	2200	2300	0000
Apr—Sept	1400	1500	1600	1700	1800	1900	2000	2100	2200	2300	0000	0100
Chicago, Dallas, Houston, New Orleans												
Oct—Mar	1200	1300	1400	1500	1600	1700	1800	1900	2000	2100	2200	2300
Apr—Sept	1300	1400	1500	1600	1700	1800	1900	2000	2100	2200	2300	0000
Denver, Salt Lake City												
Oct—Mar	1100	1200	1300	1400	1500	1600	1700	1800	1900	2000	2100	2200
Apr—Sept	1200	1300	1400	1500	1600	1700	1800	1900	2000	2100	2200	2300
Los Angeles, San Francisco, Seattle												
Oct—Mar	1000	1100	1200	1300	1400	1500	1600	1700	1800	1900	2000	2100
Apr—Sept	1100	1200	1300	1400	1500	1600	1700	1800	1900	2000	2100	2200
Honolulu	0800	0900	1000	1100	1200	1300	1400	1500	1600	1700	1800	1900
USSR												
Oct—Apr	2100	2200	2300	0000	0100	0200	0300	0400	0500	0600	0700	0800
May—Sept	2200	2300	0000	0100	0200	0300	0400	0500	0600	0700	0800	0900

For countries where the hours are sometimes changed, the months are indicated when the different times apply. The months indicated may be subject to alteration.

PERPETUAL CALENDAR

If you have the date but not the day of the week, this chart may be used to determine that particular day.																
A		**Years**		**B**						**Months**						
				Jan	**Feb**	**Mar**	**Apr**	**May**	**Jun**	**Jul**	**Aug**	**Sep**	**Oct**	**Nov**	**Dec**
	1925	1953	1981	4	0	0	3	5	1	3	6	2	4	0	2
	1926	1954	1982	5	1	1	4	6	2	4	0	3	5	1	3
	1927	1955	1983	6	2	2	5	0	3	5	1	4	6	2	4
	1928	1956	1984	0	3	4	0	2	5	0	3	6	1	4	6
1901	1929	1957	1985	2	5	5	1	3	6	1	4	0	2	5	0
1902	1930	1958	1986	3	6	6	2	4	0	2	5	1	3	6	1
1903	1931	1959	1987	4	0	0	3	5	1	3	6	2	4	0	2
1904	1932	1960	1988	5	1	2	5	0	3	5	1	4	6	2	4
1905	1933	1961	1989	0	3	3	6	1	4	6	2	5	0	3	5
1906	1934	1962	1990	1	4	4	0	2	5	0	3	6	1	4	6
1907	1935	1963	1991	2	5	5	1	3	6	1	4	0	2	5	0
1908	1936	1964	1992	3	6	0	3	5	1	3	6	2	4	0	2
1909	1937	1965	1993	5	1	1	4	6	2	4	0	3	5	1	3
1910	1938	1966	1994	6	2	2	5	0	3	5	1	4	6	2	4
1911	1939	1967	1995	0	3	3	6	1	4	6	2	5	0	3	5
1912	1940	1968	1996	1	4	5	1	3	6	1	4	0	2	5	0
1913	1941	1969	1997	3	6	6	2	4	0	2	5	1	3	6	1
1914	1942	1970	1998	4	0	0	3	5	1	3	6	2	4	0	2
1915	1943	1971	1999	5	1	1	4	6	2	4	0	3	5	1	3
1916	1944	1972	2000	6	2	3	6	1	4	6	2	5	0	3	5
1917	1945	1973		1	4	4	0	2	5	0	3	6	1	4	6
1918	1946	1974		2	5	5	1	3	6	1	4	0	2	5	0
1919	1947	1975		3	6	6	2	4	0	2	5	1	3	6	1
1920	1948	1976		4	0	1	4	6	2	4	0	3	5	1	3
1921	1949	1977		6	2	2	5	0	3	5	1	4	6	2	4
1922	1950	1978		0	3	3	6	1	4	6	2	5	0	3	5
1923	1951	1979		1	4	4	0	2	5	0	3	6	1	4	6
1924	1952	1980		2	5	6	2	4	0	2	5	1	3	6	1

How to use:

What day of the week was 9 August, 1965? Find the year 1965 in section A. Move your finger across in a horizontal line until the column marked Aug. Add the number (0) from this column to the chosen date (9). Now look for the total (9 + 0 = 9) in section C, and you will see that 9 Aug, 1965 fell on a Monday.

C				**Week Days**		
Sun	1	8	15	22	29	36
Mon	2	9	16	23	30	37
Tue	3	10	17	24	31	
Wed	4	11	18	25	32	
Thu	5	12	19	26	33	
Fri	6	13	20	27	34	
Sat	7	14	21	28	35	

HOW TO CALCULATE THE NUMBER OF DAYS BETWEEN DATES

The table below will enable you to calculate the actual number of days between two dates.

Example:
If you want to calculate the number of days between 23 November 1991 and 26 July 1992, you find November in the horizontal set of figures. Where it meets the vertical line for July it equals 242. Now add the number of days between 23 and 26, i.e. 242 + 3 = 245. There are thus 245 days between 23 November 1991 and 26 July 1992.

From any date in	Jan	Feb	Mar	Apr	May	Jun	Jul	Aug	Sep	Oct	Nov	Dec
						To same date in:						
Jan	365	31	59	90	120	151	181	212	243	273	304	334
Feb	334	365	28	59	89	120	150	181	212	242	273	303
Mar	306	337	365	31	61	92	122	153	184	214	245	275
Apr	275	306	334	365	30	61	91	122	153	183	214	244
May	245	276	304	335	365	31	61	92	123	153	184	214
Jun	214	245	273	304	334	365	30	61	92	122	153	183
Jul	184	215	243	274	304	335	365	31	62	92	123	153
Aug	153	184	212	243	273	304	334	365	31	61	92	122
Sep	122	153	181	212	242	273	303	334	365	30	61	91
Oct	92	123	151	182	212	243	273	304	335	365	31	61
Nov	61	92	120	151	181	212	242	273	304	334	365	30
Dec	31	62	90	121	151	182	212	243	274	304	335	365

People should work in a climate that is challenging, invigorating, and fun ... and the rewards should be related as directly as possible to performance

– Bim Black

IDEAS ON SELECTING GIFTS FOR ALL OCCASIONS

There are often occasions when you need to buy gifts for people at work: birthdays, anniversaries, Christmas, or even as thank you gestures or farewell presents.

It is advisable to keep a diary listing all relevant dates. This will enable you to plan ahead.

Keep a list of general "suppliers" who can always be turned to when all other ideas are rejected. This list could include your local florist and an off-licence that provides gifts specially packed such as wine or whisky.

If the occasion is the farewell of a long-standing staff-member or associate, it may make your task easier to ask the recipient if there is any gift preference. Perhaps a list of ideas could be given to you from which you can choose according to the amount you have available to spend. Don't forget a card which all contributors can sign.

Here are some gift ideas to guide you:

- If the recipient is a well-known figure, the cartoonist at your local newspaper may be able to do a cartoon of him which can be framed for presentation. Make sure the subject of the cartoon sketch has a sense of humour as this idea could backfire!

- Music in cassette, vinyl or compact disc form, is an ideal gift for a music lover. Find out what music is preferred before making any purchase.

- Calendars, diaries and desk accessories are useful items to keep on hand for spur-of-the-moment gifts.

- If someone is getting married or having a baby a whole range of gifts is available depending on the amount of money available to spend, ranging from crockery or saucepans to a buggy or baby-grows (alternatively you may decide the woman needs a present for herself – such as jewellery).

- Glassware can be a beautiful and practical gift for many occasions. Most centres usually have a specialist shop with a wide selection of gifts.

- Homecrafts are becoming increasingly popular – visit a craft fair for a surprising range of well-made, original articles.

- If the recipient is a latent (or overt) gourmet, consider a gift of food. Fruit, patés or chocolates are sure to be well-received. Or what about a complimentary dinner for two at a good restaurant. Arrangements can often be made with management for payment, and a maximum price can be agreed on if necessary.

- Always consider the hobby of the person for whom you are buying. A photographer will welcome anything from a film to a new lens. What about a subscription to a magazine specialising in a hobby?

- Theatre tickets are an ideal gift for opera, ballet, theatre or concert lovers.

- Don't overlook the garden – the source of a multitude of gift ideas.

Wedding Anniversaries

1	Cotton	9	Pottery	25	Silver
2	Paper	10	Tin	30	Pearl
3	Leather	11	Steel	35	Coral
4	Flowers	12	Linen	40	Ruby
5	Wood	13	Lace	45	Sapphire
6	Candy	14	Ivory	50	Gold
7	Copper	15	Crystal	55	Emerald
8	Bronze	20	China	60	Diamond

Birth Stones

January — Garnet	**July** — Ruby
February — Amethyst	**August** — Peridot
March — Aquamarine	**September** — Sapphire
April — Diamond	**October** — Opal
May — Emerald	**November** — Topaz
June — Pearl	**December** — Turquoise

CONVERSION TABLES

The bold figures in the central columns can be read as either the metric or the British Imperial measure. Thus 1 inch = 2.54 centimetres; or 1 centimetre = .3937 inch.
For tens, move decimal point one place to the right, for hundreds two places, etc. Then convert higher quantities thus: 2 ft. 9 in. = 33 in. = 76.2 cm. + 7.62 cm. = 83.82 cm.

Linear

Inches		Centimetres
.3937	1	2.5400
.7874	2	5.0800
1.1811	3	7.6200
1.5748	4	10.1600
1.9685	5	12.7000
2.3622	6	15.2400
2.7559	7	17.7800
3.1496	8	20.3200
3.5433	9	22.8600

Feet		Metres
3.2808	1	.3048
6.5617	2	.6096
9.8425	3	.9144
13.1234	4	1.2192
16.4042	5	1.5240
19.6850	6	1.8288
22.9659	7	2.1336
26.2467	8	2.4384
29.5276	9	2.7432

Yards		Metres
1.0936	1	.9144
2.1872	2	1.8288
3.2808	3	2.7432
4.3745	4	3.6576
5.4681	5	4.5720
6.5617	6	5.4864
7.6553	7	6.4008
8.7489	8	7.3152
9.8425	9	8.2296

Miles		Kilometres
.6214	1	1.6093
1.2427	2	3.2187
1.8641	3	4.8280
2.4855	4	6.4374
3.1068	5	8.0467
3.7282	6	9.6561
4.3496	7	11.2654
4.9710	8	12.8748
5.5923	9	14.4841

Square

Sq. Inches		Sq. Centimetres
.1550	1	6.4516
.3100	2	12.9032
.4650	3	19.3548
.6200	4	25.8064
.7750	5	32.2580
.9300	6	38.7096
1.0850	7	45.1612
1.2400	8	51.6128
1.3950	9	58.0644

Sq. Feet		Sq. Metres
10.7639	1	.0929
21.5278	2	.1858
32.2917	3	.2787
43.0556	4	.3716
53.8195	5	.4645
64.5835	6	.5574
75.3474	7	.6503
86.1113	8	.7432
96.8752	9	.8361

Acres		Hectares
2.4711	1	.4047
4.9421	2	.8094
7.4132	3	1.2141
9.8842	4	1.6188
12.3553	5	2.0235
14.8263	6	2.4281
17.2974	7	2.8328
19.7684	8	3.2375
22.2395	9	3.6422

Sq. Miles		Sq. Kilometres
.3861	1	2.5900
.7722	2	5.1800
1.1583	3	7.7700
1.5444	4	10.3600
1.9305	5	12.9500
2.3166	6	15.5400
2.7027	7	18.1300
3.0888	8	20.7200
3.4749	9	23.3100

Cubic

Cu. Inches		Cu. Centimetres
.0610	1	16.3871
.1221	2	32.7741
.1831	3	49.1612
.2441	4	65.5483
.3051	5	81.9353
.3661	6	98.3224
.4272	7	114.7095
.4882	8	131.0965
.5492	9	147.4836

Cu. Feet		Cu. Metres
35.3145	1	.0283
70.6293	2	.0566
105.9440	3	.0850
141.2587	4	.1133
176.5734	5	.1416
211.8880	6	.1699
247.2027	7	.1982
282.5174	8	.2266
317.8320	9	.2549

Cu. Yards		Cu. Metres
1.3080	1	.7645
2.6159	2	1.5291
3.9239	3	2.2937
5.2318	4	3.0582
6.5398	5	3.8228
7.8477	6	4.5873
9.1557	7	5.3519
10.4636	8	6.1164
11.7716	9	6.8810

Capacity

Gallons		Litres
.2200	1	4.5461
.4399	2	9.0922
.6599	3	13.6383
.8799	4	18.1844
1.0999	5	22.7305
1.3198	6	27.2765
1.5398	7	31.8226
1.7598	8	36.3687
1.9797	9	40.9148

Pints		Litres
1.7598	1	.5683
3.5195	2	1.1365
5.2793	3	1.7048
7.0390	4	2.2731
8.7988	5	2.8413
10.5586	6	3.4096
12.3183	7	3.9778
14.0781	8	4.5461
15.8378	9	5.1144

Quarts		Litres
.8799	1	1.1365
1.7598	2	2.2730
2.6396	3	3.4096
3.5195	4	4.5461
4.3994	5	5.6826
5.2793	6	6.8191
6.1592	7	7.9556
7.0390	8	9.0922
7.9189	9	10.2287

Weight

Ounces		Grams
.03527	1	28.3495
.07055	2	56.6990
.10581	3	85.0486
.14110	4	113.3981
.17637	5	141.7476
.21164	6	170.0971
.24692	7	198.4467
.28219	8	226.7962
.31747	9	255.1457

Power

Horsepower		Kilowatts
1.3410	1	.7457
2.6820	2	1.4914
4.0231	3	2.2371
5.3641	4	2.9828
6.7051	5	3.7285
8.0461	6	4.4742
9.3872	7	5.2199
10.7282	8	5.9656
12.0692	9	6.7113

Speed

Miles/ Hour		Kilometres/ Hour
6.2	10	16.1
12.4	20	32.2
18.6	30	48.3
24.8	40	64.4
31.1	50	80.5
37.3	60	96.6
43.5	70	112.7
49.7	80	128.7
55.9	90	144.8

Temperature Convertion

degrees Farenheit $= \frac{9}{5}°C + 32$

degrees Celsius $= \frac{5}{9}(°F - 32)$

-18°   -10°   0°   10°   20°   30°   40°

°C

°F

0°   10°   20°   32°   40°   50°   60°   70°   80°   90°   100°   110°

WEIGHTS AND MEASURES

METRIC SYSTEM

Linear Measure
10 millimetres .... 1 centimetre
10 centimetres .... 1 decimetre
10 decimetres .... 1 metre
10 metres .... 1 decametre
10 decametres .... 1 hectometre
10 hectometres .... 1 kilometre

Square Measure
100 sq. millimetres .... 1 sq. centimetre
100 sq. centimetres .... 1 sq. decimetre
100 sq. decimetres .... 1 sq. metre
100 sq. metres .... 1 sq. decametre
100 sq. decametres .... 1 sq. hectometre

Cubic Measure
1000 cu. millimetres ...... 1 cu. centimetre
1000 cu. centimetres ...... 1 cu. decimetre
1000 cu. decimetres .... 1 cu. metre

Liquid Measure
10 milliletres .... 1 centilitre
10 centilitres .... 1 decilitre
10 decilitres .... 1 litre
10 litres .... 1 decalitre
10 decalitres .... 1 hectolitre
10 hectolitres .... 1 kilolitre

Weights
10 milligrams .... 1 centigram
10 centigrams .... 1 decigram
10 decigrams .... 1 gram
10 grams .... 1 decagram
10 decagrams .... 1 hectogram
10 hectograms .... 1 kilogram
100 kilograms .... 1 quintal
10 quintals .... 1 ton

IMPERIAL SYSTEM

Linear Measure
12 inches .... 1 foot
3 feet .... 1 yard
5$\frac{1}{2}$ yards .... 1 rod
40 rods .... 1 furlong
8 furlongs .... 1 statute mile
3 miles .... 1 league

Square Measure
144 square inches .... 1 square foot
9 square feet .... 1 square yard
30 $\frac{1}{4}$ square yards .... 1 square rod
40 square rods .... 1 rood
4 roods .... 1 acre
640 acres .... 1 square mile

Cubic Measure
1,728 cubic inches .... 1 cubic foot
27 cubic feet .... 1 cubic yard
128 cubic feet .... 1 cord (wood)
40 cubic feet .... 1 ton (shipping)
2,150.42 cubic inches .... 1 standard bu
231 cubic inches ...... 1 U.S. standard gal
1 cubic foot .... about 4/5 of a bushel

Liquid Measure
4 gills .... 1 pint
2 pints .... 1 quart
4 quarts .... 1 gallon
31 $\frac{1}{2}$ gallons .... 1 barrel
2 barrels .... 1 hogshead

Apothecaries' Weight
20 grains .... 1 scruple
3 scruples .... 1 dram
8 drams .... 1 ounce
12 ounces .... 1 pound

Ounce and pound are the same as in Troy Weight.

Avoirdupois Weight
27 11/32 grains .... 1 dram
16 drams .... 1 ounce
16 ounces .... 1 pound
28 pounds .... 1 quarter
4 quarters .... 1 cwt
2,000 pounds ..... 1 short ton (mainly US)
2,240 pounds ...... 1 long ton (mainly UK)

Troy Weight
24 grains .... 1 pwt
20 pwt .... 1 ounce
12 ounces .... 1 pound
Used for weighing gold, silver and jewels.

Angular Measure
60 seconds .... 1 minute
60 minutes .... 1 degree
30 degrees .... 1 sign
90 degrees .... 1 quadrant
4 quadrants, or 360 degrees ....1 circumference or great circle

The earth rotates at a velocity of 15 degrees and hour (about 17,366 miles a minute at the Equator); 1 degree is therefore equal to 4 minutes.

Dry Measure
2 pints .... 1 quart
8 quarts .... 1 peck
4 pecks .... 1 bushel
36 bushels .... 1 chaldron

Mariners' Measure
6 feet .... 1 fathom
120 fathoms .... 1 cable length
7 $\frac{1}{2}$ cable lengths .... 1 mile
5,280.2 feet .... 1 statute mile
6,080.2 feet .... 1 nautical mile

Surveyors' Measure
7,92 inches .... 1 link
25 links .... 1 rod
4 rods .... 1 chain
10 square chains or 160 square
  rods .... 1 acre
640 acres .... 1 square mile
36 square miles
(6 miles square) .... 1 township

Time Measure
60 seconds .... 1 minute
60 minutes .... 1 hour
24 hours .... 1 day
7 days .... 1 week
28,29,30 or 31 days .... 1 cal. month
30 days ..... 1 month ..... in comp. interest
365 days ...... 1 year, 366 days 1 leap year

GLOSSARY OF COMMON ADMINISTRATIVE AND BUSINESS TERMS

A

Acceptance:
(1) The act of a person who, by signing his name on a bill of exchange as acceptor, agrees to comply with the order of the drawer expressed in the bill.
(2) A bill of exchange which has been accepted.

Acceptance credit:
A letter of credit stating that the issuing bank is prepared to accept and pay bills of exchange drawn upon it in accordance with the conditions specified by the person in whose favour the credit is issued.

Accommodation bill:
A bill of exchange that is drawn and accepted for no consideration, with the object of providing financial accommodation for one of the parties thereto.

Accountability:
The obligation of a subordinate in an organisation to answer to a superior for the due performance of a task or function for which he is responsible.

Account Current:
A statement giving the particulars of the transactions which have been carried on between two persons or firms for a period of time.

Account Sales:
A statement made by an agent who has sold his principal's goods, detailing the prices obtained and the expenses incurred.

Active Partner:
One who takes an active part in the running of a business which partly belongs to him.

Administration:
The aspect of management that is concerned with the interpretation of policy and its practical implementation in action.

Ad valorem:
The Latin phrase meaning "according to value" indicating that a charge is based on the value of the goods rather than on their weight, size or quantity.

Advice note:
A document notifying the receiver that a particular transaction has been or shortly will be carried out on his behalf. It generally indicates that goods ordered have been despatched.

After date:
A bill of exchange that is drawn a given number of days "after date" falls due the stated number of days after the date on the bill.

After sight:
A bill of exchange that is drawn a given number of days "after sight" falls due the stated number of days after the date on which the bill is accepted.

Agenda:
A list of items of business, arranged in the order in which they will be dealt with at a meeting.

Allonge:
A slip of paper attached to a bill of exchange for the purpose of taking additional endorsements when there is no further space on the back of the bill itself.

Amendment:
A proposal to alter the terms of an original motion by addition, deletion or substitution of words or groups of words. The amendment must be proposed, seconded and placed before a meeting.

Amortisation:
The gradual repayment of a debt, often by periodic drawings from a sinking fund (q.v.) established for this purpose.

Annuity:
An annual payment of a specified sum of money for a stated number of years or until the death of the beneficiary, who is known as the annuitant.

Arbitrage:
The operation of buying commodities, stocks or foreign exchange in a market where the price is relatively low, and selling them in another market where the price is higher, in order to take advantage of the difference in the prices.

Arbitration:
A method of settling a dispute by referring the matter to an independent person for adjudication, instead of bringing an action in court.

Assets:
All property and possessions belonging to an individual or business.

Assurance:
(1) A contract between a life assurance company or a member of Lloyd's (the "assurer") and a policy holder (the "assured") whereby the assurer undertakes to pay a specified sum of money (an "endowment") or a series of annual payments (an "annuity") to the assured, his estate or a named beneficiary, on the death of the assured or when he reaches a specified age.
(2) A positive declaration that a statement is true.

At sight:
A bill of exchange drawn "at sight" is payable immediately it is accepted.

Attorney:
(1) An agent duly appointed to act for another.
(2) A solicitor/lawyer.

Audit:
The examination and inspection of accounting records with a view to certifying their correctness.

Authority:
The right to discharge the duties attaching to the performance of a task to which an individual has been assigned.

Autocratic management:
The style of management in which authority is highly centralised in top management (cf. *Democratic management*).

Automation:
The use of electronic equipment to perform a function without human intervention.

Average:
(1) General average: The principle whereby a partial loss incurred to prevent a total loss while goods are being transported by sea is shared by all the parties involved.
(2) The principle of fire insurance whereby, in the event of under-insurance, the insured is deemed to be his own insurer in respect of the amount under-insured.

B

Bad Debts:
Sums of money owing by debtors which are unlikely to be, or are never paid.

Balance sheet:
A statement of the assets, liabilities and capital of an enterprise as at a specified date.

Bank draft:
A document issued by a bank instructing another bank, or another branch of the same bank, to pay a specified sum of money to a named payee.

Bankrupt:
The term used for a person who has been declared insolvent.

Bill broker:
One who deals in bills of exchange, acting as a middleman between the public and various financial institutions which are prepared to discount such bills.

Bill discounter:
One who is prepared to purchase a bill of exchange at its face value, less simple interest reckoned on that value at an agreed rate per cent for the period that the bill has still to run before maturity.

Bill of exchange (B/E):
A legally enforceable written order signed by the drawer requiring the addressee to pay on demand or at a specified future time, a certain sum of money to a named person, or to his order, or to bearer.

Bill of lading (B/L):
A freight contract setting out the terms on which goods specified therein are to be transported by ship, and constituting the document of title thereto.

Bill of sale:
A document by which the owner of property transfers it to another. Under a conditional bill of sale the original owner can reclaim possession after meeting certain conditions, such as paying money back to the second party.

Blank endorsement:
An endorsement on a negotiable instrument consisting of the signature of the holder only, without specifying the name of the endorsee.

Bond:
A document stating the existence of a debt owed by the issuer to the holder.

Break-even point:
The volume of output at which the total of fixed and variable costs equals total revenue.

Broker:
An agent who enters into contracts of purchase and sale on behalf of a principal, such as an insurance broker.

Brokerage:
The remuneration payable to a broker for effecting a contract of purchase and sale on behalf of a principal.

Budget:
A statement in financial and/or physical terms of the operational plans of an enterprise, or a specific facet thereof, for a fixed future period.

Budgetary control:
A management technique involving a comparison of the projections of various items in a budget with actual performance.

By-Law:
A regulation made by a local government authority or public corporation using powers granted by an Act of Parliament.

C

Call money:
Money lent on the money market by financial institutions repayable at call.

Capital:
The excess of the assets of an enterprise over its liabilities, consisting of fixed capital and working capital (q.v.).

Capital commitments:
Contracted and authorised capital expenditure commitments.

Capital employed:
Total shareholders' funds plus deferred tax and long-term debt, plus all current liabilities – equal to total assets.

Capitalism:
The basic principle of an economy in which invested capital is owned and controlled by individuals and companies.

Carriage forward:
When goods are sold "carriage forward" the cost of delivery is to be borne by the buyer.

Cash flow statement:
A statement in summary form of cash receipts and payments for a specified period.

Cash with order:
The goods are to be paid for at the time of order.

Centralisation:
The principle of organisation whereby resources and/or decision-making authority are concentrated.

Certificate of origin:
A document stating place of origin, growth or manufacture of goods being exported.

Chart:
A graphic presentation of quantitative data designed to facilitate comprehension and interpretation.

Charterer:
One who hires a ship or aircraft or a part thereof either for a specified journey or for a stated period of time, or for both.

Charter party (C/P):
The contract of hire of a ship or aircraft or part thereof as above.

Cheque:
A bill of exchange drawn on a banker and payable on demand.

Circular letter of credit:
A document issued by a bank to a customer requesting other banks or branches of the same bank to allow the customer to draw money up to a stated amount.

Circulating capital:
The portion of the capital (q.v.) of a business which consists of current assets which are con-

stantly changing, e.g. stock in trade.

Clean bill of exchange:
One that is not accompanied by the relevant documents in regard to which the bill is drawn.

Clean bill of lading:
A bill of lading that contains no adverse qualifying clause regarding the condition of the goods to which it relates.

Clean credit:
An undertaking by a bank to accept and pay all bills of exchange drawn upon it without requiring attachment of the relevant documents in regard to which the bill is drawn.

Coercive controls:
Procedures, rules and regulations that require actions or restraint from actions to avoid penalties for non-compliance; the "big stick" approach to management (cf. *Inducive controls*).

Co-insurance:
The sharing of a risk between two or more insurers with a view to limiting the liability of each.

Collateral security:
Security, additional to the creditor's personal right of action, that is pledged by the debtor as security for a loan.

Collegial management:
A management style that recognises fellow workers in an organisation as colleagues or co-equals rather than as subordinates.

Command:
The area of authority of a manager comprising:
(a) his "immediate command", i.e. the group of subordinates who are immediately accountable to him; and
(b) his "extended command", i.e. all the members of the organ-

isation who are ultimately under his control.

Commercial bank:
A bank which deals with the public, and specialises in the acceptance of deposits which are withdrawable on demand, and in lending money on short term.

Committee:
One or more persons, appointed by authority or elected to represent others, who are collectively accountable for their decisions and/or their recommendations to those who have appointed or elected them.

Communication:
The interchange of thoughts and information between two or more persons.

Company:
A corporate body having a legal identity separate and distinct from that of the persons who constitute its membership.

Computer:
An electronic data processor that can perform complex calculations and logical operations without human intervention.

Condition:
In the law of contract, an essential duty, failure to carry out which will allow the other party to treat the contract as ended (cf. *Warranty*).

Confirmed letter of credit:
An undertaking by a bank to accept and pay any bills of exchange drawn against the credit, subject to certain specified conditions.

Consignment note:
The form on which the consignor of goods by rail or boat gives particulars of the goods he is despatching. It includes details of the name of the consignor and the consignee, weight, etc., and is

handed to the carrying company. Also known as a way-bill.

Constructive total loss:
Loss resulting from the abandonment of a ship or cargo which is so damaged that it would cost more to recover it than it is worth.

Control:
The aspect of management that is concerned with ensuring that performance matches plans and that appropriate remedial steps are taken to reduce or eliminate any significant adverse variance.

Copying:
The process whereby copies of a document are obtained (cf. *Duplicating*).

Copyright:
The legal right of an author, artist or poet to his original work.

Cost/benefit analysis (CBA):
The systematic comparison of the cost of a proposed course of action with the benefit or advantages, expressed in monetary terms, to be derived.

Costing:
A technique for determining the cost of a unit of production or operation used to assist management in achieving optimum cost effectiveness.

Credit card:
A plastic card issued by commercial banks and certain large retail organisations entitling customers to purchase goods on credit up to a specified limit.

Critical Path Method (CPM):
An extension of the Gantt Chart (q.v.) to determine the most logical and economical sequence for the performance of the various operations involved in the completion of a complex project. Also known as Critical Path Analysis (CPA).

Currency:
(1) The legal medium of exchange comprising (usually) coins and notes.
(2) The period which a bill of exchange has still to run before it matures.

Current ratio:
Current assets divided by current liabilities.

Cybernetics:
The science of automatic communication and control systems in men and machines. Of most relevance to business in the area of automating industrial processes.

D

Data:
"The things given" (i.e. the facts).

Debt cover:
Gross cash flow expressed as a multiple of interest-bearing debt.

Debt:equity ratio:
All interest-bearing debt expressed as a ratio of total shareholders' funds.

Decentralisation:
The dispersion of resources or decision-making authority (cf. *Centralisation*).

Del credere agent:
One who holds himself personally liable for default of customers he introduces to his principal. For taking this additional risk he earns himself extra commission, called "del credere commission".

Delegation:
The principle of organisation whereby a task or decision-making authority is passed by a superior to a subordinate in respect of a matter which lies within the responsibility of the superior.

Democratic management:
The management style in which authority and control are disseminated among lower levels of the organisational hierarchy (cf. *Autocratic management*).

Demurrage:
Undue delay or detention of a ship, barge or railway truck. Compensation for such delay.

Depreciation:
A decline in the value of assets due to wear and tear, or obsolescence, or alternatively, sums set aside from profits to replace worn-out or obsolete assets.

Direct debit:
A standing instruction to a bank to pay on due date various accounts on which regular but variable amounts become payable.

Directing:
Interpreting policies and plans and giving instructions on how they are to be carried out.

Directive:
A written instruction given by a member of top management to his immediate subordinate(s) which will have long-term application.

Dirty bill of lading:
A bill of lading bearing a qualifying clause, such as "one case damaged".

Discounted cash flow (DCF):
The technique of calculating the true present value of an asset by adding together the present values of the anticipated annual future payments, on the principle that a given sum invested now will earn interest during the life of the investment.

Discretionary income:
The portion, if any, of disposable income that remains after the necessities of life have been paid for.

Dividend cover:
Earnings attributable to ordinary shares divided by ordinary dividends paid.

Dividend yield:
The relation of the declared dividend on a share to the current market price of the share, expressed as a percentage (cf. *Earnings yield*).

Documentary bill:
A bill of exchange accompanied by various documents such as the export invoice, the bill of lading, the policy of insurance and a letter of hypothecation, relating to the goods in connection with which the bill has been drawn.

Documentary credit:
A letter of credit which requires bills of exchange drawn in pursuance thereof to be accompanied by the relevant documents as above.

Document of title:
A document which gives the holder the right to deal with specified goods or property as if he owned them, e.g. bill of lading.

Draft:
(1) A bill of exchange which has not yet been accepted or, in the case of a bank draft, does not need acceptance.
(2) A preliminary form of a document.

Drawback:
Foreign goods imported into a country are usually subject to customs import duty. If, however, the goods are not consumed in that country, but are re-exported, the duty may be refunded. This is called drawback.

Dunnage:
Mats, wood, etc., used in stowing cargo.

Duplicating:
The process of reproducing many facsimiles of a document by mechanical means.

E

E. & O.E.:
Errors and omissions excepted. These letters at the foot of an invoice mean that the business sending the invoice reserves the right to correct any errors or omissions which may be afterwards discovered. These letters have no legal significance.

Earnings yield:
The relation of the total profits available for distribution to the total value of the ordinary shares at market price, expressed as a percentage.

Embargo:
An order placing a stoppage on trade between certain countries, or forbidding a ship to leave port before a certain time.

Employee-centred:
An attitude of a manager in which concern for the employee's welfare overrides concern for output, which is deemed to be of secondary importance.

Endorse:
To sign a name on the back of any commercial or legal document, thereby assigning or giving sanction to the paper.

Endowment policy:
A life assurance policy which provides for a specified sum of money to become payable after the expiry of a stated number of years or on the death of the assured, whichever is earlier.

Equity:
(1) The right of a shareholder to participate in the profits of the company of which he is a member.
(2) The ordinary shares of a company, i.e. excluding the portion, if any, of the share capital which carries no right to participate beyond a specified percentage in the distribution of dividends or in the return of capital.
(3) Principles of fairness in human relationships.

Ergonomics:
The science of the relationship between man and his working environment, aimed at achieving optimum productivity by ensuring satisfactory working conditions, tools, equipment, etc.; also known as *Human engineering*.

Escrow account:
An account opened with a bank or other financial institution in which funds are lodged for release to a third party only on the performance of certain specified conditions.

Exception principle:
The principle of control by concentrating attention only upon significant variances between planned and actual performance.

Excise duty:
Taxes on goods manufactured or consumed in a country.

Ex Quay:
The term means that the buyer has to take the delivery of the goods when they are landed on the wharf.

Extempore:
Without preparation or notes.

Extended command:
The entire range of subordinates for whose work activities a superior is accountable.

Extrinsically significant incentives:
Intangible work incentives; incentives of a social, non-monetary nature.

F

Face value:
The value stated on the face of a document such as a share certificate or bill of exchange as distinct from its market value at any particular time.

F.A.S. (Free alongside ship):
The buyer must therefore pay the costs involved in putting the goods on board.

Feasibility study:
A detailed enquiry into the practicality of pursuing a proposed course of action.

Fidelity insurance:
Insurance against loss resulting from an employee's dishonesty or breach of contract.

Fixed capital:
The permanent assets of an undertaking intended for retention and use in pursuing the objects of the enterprise and not for resale.

Flotsam:
Wreckage of a ship found floating on the sea, including cargo from the ship.

Flow chart:
A diagram that shows, by means of symbols and interconnecting lines, the general sequence of operations in a particular routine.

F.O.B. (Free on board):
The seller pays the cost of delivering the goods into the hold of the ship.

F.O.R. (Free on rail):
The seller pays the costs incurred up until the time the goods are loaded on the train, all further costs are for the account of the buyer.

Forecasting:
Predicting probable results of decisions or of changes in prevailing circumstances.

Foreclosure:
The seizing of property pledged in a mortgage, for payment of the debt secured thereby.

Foreign bill:
A bill of exchange which is either drawn by a non-resident of the UK, or drawn by a resident upon a non-resident for payment outside the UK.

Foul bill of lading:
Same as a dirty bill of lading (q.v.).

Franking:
The process of machine stamping postal matter instead of affixing adhesive postage stamps.

Free enterprise:
The basic principle of an economy in which production is undertaken by individuals and companies acting on their own initiative and not at the instigation of the State (cf. *Socialism*).

Freehold:
Ownership of land in perpetuity.

Free rein management:
A *laissez faire* style of management that leaves decision-making in the hands of subordinates.

Functional authority:
Authority exercised across organisational lines rather than through the normal chain of command by executives performing a staff or service function.

Funding:
(1) The conversion of a floating debt into formal definitive securities.
(2) The financing of a project.

Futures contract:
A deal on an organised market or exchange involving delivery of the subject-matter on a future date.

G

Gantt chart:
A bar diagram used to schedule work by portraying, against a time scale, the periods of time allocated to the performance of major tasks involved in the completion of a complex project.

Garnishee order:
An order of the court to a person who owes money to a judgement debtor (e.g. wages or salary) to retain the money for the benefit of a judgement creditor.

General average loss:
The cost of any deliberate action (e.g. jettisoning cargo) in order to save a ship and/or the balance of the cargo. Such loss must be shared proportionately by all parties benefiting from the action.

Gilt-edged security:
A first-class security; a term generally applied to government stocks.

Goodwill:
An intangible asset of a business representing its reputation or image and its business connections.

Grid organisation:
An alternative term for line and staff organisation (q.v.).

Gross cash flow:
Profit after tax and redeemable preference dividends, but before minorities, plus depreciation and deferred tax.

H

Hedge:
A contract entered into to cover the risk of loss.

Hierarchy:
The different levels of authority in an organisational structure.

Human engineering:
See *Ergonomics*.

Hypothecation:
The act of pledging or mortgaging goods as security for a debt.

I

Implied term:
A term of a contract which, though not explicitly stated, is clearly understood.

In Bond:
Imported goods which have not been cleared through customs but are being held until duty has been paid on them.

Incentive:
An inducement to maximise performance.

Income statement:
A profit and loss account (or, in the case of a non-profit-earning undertaking, an income and expenditure account) in which items of income are set out and totalled, followed by items of expenditure which are similarly totalled, revealing the nett profit or loss (or the nett surplus or deficit).

Indemnity:
A written undertaking whereby the giver agrees to reimburse another in the event of loss or damage which might accrue to him as a result of the occurrence of some specified contingency.

Inducive controls:
Programmes or procedures that offer rewards for compliance; the "carrot" approach to management (cf. *Coercive controls*).

In extenso:
"At full length" (Latin).

Inflation:
A general rise in prices resulting from an increase in purchasing power in an economy without a corresponding increase in goods and services available for purchase.

Information:
Data that is pertinent to the administration of an enterprise.

Inland bill:
A bill of exchange drawn and payable within the British Isles, or drawn within the British Isles, upon a person resident therein.

In situ:
"On the site", i.e. on the premises (Latin).

Insolvent:
(1) The condition in which liabilities exceed assets.
(2) A person who has been declared by the court to be in that condition.

Insurable risk:
A contingency which can be insured against.

Insurance:
A contract of indemnity whereby the insurer (i.e. the insurance company) undertakes to reimburse the insured (i.e. the policy holder) for any loss incurred as a result of the happening of a specified event.

Interest & leasing cover:
Pre-interest profit plus leasing charges expressed as a multiple of interest and lease payments.

Internal audit:
The continuous examination and inspection of the accounting records of an enterprise with a view to verifying their correctness and minimising the risk of loss from fraud or defalcation, undertaken in accordance with instructions issued by top management, to whom alone the internal auditor is answerable.

Internal check:
The system of checks incorporated in routines and procedures whereby the work of one member of the staff is checked by another and designed to minimise errors and to reduce the risk of fraud, pilferage and defalcation.

Internal control:
The complete system of internal check and internal audit in operation in a concern.

Intrinsically significant incentives:
Incentives of a personal nature.

Inventory:
A detailed list of raw materials and finished and partly finished stocks on hand.

Inventory capital:
That part of the capital of an enterprise that is represented by raw materials, purchased parts, work in progress and partially finished and finished goods available for sale.

Investment:
An outlay of funds on an asset with a view to deriving income therefrom.

J

Jetsam:
Goods that have been thrown overboard at a time of peril with a view to saving a ship by reducing the amount of cargo on board (cf. *Flotsam*).

Jettison:
The act of throwing goods overboard with a view to saving a ship by reducing the amount of cargo on board.

Job:
An amount of work to be performed in a specified period of time.

Job-centred:
A management attitude in which concern for output and performance of the job takes precedence over employee welfare (cf. *Employee-centred*).

Job definition:
A detailed statement of a job, comprising the job description and the job specification (q.v.).

Job description:
A written statement specifying the training, skill, experience and initiative demanded by a job for its efficient performance.

Job enlargement:
See *Job enrichment*.

Job enrichment:
The purposeful extension of individual freedom, responsibility and challenge involved in a job with the object of increasing job satisfaction (q.v.).

Job evaluation:
A systematic method of determining the monetary value of each job in terms of its job description.

Job satisfaction:
The sense of pleasure and self-fulfilment derived from the performance of a job.

Job specification:
A written statement defining the responsibility, authority and relationships with other positions, of a particular position in an organisation; also known as a "position guide".

L

Leadership:
The ability to influence or inspire subordinates to exert themselves willingly in the achievement of an objective.

Lease:
A contract whereby one party

(the "lessor") agrees to allow the other party (the "lessee") the use of an asset for a specified period in return for a periodical payment called a rent.

Lease-back:
The sale of an asset to a financial institution, immediately followed by its lease back to the vendor who thus retains the use thereof subject to payment of rent without tying up working capital.

Leasehold:
Tenure of land and/or buildings in terms of a lease (cf. *Freehold*).

Lending rate:
The prevailing rate of interest at which financial institutions are prepared to lend money against appropriate security.

Letter of credit (L/C):
A document issued by a bank authorising another bank, or another branch of the same bank, to pay money up to a specified amount to the person in whose favour the letter of credit is issued.

Letter of hypothecation (L/H):
A letter pledging property, goods or securities in consideration of a loan.

Letter of indemnity:
A written guarantee against loss should a specified act be performed or a certain event occur.

Letter of subrogation:
A document conveying the right of subrogation (q.v.).

Lien:
The right of a creditor who is in possession of property of his debtor in respect of which he has incurred expenditure, to retain that property until he has been reimbursed in respect of the expenditure.

Line and staff organisational structure:
The structure in which both line and staff functions are co-ordinated to form a single organic whole.

Line function:
An activity that is essential to the attainment of the objects of an enterprise (cf. *Staff function*).

Line graph:
A chart presenting data in a readily comprehensible form by means of lines joining points plotted on graph paper.

Line organisation:
The type of organisational structure in which authority flows in a direct line from superior to subordinate through a succession of levels of authority.

Liquid assets:
The assets of an enterprise which are in the form of cash or are readily realisable into cash, such as securities which can be sold on the Stock Exchange.

Lloyd's:
An association of insurance underwriters and brokers whose headquarters were originally at Lloyd's coffee house in London.

Lloyd's policy:
The standard form of insurance policy authorised by the committee at Lloyd's.

Lloyd's Register:
A complete register of all ships which have been built under Lloyd's inspection; ships of first-class construction and in first-class condition are known as "A1 at Lloyd's".

M

Management:
(1) The administration of an

enterprise or any part thereof.

(2) A generic term applied to the group of top level managers who together are responsible for the work of the enterprise.

Management by exception (MBE):
The management technique which concentrates upon elements the performance of which reveals a significant adverse variance as compared with the target, standard or budget figure laid down.

Management by objectives (MBO):
The method of management in which the objectives to be achieved are established by consultation between a manager and his subordinates, but in which the means to be utilised are determined by the subordinates.

Management job description (MJD):
A written statement specifying the functions, responsibilities and authority of a particular managerial position.

Manager:
A member of an organisational structure having authority to appoint and dismiss subordinates and to determine their duties, and for whose work he is accountable to some higher authority.

Manifest organisation:
The organisational structure of an enterprise as it is portrayed in an organisation chart.

Manpower planning:
The long-term planning of the personnel of an enterprise with the object of ensuring the availability of staff of the calibre and in the numbers that will be required to fill vacancies at different levels and to meet the demands of expansion, as these occur in the future.

Marginal costing:
The costing technique which is concerned with the changes in unit prime cost resulting from changes in the volume of output.

Marked cheque:
A cheque certified by the bank on which it is drawn that it is good for the amount for which it is drawn at the time that it is so marked.

Market capitalisation:
Number of ordinary shares and convertible preference shares multiplied by their latest market price.

Market research:
The collection of information regarding the potential of a particular market with the object of forecasting the demand for a product or service.

Marxism:
The political and economic theories propounded by Karl Marx, advocating the abolition of the private ownership of the means of production and the substitution of State ownership and direction of economic activity by the State.

Measurement:
The element of the control function of management that provides information regarding the quantity and quality of output and the economical use of resources in the performance of a task.

Mechanisation:
The use of mechanical appliances to replace physical effort.

Mediation:
The action of a third party who brings about an agreement between two parties in dispute (cf. *Arbitration*).

Method study:
The first phase of work study designed to discover the most

effective way in which to perform a task or operation.

Milestone:
A stage in the completion of a complex project.

Mixed policy:
A marine insurance policy providing cover both for a specified period of time and for a stated voyage.

Morale:
The willingness of the members of a group to co-operate in the achievement of an objective.

Mortgage:
The right over fixed property given by a borrower by way of security for a loan on condition that the property may be redeemed on repayment of the loan.

Motion:
A formal proposal put before a meeting for the purpose of arriving at a decision on that matter.

Motivation:
(1) The urge to perform a task.
(2) The arguments in favour of a particular course of action.

Motive:
An inner conscious or subconscious urge or drive based on one or more unfulfilled desires or fears.

N

Negotiability:
The property of certain documents whereby an indisputable title can be transferred, provided the transferee takes delivery in good faith.

Nett asset value:
Nett assets attributable to ordinary shareholders after adjustment for market and/or directors' valuation of investments, less intangibles.

Nett present value:
The current value of an investment after taking account of the discounted cash flow (q.v.) of its anticipated future yield.

Network:
The interrelationship of the various tasks or "milestones" involved in the completion of a project.

No carbon required (NCR):
Specially impregnated paper that produces copies without the intervention of carbon paper.

O

Objective:
The declared goal to which activities are directed.

Open credit:
An unconditional letter of credit (q.v.).

Opened cheque:
A cheque on which the crossing has been cancelled by the drawer.

Open policy:
A marine insurance policy in which the value of the goods insured is to be declared later.

Organisation:
(1) The command structure of an enterprise in which the roles of the various members are co-ordinated with a view to achieving common objectives.
(2) The function of assembling the human and material resources required to achieve the objectives of an enterprise and of integrating them into a structure of relationships that will enable them to perform effectively the planned activities of the enterprise.

Organisation and methods (O & M):
The analytical study of the organisational structure and operational methods of an enterprise with the object of simplifying and improving them.

Organogram:
A diagrammatic chart portraying the organisational structure of an enterprise as it is believed to exist at a particular time, i.e. its "manifest organisation".

Over-capitalised:
The state of a business of which the capital is too large in relation to the profits made to enable a satisfactory yield to be earned thereon.

Overhead expenses:
The fixed costs of running a business; those which do not vary with output or turnover.

Overtrading:
Undertaking more business or investing in more fixed assets than the available capital warrants if the enterprise is to maintain a reasonably liquid position.

P

Paternalistic management:
The management style that tends to be fatherly and benevolent in its attitude towards the workers (cf. *Democratic management*).

PE ratio:
The present market price of an ordinary share divided by the company's nett earnings.

Per Procuration (Per Pro; PP):
Used before the signature of a person having limited authority to sign on behalf of another.

Personal Assistant (PA):
One whose function is to assist the executive to whom he is attached in whatever capacity the executive may require, but having no personal authority in the organisational structure of the enterprise.

PERT (Progress Evaluation and Review Technique):
A method similar to the Critical Path Method (q.v.) for arriving at the most efficient routes for the performance of the various operations involved in the completion of a complex project, with particular reference to the duration of each operation.

Photostat:
A photocopy of a document.

Planned economy:
A society in which the free operation of market forces is superseded by controls exercised by the State in the implementation of a policy of planned economic development.

Pledge:
The lodgement with a creditor of movable assets or documents of title by way of security for a loan upon the understanding that the objects pledged will be redeemed on repayment of the loan (cf. *Mortgage*).

Policy:
(1) A statement laid down by authority and specifying in broad terms the appropriate behaviour for dealing with a recurring problem for which there is no routine solution, by requiring the organisation to recognise particular objectives and to work towards their fulfilment.
(2) A document setting out the terms of a contract of insurance.

Pool:
A group of typists or other workers, any of whom may be called upon to undertake the work of a particular executive.

Power:
The ability to enforce managerial authority.

Power of Attorney (P/A):
A formal document appointing an agent and authorising him to act on behalf of the principal in certain prescribed circumstances and subject to certain specific conditions. It may be either a "special power" authorising the agent to perform a single specified act or group of acts, or a "general power" which in effect is merely "a bundle of special powers enumerated in a single document".

Pre-interest margin:
Pre-interest profit less dividend income as a percentage of turnover.

Pre-interest profit:
Pre-tax profit plus all interest paid.

Private enterprise:
Same as *Free enterprise* (q.v.).

Processing:
The manipulation of data fed into a computer in order to provide a required answer or result.

Pro-forma invoice:
A document showing the details of a proposed transaction, sent as a matter of form, and not committing either the sender or the recipient to the deal.

Project:
A detailed plan involving a number of interrelated tasks, usually having a specified completion date and often constituting part of a broader plan designed to achieve a stated objective.

Projected cash flow (PCF) statement:
A forecast of expected cash receipts and payments during a specified future period.

Projected source and application of funds statement:
A forecast of the funds from various sources that are expected to be available to an enterprise during a specified future period, and of the manner in which these funds will be utilised.

Projection:
A quantitative forecast used as a basis of planning.

Promissory Note:
A written promise to pay an amount of money on a certain day.

Prospectus:
The printed announcement of a limited company giving details of the enterprise and a form of application for shares.

Q

Quality control:
The regular and systematic inspection of products to ensure that variances from prescribed standards do not exceed specified limits.

Quorum:
A specific number of members or directors of a company or other body or organisation who have power to act. If a quorum is not present at a meeting, those present cannot make legally binding decisions.

Quota:
Control on the quantity of a certain product that may be imported.

R

Redemption:
The repayment of a loan.

Reinsurance:
The procedure whereby an insurer passes on the whole or a part of a risk insured to one or more other insurers.

Reporting:
The transmission of information by a subordinate to a superior to whom he is answerable in a line relationship, or laterally to an executive with whom he is in a staff relationship.

Reporting by responsibility:
The system whereby reports are submitted only to those executives who are responsible for taking action thereon, thus avoiding the danger of overwhelming them with unnecessary paperwork.

Requisite organisation:
The pattern of organisation as it would have to be represented in an organisation chart if the chart were accurately to reflect the true situation as it exists at a particular moment in time.

Research and development (R & D):
The function of keeping up to date with new materials, processes, design, and production techniques.

Resolution:
A motion passed at a meeting after being proposed and seconded.

Responsibility:
(1) The obligation to perform the tasks that have been acceptd.
(2) The obligation of a member of a line organisation to ensure that the tasks delegated to subordinates are duly performed.

Resumé:
A summary; an abstract.

Return on equity:
Earnings per share as a percentage of net asset value.

Return on capital:
Pre-interest profit as a percentage of capital employed.

Risk:
The possibility of loss resulting from the occurrence of a contingency.

Role:
The function of a member in an organisational structure.

S

Salvage:
(1) Property saved from loss either in a fire or at sea.
(2) The allowance paid to one who saves property from loss in a fire or at sea when he has no legal obligation to take such action.

Salvage loss:
The amount paid by underwriters for the loss of property insured less the value of what has been salvaged.

Sampling:
The selection of random units from a larger bulk with a view to judging therefrom the quality of the bulk.

Scalar:
The principle whereby managerial authority scales downwards by degrees from top level through successively lower levels in an organisational structure.

Scheduling:
The detailed planning of the time sequence of a series of operations or tasks in a project.

Security:
(1) Protection against the risk of loss from malicious damage.
(2) A document of title evidencing an investment, such as a share certificate.
(3) An asset, or document of title to an asset, lodged with a bank or other financial institution as a pledge for the repayment of a loan.

Self-insurance:
The acceptance of a risk in preference to taking out insurance cover, with or without the creation of a fund out of which to meet such losses.

Sequestration:
The assignment of the estate of a bankrupt person into the hands of a trustee on his being declared bankrupt by the court.

Shareholders' interest:
Total shareholders' funds expressed as a ratio of capital employed.

Sight credit:
A letter of credit (q.v.) in which the issuing bank undertakes to accept and pay all bills of exchange drawn in accordance with the conditions specified therein.

Sinking fund:
Money set aside for the purpose of liquidating a liability by degrees.

Socialism:
The basic principle of an economy in which the means of production are owned by the State, which also undertakes all production in what are held to be the best interests of the society.

Source and application of funds statement:
A statement in summary form of the funds from various sources which have been available to an enterprise during a stated period, and of the manner in which they have been utilised; also known as a "funds flow statement".

Span of control:
The number of subordinates answerable to a superior in a line organisational structure; also known as "span of management" or "span of authority".

Staff:
The white-collar employees of an enterprise, usually remunerated by monthly salary.

Staff function:
The duty to advise and assist, but not to issue orders to, those constituting the line organisation of an enterprise.

Stale cheque:
A cheque that is not presented for payment within a period of six months from the date thereof.

Standard:
A norm or accepted level of performance against which actual achievement is measured.

Standard costing:
The system of costing based upon the cost of producing a standard product in standard quantities under standard conditions.

Standing order:
An instruction by a customer to his bank to pay at regular intervals a specified sum of money to the bank account of a named party.

Statistical quality control:
The technique of measuring the quality of production by using statistical methods based on sampling and the laws of probability.

Status:
The rank or degree of prestige enjoyed by a member of an organisational hierarchy.

Stock:
(1) Goods purchased in the course of business with a view to their resale at a profit.
(2) Fully paid shares which have been consolidated and which can be dealt in on the Stock Exchange in any amounts.
(3) Securities issued by a government or other public authority in acknowledgement of a loan.

Stock turnover:
Turnover divided by the year-end stock figure.

Stop order:
A notice to a bank by the drawer of a cheque or bill of exchange that it must not be paid should it be presented.

Subrogation:
The right of one party (e.g. an insurance company) to stand in the shoes of another (e.g. the insured) and to exercise all his legal rights and remedies.

Supervisor:
A person to whom a superior delegates authority to assign work to subordinates and to undertake responsibility for the due completion of such work.

Supportive management:
A management style that encourages participative activities by subordinates; same as *Democratic management* (q.v.).

Surrender value:
The amount which a life assurance company is prepared to pay to an endowment policy holder in consideration of his relinquishing his rights under the policy before it has matured.

Synergy:
The combination of the efforts of two or more persons or productive units to achieve a result greater than the sum of the results of their individual efforts.

T

Tare:
The weight of the container of goods, e.g. crate, cask, box, etc.

Tariff:
List of imports upon which custom duties are payable.

Telecommunication:
The transmission of signals over long distances, such as radio or telegraph.

Telegraphic transfer (TT):
A telegraphically transmitted order by one bank to another, or to another branch of the same bank, to pay a stated sum of money to a specified person.

Telex:
A system of telegraphy whereby printed messages are sent from and to teleprinters connected to the public telephone network.

Tenor of a bill:
The period for which a bill of exchange has to run from the date of drawing to the date of maturity.

Time and motion study:
The analytical examination of the time involved and the movement required to perform each part of a task, with a view to ascertaining the most effective way of performing the task with the minimum of wasted time and effort.

Time graph:
A diagram presented on graph paper in which time is one of the variables, plotted along the horizontal (OX) axis.

Time policy:
A marine insurance policy which runs for a fixed period only, as distinct from one covering a particular voyage.

Time series analysis:
The critical examination of past data covering a period of time with a view to identifying seasonal and cyclical fluctuations and the long-term trend, on the basis of which future projections of probable movements may be made on which to base policy decisions.

Total shareholders' funds:
The total of ordinary, minority and irredeemable preference shares plus all capital convertible into equity, less intangibles and adjusted for the market and/or directors' valuation of investments.

Turnover:
Nett sales, i.e. gross sales minus returns.

U

Underwriter:
(1) An insurer, particularly a marine insurer.
(2) A person or financial institution who guarantees a public issue of shares or debentures, and undertakes to take up any securities not applied for by members of the public.

Unfunded debt:
Short-period government borrowings which are not evidenced by formal definitive securities such as government stock.

Uniform costing:
A costing system uniformly adopted throughout a particular industry in order to achieve standardisation and to facilitate inter-firm comparisons.

Unity of command:
The principle that every subordinate in an organisational structure should be accountable to, and subject to the authority of, one and only one superior.

Unvalued policy:
An insurance policy in which the value of the property insured is not assessed until a loss has occurred.

Usance:
The customary period for which bills of exchange between two particular countries are drawn.

V

Value analysis:
The critical examination of procedures, proposed purchases of equipment and other projects to determine whether the cost involved is justified by the results achieved or anticipated (cf. *Cost/benefit analysis*).

Valued policy:
An insurance policy in which the value of the property insured is stated.

Variance:
The deviation of actual results achieved from the prescribed standard.

Voucher:
A document attesting a transaction recorded in the books of account.

Voyage policy:
A marine insurance policy which covers a specified voyage irrespective of the time taken.

W

Warranty:
(1) In general, a stipulation in a contract, breach of which gives a right of action for damages but not for the cancellation of the contract (cf. *Condition*).
(2) In marine insurance, a stipulation in a policy which must be strictly complied with, breach of which gives the underwriters the right to avoid the policy, irrespective of whether the warranty affects the quality of the risk.

Waybill:
See *Consignment note*.

Working capital:
The amount by which the current assets of an enterprise exceed its current liabilities.

Work study:
The systematic examination of a job or operation, embracing method study and work measurement, and aiming at increased effectiveness, greater economy of time, material and effort, and hence lower costs.

Y

York-Antwerp Rules:
A set of rules drawn up at a conference of marine insurance underwriters at Antwerp in 1877 to unify the practice of adjusting general average losses (q.v.).

When I was a boy of fourteen, my father was so ignorant I could hardly stand to have the old man around. But when I got to be twenty-one I was astonished at how much the old man had learned in seven years

– Mark Twain

BIBLIOGRAPHY

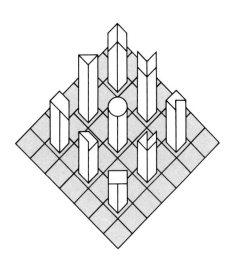

BIBLIOGRAPHY

In the publishers' quest to cover a broad scope of practical facets experienced daily by all levels of management worldwide, numerous books, journals, speeches, etc. were consulted. Considerable trouble has been taken to trace and contact owners of possible copyright material in this publication. Should any omission have occurred in this respect, the publishers will be pleased to be informed so that the matter can be rectified.

In addition, our editors interviewed authors, consultants, publishers, lecturers and managers on a wide range of topics concerning the art of communication and management. We have pleasure in listing here, as comprehensively as possible, our list of references.

Adair, J. *The Action Centred Leader*. The Industrial Society, London.
Alexander Hamilton Institute. *An Executive's Guide to Effective Writing*.
Alberti, Robert E. and Emmons, Michael L. *Assert yourself – It's Your Perfect Right*. Impact.
Alberti, Robert E. and Emmons, Michael L. *Stand Up, Speak Out, Talk Back!* Pocket Books.
A Manual of Style. University of Chicago Press.
Anger, B.Y. *How To Run Better Business Meetings*. Amacom.
Appleby, Robert C. *Modern Business Administration, 5th edition*. Pitman.
Armstrong, M. *How to be a Better Manager*. Kogan Page.
Avis Rent-a-Car.
Barrett, R. *How To Succeed By Setting Your Goals*. CTP.
Bassin, Marc S. *Developing Executive Leadership: A General Foods Approach*. Personnel.
Beasley, D. Teltron.
Biz Com. Useful forms.
Borgelt, Tersia. Consultant, Top Secretary Training.
Bosticco, M. *Personal Letters for Businessmen*. Business Publications Limited.
Brill, L. *Business Writing Quick and Easy*. Pan Books.
British Institute of Management.
Bunning, Richard L. *A Comprehensive Approach to Improving Attendance*. Personnel Journal.
Burger, C. *Survival in the Executive Jungle*. MacMillan.
Butt, Margot. *Dictionary of English Usage*. Collins.
Callihan, E.L. *Grammar for Journalists*. Chilton Book Company.
Calonius, Erik. *How Top Managers Manage Their Time*.
Castledex Business Systems.
Cooper, M.C. *Writing Technical Reports*. Pelican.
CSIR Newsletter on occupational health.
Dale Carnegie Training.
Davidson, Jeffrey P. and Allessandra, Anthony. *Dealing with High Absenteeism*.
De Becker, Gavin. *Managing the Violent Employee*. Security Management.
Delaney, W.A. *Tricks of the Manager's Trade*. AMACOM.
Dely, Renè. Executive Image.
Drake Business Review: Various issues.
Eddings, C.N. *Secretary's Complete Model Letter Handbook*. Prentice-Hall, Inc.
Elliot-Afrovan.
Executive Health: Various issues.
Falkenberg, Randall. Managing Director, Contact Group.
Fearns, Peter. *The Business Companion*. Hodder & Stoughton.
Fellons, H. and Ikeda, F. *Business Speaking and Writing*. Prentice-Hall.
Fisher, Carol E. and Olham, Anne-Rose. *Secretary's Correspondence Guide*. Shuter & Shooter.
Fletcher, John. *Effective Interviewing*. Kogan Page.
Fortune, USA: Various issues.
Fowler, H.W. *A Dictionary of Modern English Usage*. Oxford University Press.
Gowers, E. *The Complete Plain Words*. Penguin.
Graham, H.T. *Human Resources Management 4th ed*. Macdonald and Evans.
Grant, Sue. Managing Director, Markinor.
Grice, G.L. and Skinner, J.F. *Delivering Your Speech: Using Body, Voice and Language*. Prentice-Hall.
Harrison, R.P. *Beyond Words*. Prentice-Hall.
Harvard Business Review, USA: Various issues.
Hill, N.C. *How to Increase Employee Competence*. McGraw-Hill.
Holmes, Ann E. and Painter, Richard W. *Employment Law*. Blackstone Press.
Hopkins, R.E. *Speak Up*. Pan Books.
Hopper, R. *Between You and Me: The Professional's Guide to Interpersonal Communication*. Scott, Foresman & Co.
Huseman, Richard C., Lahiff, James M. and Hatfield, John D. *Business Communication*. Holt-Saunders.
IMS International Inc.
Inglis, S. and Kobusska, J. *Making Presentations*. Simon & Schuster.
Janis, J.H., Kilduff, E.J. & Dressner, H.R. *Business Writing*. Barnes & Noble Inc.
Jenks, James M. and Kelly, John M. *The Secret Power of the Successful Manager*. Kogan Page.
Jennings, L.M. *Secretarial and Administrative Procedures*. McGraw-Hill.
Jewellery Council.
Keenon, Dennis & Riches, Sarah. *Business Law*. Pitman.

Knapp, Mark. *Non-verbal Communication in Human Interaction*.

Labich, Kenneth. *The Seven Keys to Business Leadership*.

Le Boeuf, M. *The Greatest Management Principle in the World*. GP Putnam.

Little, G. *101 Ways to be a Better Manager*. Reed Methuen Publishers.

Logan, A.L. *Remembering Made Easy*. Arco Publishing.

Lundberg, L.B. *The Art of Being An Executive*. Collier MacMillan.

Lufthansa Business Service: *Fitness in the Chair*.

Mager, N.H. and S.K. *What To Say ... How To Say It*. William Morrow & Company.

Management Communications Handbook, South Africa.

Management Planning, USA: Various issues.

Management World, USA: Various issues.

Margerison, Charles & Smith, Barry. *Time Management, Acting Justly, Counselling, Inspired Leadership*. In Shakespeare and Management.

Marino, Michael. *Are you posture perfect?* Mademoiselle.

Marketing, *Constructing a table*.

Marsh, Cynthia E. *Address the Cause – Not the Symptons – of Behavior Problems*. Personnel Journal.

Newstrom, J.W. *Reward Solid Solutions*. Training and Development Journal.

Nieman, Jean. *A World of Travel Tips*.

Oches, Norman. *Cross-cultural presentations – How to make them more effective*.

Office Administration & Automation, U.S.A.: Various issues.

Osgood, Don. *How Your Personal Attitudes Can Make or Break You*. Harper & Row.

Pace, R. Wayne, Peterson, Brend D. & Dallas Burnette M. *Conflict Management in Techniques for Effective Communication*. Addison-Wesley.

Paxson, W.C. *The Business Writing Handbook*. Bantam Books.

P E Corporate Services.

Peel, M. *How To Make Meetings Work*. Kogan Page.

Perry, P.J.C. *Hours into Minutes*. British Association for Commercial and Industrial Education.

Phillips Dictation Equipment: Manual.

Presenting Yourself. Kodak.

Professional Learning Systems: Various publications.

Public Relations Journal: Various issues.

Puth, G. Professor of Management.

Reader's Digest. *Write Better, Speak Better*.

Roaf, R. *In Support of Good Posture*. Pan Books.

Rowntree, D. *The Manager's Book of Checklists*. Corgi.

Rutherford, Robert D. *Just In Time: Immediate Help for the Time-pressured*. John Wiley & Sons.

Saifullah, Ed & Kleiner, Brian H. *Effective Time Management*.

Sarnoff D. *Speech Can Change Your Life*. Prentice-Hall.

Scott, Deanna. Consultant for Whitehead Morris.

Sigland, M.B. and Bateman D.N. *Communicating in Business*. Prentice-Hall.

Sims, Frank. The Security Association.

Smith Ken J. *The Power of Good Management*. William Morrow & Co.

Sorrels, B.D. *Business Communication Fundamentals*. Charles E. Merrill.

Specialised Exhibitions.

Speech-making, More Than Words Alone. Kodak.

Successful Salesmanship: Various issues.

Supervisory Management: AMACOM, New York: Various issues.

The Director, U.S.A.: Various issues.

The Office, U.S.A.: Various issues.

The Secretary's Handbook, Australian, Singapore and South African editions.

The Secret Power of the Successful Manager. Kogan Page.

Thomas Cook.

Thouless, R.H. *Straight and Crooked Thinking*. Pan Books.

TIM (Travel Information Manual).

Tomkins, Sandra. *The Secretary's Survival Manual*.

Training and Development Journal, UK: Various issues.

Treble, H.A. and Vallins, *The ABC of English Usage*. Clarendon Press.

UNISA: Bureau of Market Research: Various publications.

US News & World Report.

Van Grundy, Arthur B. *108 Ways to Get a Bright Idea*. Prentice-Hall Inc.

Viljoen, P du T. Management Consultant.

Wells, G. *How to Communicate*, McGraw-Hill.

Wilcox, A. *The Right Way to Apply for a Job*. Elliot Right Way Books.

Winkler, John. *Bargaining for Results*. William Heinemann.

Woman's Day: Various issues.

Yate, M.J. *Great Answers to Tough Interview Questions 2nd ed.* Kogan Page.